Celebrating African-American Achievements

WHO'S WHO
in BLACK
Washington, D.C.®
THE INAUGURAL EDITION

Celebrating African-American Achievements

WHO'S WHO
IN BLACK
Washington, D.C.®

THE INAUGURAL EDITION

Who's Who In Black Washington, D.C.®
is a registered trademark of
Real Times Media

Purchase additional copies online @
www.whoswhopublishing.com

Corporate Headquarters
Who's Who Publishing Co.
1801 Watermark Drive, Suite 250
Columbus, Ohio 43215

All Credit Cards Accepted
*Inquiries for bulk purchases for youth
groups, schools, churches, civic or
professional organizations, please call
our office for volume discounts.*

Corporate Headquarters
(614) 481-7300

Copyright © 2009 by Real Times Media
ISSN Number: 1938-8268

Inside Photo Credits
Donald L. Baker, John Ellis, C. Sunny Martin,
Monica Morgan, Rob Roberts, and Mike Styles

Cover Design: Monica Sherchan
Cover Photos: Monica Morgan

ISBN # 1-933879-87-4 Hardback
$50.00 each-U.S. Hardback
Commemorative Edition

ISBN # 1-933879-86-6 Paperback
$34.95 each-U.S. Paperback

Table of
CONTENTS

MEET THE TEAM

WHO'S *WHO*

A Real Times Media Company

Carter Womack
Washington, D.C. Associate Publisher

Cassandra Bozeman
Chief Operations Officer

Ernie Sullivan
Senior Partner

Melanie Diggs
Executive Editor

Paula Gray
V.P. Customer Care

Tamara Allen
Production Manager

Steve Clark
Sales Representative

Nathan Wylder
Senior Editor

Alicia Dunlap
Production Assistant

Corey E. Favor
Sr. Graphic Designer

John Glover
Senior Account Executive

Monica Sherchan
Graphic Designer

Kimberly Byers
Graphic Designer

Earron West
Graphic Designer

Rachel Bobak
Copy Editor

Lester Davis
Account Executive

Danielle Solomon
Copy Editor

Amanda Forbes
Copy Editor

Meagan Culley
Customer Service Rep.

Vercilla Brown
Account Executive

Sarah Longacre
Executive Assistant

Stephanie Longacre
Administrative Assistant

CORPORATE OFFICE
1801 Watermark Drive, Suite 250 • Columbus, Ohio 43215 • (614) 481-7300

Visit Our Web Site - www.whoswhopublishing.com

Foreword by

DOROTHY I. HEIGHT

Chair/President Emerita
National Council of Negro Women, Inc.

This premier edition of *Who's Who In Black Washington, D.C.*® is a tribute to the rich history of African-American achievement in the nation's capital. Despite barriers of slavery, racial segregation, Jim Crow laws, and the continued absence of full voting representation in Congress, there is an enduring African-American legacy in Washington, D.C.

While mathematician and inventor Benjamin Banneker is credited with playing a pivotal role in creating one of the world's most beautiful cities, many of its greatest monuments, the Capitol and other government buildings, were built by enslaved Africans who were never acknowledged for their contributions. Yet, in every area of human endeavor, can be found the names of black Washingtonians who have made their mark not only locally, but nationally and internationally.

Following in the footsteps of families such as Drew, Holmes, Syphax and Quander, came "The Black Cabinet," whose titular head was Mary McLeod Bethune and individuals such as Anna J. Cooper, Charles Hamilton Houston, Mordecai Johnson, Montague Cobb, Mary Church Terrell, Duke Ellington, Elizabeth Catlett and Addison Spurlock. Those and many others are the accomplished and dedicated men and women chronicled in the 21st century *Who's Who In Black Washington, D.C.*®, whom I am proud to salute.

This book is published in an era of significant change under President Barack Obama, who leads a country where scores of black Americans serve in the Cabinet, in appointive offices, the halls of Congress, and the District of Columbia government with Mayor Adrian Fenty. Others hold high positions in corporations, businesses, faith-based institutions and community-based health, advocacy and service organizations.

Permanent recognition of the historic contributions of black Americans to the country and world are evident

> *"Yet, in every area of human endeavor, can be found the names of black Washingtonians who have made their mark not only locally, but nationally and internationally."*

in Washington, D.C. Among its many monuments are the Bethune Memorial in Lincoln Park, spearheaded in 1974 by the National Council of Negro Women – the first monument to an African American or to a woman of any race erected on public land in the nation's capital – and the monument to Martin Luther King, Jr., organized by Alpha Phi Alpha Fraternity, Inc.

Share this directory with young people everywhere. Use it as a teaching tool to help them understand that achieving their highest potential is within their grasp if they develop their God-given abilities through education and pursue a life of service to their community. My mentor, Mary McLeod Bethune, taught me the value of knowing black history, affirming my sense of living with purpose and being a part of an organization with a unity of purpose, unity of action and a strong presence in the nation's capital. In my lifetime, I have had the honor of holding national leadership in the United Christian Youth Movement of North America, The YWCA of the USA, Delta Sigma Theta Sorority, Inc., the Leadership Conference on Civil Rights and the National Council of Negro Women.

I pay profound tribute to the dedicated men, women and youth history makers presented in this edition of *Who's Who In Black Washington, D.C.*®. May they inspire the present, the next generation, and those yet unborn to follow in their footsteps.

Sincerely,

Dorothy Height

Dorothy I. Height
Chair/President Emerita
National Council of Negro Women, Inc.

OBAMA'S
Presidential

HISTORIC
Campaign

THIS BOOK WAS MADE POSSIBLE BY THE GENEROUS SUPPORT OF OUR

SPONSORS

OFFICIAL AIRLINE

△ DELTA

DIAMOND SPONSORS

EST. 1892
Abercrombie & Fitch
NEW YORK

EMERALD SPONSORS

DELTA SIGMA THETA

UNVEILING SPONSORS

Congressional Black Caucus Foundation, Inc.

THE POWER OF INCLUSIVE LEADERSHIP

EDUCATIONAL SPONSORS

MEDIA SPONSORS

MORGAN STATE UNIVERSITY

1867
HOWARD UNIVERSITY

BLACK *Leadership* FORU

LINKING LEADERSHIP TO LEGISLA

Inspired by Dr. Dorothy Height (Chair and President Emeritus of the National Council of Negro Women) and the "Big 6" (*) civil rights leaders of the 1960's, the Black Leadership Forum, Inc. (BLF) is an alliance of over thirty national African American civil rights and service organizations in the United States of America. Member organizations are strategically linked together to stategically advocate for the legislative and policy interests of Black people on the international, congressional, state, county, and municipal level.

In 1977, led by Dr. Dorothy Height, Vernon Jordan (National Urban League), Dr. Joseph Lowery (Southern Christian Leadership Conference), Eddie Williams (Joint Center for Political and Economic Studies), Bill Lucy (Coalition of Black Trade Unionists), Dr. Ramona Edelin (National Urban Coalition), and Dr. Yvonne Scruggs-Leftwich (first executive director), BLF was formed with 11 organizations (**) as a clearinghouse for national Black organizations.

Today's BLF national leaders continue the legacy of leadership passed to them from past advocates of progressive public policy.

* 1960's "Big Six": Dr. Martin Luther King, Jr. - Southern Christian Leadership Conference; Whitney Young - National Urban League; Roy Wilkins - National Association for the Advancement of Colored People; A. Philip Randolph - Brotherhood of Sleeping Car Porters; James Farmer - Congress of Racial Equality; and John Lewis - Student Nonviolent Coordinating Committee.

** 1977 original members of the Black Leadership Forum: Congressional Black Caucus, Joint Center for Political and Economic Studies, Martin Luther King Center for Non-Violent Social Change, NAACP Legal Defense and Educational Fund, National Business League, National Conference of Black Mayors, National Council of Negro Women, National Urban Coalition, National Urban League.

www.blackleadershipforum.org/home.html

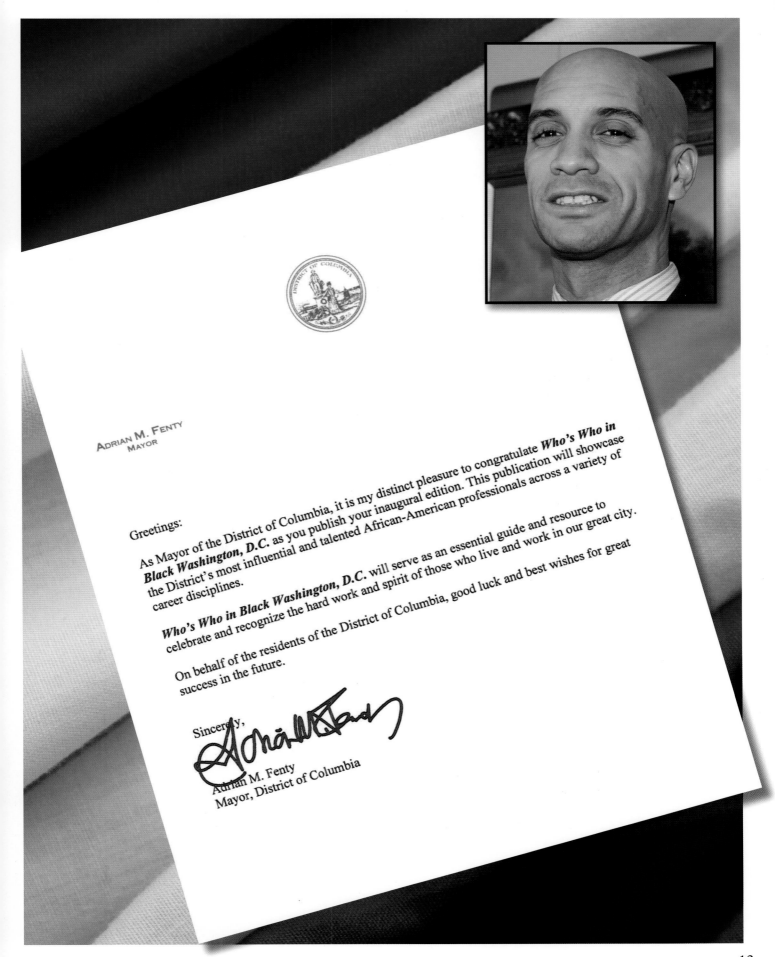

ADRIAN M. FENTY
MAYOR

Greetings:

As Mayor of the District of Columbia, it is my distinct pleasure to congratulate *Who's Who in Black Washington, D.C.* as you publish your inaugural edition. This publication will showcase the District's most influential and talented African-American professionals across a variety of career disciplines.

Who's Who in Black Washington, D.C. will serve as an essential guide and resource to celebrate and recognize the hard work and spirit of those who live and work in our great city.

On behalf of the residents of the District of Columbia, good luck and best wishes for great success in the future.

Sincerely,

Adrian M. Fenty
Mayor, District of Columbia

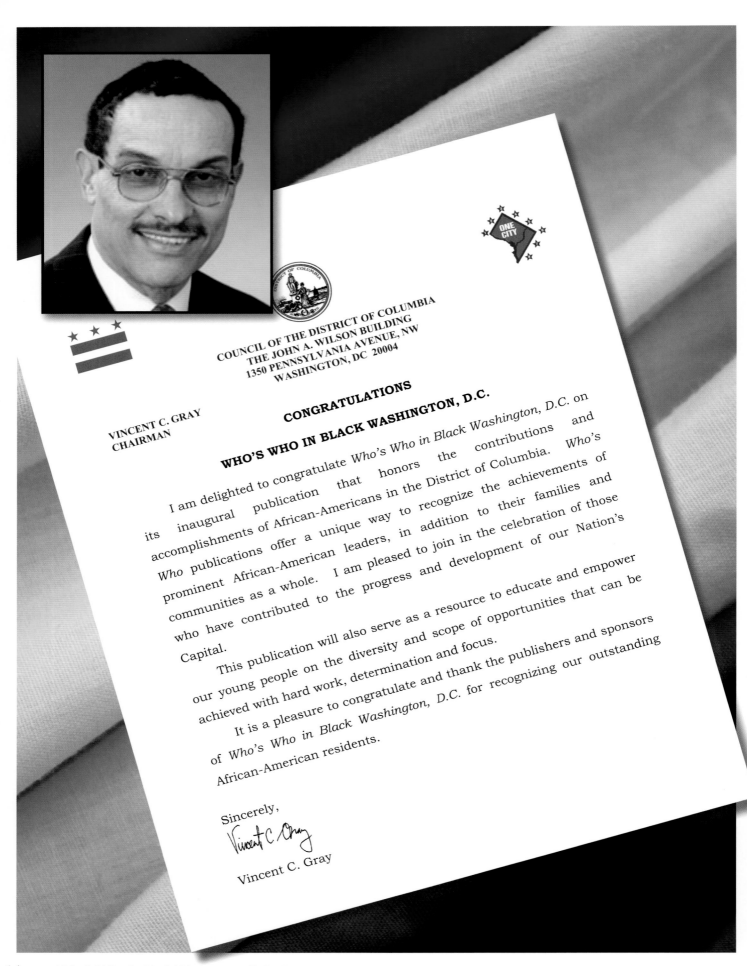

COUNCIL OF THE DISTRICT OF COLUMBIA
THE JOHN A. WILSON BUILDING
1350 PENNSYLVANIA AVENUE, NW
WASHINGTON, DC 20004

VINCENT C. GRAY
CHAIRMAN

CONGRATULATIONS

WHO'S WHO IN BLACK WASHINGTON, D.C.

I am delighted to congratulate *Who's Who in Black Washington, D.C.* on its inaugural publication that honors the contributions and accomplishments of African-Americans in the District of Columbia. *Who's Who* publications offer a unique way to recognize the achievements of prominent African-American leaders, in addition to their families and communities as a whole. I am pleased to join in the celebration of those who have contributed to the progress and development of our Nation's Capital.

This publication will also serve as a resource to educate and empower our young people on the diversity and scope of opportunities that can be achieved with hard work, determination and focus.

It is a pleasure to congratulate and thank the publishers and sponsors of *Who's Who in Black Washington, D.C.* for recognizing our outstanding African-American residents.

Sincerely,

Vincent C. Gray

A Legacy Renewed
HOWARD UNIVERSITY

Howard University is a living symbol of the determination of a people to free themselves of oppression and enjoy the fruits of life, liberty, happiness and prosperity as responsible citizens in an equal society.

For 140 years, the Howard University School of Law has been a champion of civil rights and social justice. The School of Law has a proud tradition of producing leaders and social engineers. These leaders include Supreme Court Justice Thurgood Marshall ('33), Virginia Governor L. Douglas Wilder ('59) and Mayors of the nation's capital, Sharon Pratt Kelly ('68) and Adrian Fenty ('96).

As a leading research university, it is dedicated to attracting and developing the best and brightest students. We produce more on-campus African-American doctoral degrees than any other university in the United States.

1867
HOWARD
UNIVERSITY

2400 Sixth Street, NW, Washington, DC 20059 • 202-806-6100 • www.howard.edu

A MESSAGE FROM THE

Chief Executive Officer

HIRAM E. JACKSON

REAL TIMES MEDIA

Welcome to our inaugural edition of *Who's Who In Black Washington, D.C.*®!

It is fitting that we launch this publication in the same year as the inauguration of our first African-American president, Barack Obama, to whom we pay tribute. While many viewed this historic event as improbable, we knew it was not impossible. Not only are we witnesses to history, we are participants of a movement of people that began centuries ago. The same buildings constructed by our forefathers are now inhabited by those who serve in some of the highest offices in our land, and who govern, advocate and educate on our behalf. Their combined efforts ensure the success of the next generation of leaders. It is my sincere hope that our past victories are not forgotten, but used to forge new paths.

Moreover, I am humbled that Dr. Dorothy Height, president emerita of the National Council of Negro Women and past national president of Delta Sigma Theta Sorority, Inc., has penned the foreword. With strength and grace, she represents the countless men and women who worked to see change come to our land in ways that decreased the number of women and children in poverty, secured fair representation of legislative issues and brought parity to our communities. We thank her for the vision and fortitude that she and so many others held throughout the years.

I am honored to salute those featured in this publication. Your work in the halls of government, community-based organizations, educational institutions, corporations and cultural centers makes our nation's capital a dynamic kaleidoscope of talent and resources. Our strength lies not merely in numbers, but in the force of our collaborative efforts. Therefore, I encourage our readers to share this great chronicle of Washington, D.C.'s African-American history. Do your best to get this and future volumes into the hands and onto the desks of our youth, the bright young minds who are our next generation of civil rights activists, global leaders, entrepreneurs, pastors, educators and parents.

Who's Who In Black Washington, D.C.® | The Inaugural Edition

A MESSAGE FROM THE *Chief Executive Officer*

With a legacy that journeys back more than 100 years, Who's Who Publishing Co.'s parent company, Real Times Media, strives to become the leading source of news, entertainment and lifestyle information from the African-American perspective. Our acquisition of Who's Who Publishing Co. in 2009 was a natural evolution of this mission.

Real Times Media provides comprehensive news and information that helps our communities continue to not only thrive and grow, but also chronicles the events and individuals who are making history. We accomplish this through our family of companies, which includes the most extensive African-American newspaper collective in the nation – the *Chicago Defender*, the *Michigan Chronicle*, The *Michigan FrontPage*, *The New Pittsburgh Courier* and the *Tri-State Defender* (Memphis) – and RTM Digital Studios, an unparalleled archive of historical photographs and other artifacts of the African-American experience throughout the past century. Additionally, we are proud to offer our communities access to a series of events across the country where we pay honor to unsung community and religious leaders.

I invite you to learn more about us online at realtimesmedia.com and whoswhopublishing.com.

Sincerely,

Hiram E. Jackson

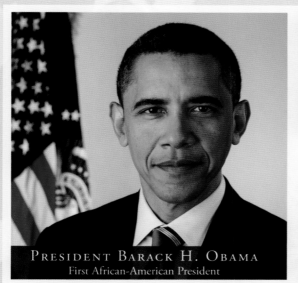
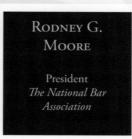

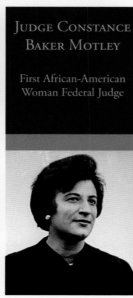

Criteria for Inclusion

Who's Who In Black Washington, D.C. is an opportunity for us to afford a measure of recognition to the men and women who have made their mark in their specific occupations, professions, or in service to others in the Washington, D.C. community.

A sincere effort was made to include those whose positions or accomplishments in their chosen fields are significant and whose contributions to community affairs, whether citywide or on the neighborhood level, have improved the quality of life for all of us.

The names of those brief biographies included in this edition were compiled from customary sources of information. Lists of a wide variety were consulted and every effort was made to reach all whose stature or civic activities merited their inclusion.

In today's mobile society, no such publication could ever claim to be complete; some who should be included could not be reached or chose not to respond, and for that we offer our apologies. Constraints of time, space and awareness are thus responsible for other omissions, and not a lack of good intentions on the part of the publisher. Our goal was to document the accomplishments of many people from various occupational disciplines.

An invitation to participate in the publication was extended at the discretion of the publisher. Biographies were invited to contribute personal and professional data, with only the information freely submitted to be included. The editors have made a sincere effort to present an accurate distillation of the data, and to catch errors whenever possible. However, the publisher cannot assume any responsibility for the accuracy of the information submitted.

There was no charge for inclusion in this publication and inclusion was not guaranteed; an annual update is planned. Comments and other concerns should be addressed to:

Who's Who Publishing Co.
1801 Watermark Drive, Suite 250
Columbus, Ohio 43215
Phone: (614) 481-7300

www.whoswhopublishing.com

A MESSAGE FROM THE

Washington, D.C.

ASSOCIATE PUBLISHER

Carter Womack

As we launch this inaugural edition of **Who's Who In Black Washington, D.C.**®, historic as it is, it is truly a continuation of a story. Our ancestors designed and built this city, and it was their hard work that brought it to life. Their pain and tears turned a swamp into the capital city of the world's most powerful country. The story continues as these men and women built the most famous house in the world, the White House, for centuries the home of presidents and first families. This historic edition of **Who's Who In Black Washington, D.C.**® is a tribute to the exceptional African-American men and women of Washington, D.C. It is a celebration of the hard work of generations of African-American people who paved the way for us to honor them and their past accomplishments.

As we commemorate the many historic events that have occurred in America, most recently with the election of Barack Obama as the first African-American president, I know that our ancestors who helped build the White House never thought that a black man would ever live there as president of the United States. His election and the presence of an African-American family in the White House are an inspiration for young people everywhere.

In celebrating our achievements, we now have a great opportunity to be strong role models for our young brothers and sisters. It is our responsibility to ensure that high school and college graduation rates increase, crime rates in our community are reduced, the impact of HIV/AIDS is confronted, and that we teach our young people the importance of being responsible and respectful.

I want to thank Dr. Dorothy I. Height for her support and agreeing to write the foreword for this edition. To my local publishing team of John Glover, Lester Davis, Vercilla Brown, and the writers and the photography team – the success of this book would not have been possible without your support. Thank you!

Please enjoy this inaugural edition of **Who's Who In Black Washington, D.C.**®. Share it with others, for truly, the story continues...

Sincerely,

Carter D. Womack

WHO'S WHO
A Real Times Media Company

Salutes the Members of
THE CONGRESSIONAL
BLACK CAUCUS

The Honorable G.K. Butterfield

The Honorable Sanford D. Bishop, Jr.

The Honorable Corrine Brown

The Honorable Roland W. Burris

The Honorable Andre Carson

The Honorable Donna M. Christensen

The Honorable Yvette Clarke

The Honorable William Lacy Clay, Jr.

The Honorable Emanuel Cleaver II

The Honorable James E. Clyburn

The Honorable John Conyers, Jr.

The Honorable Elijah E. Cummings

The Honorable Artur Davis

The Honorable Danny K. Davis

The Honorable Donna Edwards

The Honorable Keith Ellison

The Honorable Chaka Fattah

The Honorable Marcia L. Fudge

The Honorable Al Green

The Honorable Alcee L. Hastings

The Honorable Jesse L. Jackson, Jr.

The Honorable Sheila Jackson Lee

The Honorable Hank Johnson

The Honorable Eddie Bernice Johnson

The Honorable Carolyn Cheeks Kilpatrick

The Honorable Barbara Lee

The Honorable John Lewis

The Honorable Kendrick B. Meek

The Honorable Gregory W. Meeks

The Honorable Gwendolynne Moore

The Honorable Eleanor Holmes Norton

The Honorable Donald M. Payne

The Honorable Charles B. Rangel

The Honorable Laura Richardson

The Honorable Bobby L. Rush

The Honorable David Scott

The Honorable Robert C. Scott

The Honorable Bennie Thompson

The Honorable Edolphus Towns

The Honorable Maxine Waters

The Honorable Diane E. Watson

The Honorable Melvin L. Watt

THE CONGRESSIONAL BLACK CAUCUS FOUNDATION, INC.
The Premier Public Policy, Education and Research Organization

EDUCATING FUTURE LEADERS | INVESTING IN YOUNG LEADERS
ADVANCING ECONOMIC DEVELOPMENT | NARROWING HEALTH DISPARITIES

CBCF was established in 1976 as a nonpartisan, nonprofit, public policy, research and education institute to help improve the socio-economic circumstances of African Americans and other underserved communities. Led by our Chairman of the Board, Rep. Kendrick B. Meek of Florida, and our President and Chief Executive Officer, Elsie L. Scott, Ph.D., CBCF helps to bring powerful ideas and proposals to our nation's leaders and policymakers.

Black Health Empowerment Project

Internship & Fellowship Programs

CBC Spouses

Annual Legislative Conference

SHOP for Wealth

Economic Empowerment Forums

To learn more about the Congressional Black Caucus Foundation, please visit our web site at www.cbcfing.org

CONGRESSIONAL BLACK CAUCUS FOUNDATION, INC. | 1720 Massachusetts Avenue NW, Washington, D.C. 20036 | 202.263.2800

Chapter Membership ⁝•

Student Membership ⁝•

Early Career Membership ⁝•

Associate Membership ⁝•

Intitutional Membership ⁝•

National Association of Health Sevices Executives

⁝• NAHSE will be recognized globally as the premier professional membership society for Blacks in health care management. NAHSE strives to improve the health status, economics opportunities and educational advancement of the communities we serve.

www.nahse.org

Any Questions..Contact our national headquarters

1140 Connecticut Ave. NW Suite 505
Washington, D.C. 20036

Tel 202.429.6060
Fax 202.429.6767

OUR MEMBER BENEFITS INCLUDE:

⁝• Affiliation with one of NAHSE's 26 local chapters which allows for great educational and networking opportunities.

⁝• Annual Educational Conference with healthcare related programs and well-known speakers eligible for up to nine category II ACHE credits.

⁝• An annual CEO/Senior Executive Conference that focuses on the leader's role in healthcare.

⁝• Emerging Leaders Health Care Forum For students and early careerists.

A CHANGE HAS COME TO *America*

By A. Christine Dunlap

"Change will not come if we wait for some other person, or if we wait for some other time. We are the ones we've been waiting for. We are the change that we seek. "
— President Barack Obama

With confidence, yet humility, Barack Hussein Obama has made historical strides that will pave the way for a stronger, more empowered generation. Through his words of hope, spirit of determination, love for his family and never ending drive, Obama, now the 44th President of the United States, has shown the world change has come.

As a symbolism of change, Obama's journey has been a long and tireless road to the White House. This journey, which began even before he was born, would enable him to draw strength from the forerunners of this decade, and with the help of a nation, make their dreams of "one day" a reality.

"One day this nation will rise up and live out the true meaning of its creed. We hold this truth to be self evident that all men are created equal."- *Dr. Martin Luther King, Jr. "I Have a Dream" speech*

Through the life and words of such civil rights martyrs as Dr. Martin Luther King Jr., Malcolm X, Rosa Parks and Medgar Evers, to name a few, Obama began stepping into footsteps divinely created for this moment in time, his moment in time. The inspiration of such pioneers not only paved the way for his journey but also inspire him to inspire others.

"Dr. King inspired with words, not of anger, but of urgency. A fierce urgency that still speaks to us today," states President Obama. "Unity is the great need of the hour."

mother went on to marry Lolo Soetoro, another East-West Center student from Indonesia. After moving to Jakarta, the family welcomed little sister Maya Soetoro Ng.

At the age of 10 Obama returned to Hawaii to live with his maternal grandparents, Madelyn and Stanley Dunham, and later his mother who died of ovarian cancer in 1995. Enrolled in the esteemed Punahou Academy, this move became the shift that would bring the consciousness of racism to the forefront in his life, showing him the impact of what it means to be African American.

Barack Hussein Obama Jr. began his life journey August 4, 1961 in Honolulu, Hawaii, born to parents Barack Obama Sr. and Ann Dunham. Born into a multiracial family, a father of Luo ethnicity in Nyanza Province, Kenya, and a mother who grew up in Wichita, Kansas, he learned from birth the impact of love and true meaning of family. This lesson would not only impact who he was, but would enable him to walk with understanding and embrace who he was to become.

At the age of 4 his parents divorced and his father went to Harvard to pursue Ph.D. studies and then returned to Kenya. His

After high school, he studied at Occidental College in Los Angeles for two years, transferring to Columbia University in New York, where he graduated in 1993 with a degree in political science. Upon graduation he worked for Business International Corporation before moving to Chicago in 1985. There, he worked as a community organizer with low-income

residents in Chicago's Roseland community and the Altgeld Gardens public housing development on the South Side.

Just beginning the journey that would equip him to become the leader of "change," Obama entered Harvard Law School in 1988 where he would become the first African-American editor of the *Harvard Law Review*. After graduating, magna cum laude, in 1991, he returned to Chicago to practice as a civil rights lawyer, joining the firm of Miner, Barnhill & Galland. His organizational skills and the impact of his genuine concern for the community were already being felt nationwide. He had been a community organizer in Harlem, a full-time community organizer with faith-based group Developing Communities Projects and helped organize voter registration drives during Bill Clinton's 1992 presidential campaign.

While professionally, his love for community had him headed in the right direction, it would be his love for a certain young lady that would complete what he needed to go full steam ahead. Starting their history in Chicago, Michelle was assigned as an advisor to the summer intern, Barack Obama. After two years of dating, he proposed in a most memorable manner. "We were at a restaurant having dinner to celebrate the fact that he had finished the bar," Michelle remembers. "Then the waiter came over with the dessert and a tray. And there was the ring. And I was completely shocked."

On October 18, 1992, Obama and Michelle Lavaughn Robinson became what would later be called the "power couple in the

White Hou Sharing a love community family, they bega journey that wo not only inspir nation, but wo impact a world.

Empowered educated in her own right, Michelle's succ much like that of her husband, was evident fr the beginning. Her natural gift allowed her skip the second grade, pushing her forwarc an accelerated rate. While in the sixth grade, was chosen for the "gifted student" progr This program opened the door for her to t advanced biology and French classes at Kenne King Community College. Based on her acade excellence, she was given the opportunity to attend the first "magnet" high school in Chicago. This institution afforded students a greater depth and breadth of study with a focus on college preparedness. Here she was enrolled in advanced placement classes and was invited to join the National Honor Society. She also served as Student Council treasurer. From there Michelle attended Princeton University, where she received a bachelor's degree in Sociology with a minor degree in African-American studies. She worked with the Third World Center and belonged to the Organization of Black Unity, an African-American student group. She also graduated cum laude from this institution.

Continuing her educational career, Michelle went on to attend Harvard Law School, obtaining a juris doctorate degree. While in attendance, she joined the Black Law Students Association. This organization would help to enhance her speaking skills while addressing

legal issues and career guidance.

Transitioning from her educational path to her professional destiny, Michelle continued to make strides that would place her in positions of influence, allowing her to implement change. She would hold such positions as executive director for the Chicago office of Public Allies, associate dean of student services for The University of Chicago, executive director of community relations at The University of Chicago Hospitals and vice president of community relations and external affairs at The University of Chicago Medical Center. She also manages the business diversity program and sits on six boards, including the prestigious Chicago Council on Global Affairs and The University of Chicago Laboratory Schools.

In 1996 Obama was elected to his first to two terms in the Illinois State Senate and the world began to stand up and take notice. The senator from Illinois elected from the South Side neighborhood of Hyde Park would break traditional political guidelines, working with both Democrats and Republicans in drafting legislation on ethics, expanding health care services and early childhood education programs for the poor. He also created an earned-income tax credit for the working poor, magnifying his concern for the welfare of all people. After a number of inmates on death row were found innocent, he worked with law enforcement officials to require the videotaping of interrogations and confessions in all capital cases.

During his terms in office, it became very evident that Obama's commitment to the people of Illinois was heartfelt and true. His hands on approach to changing lives was seen and felt throughout the state. While the state of Illinois understood the impact of his influence, it would be his 2004 keynote address at the Democratic National Convention that would mark him as the man for change.

"I stand here today, grateful for the diversity of my heritage, aware that my parents' dreams live on in my precious daughters. I stand here knowing that my story is part of the larger American story, that I owe a debt to all of those who came before me, and that, in no other country on earth, is my story even possible. Tonight, we gather to affirm the greatness of our nation, not because of the height of our skyscrapers, or the power of our military, or the size of our economy. Our pride is based on a very simple premise, summed up in a declaration made over 200 years ago, 'We hold these truths to he self-evident, that all men are created equal. That they are endowed by their Creator with certain inalienable rights. That among these are life, liberty and the pursuit of happiness."

In 2007 he entered the race for the White House, facing critics who labeled him as unqualified, too young and simply not ready. But as Dr. King spoke to the heart of the people, for the people, as did Obama. With a personal touch, motivating speeches, inspirational commercials and "cool" debates, he has broken the stereotype connected to Black America, paving the way for the next generation to succeed. With chants of "Yes We Can!" and campaigns labeled "Get out the Vote,"

the world witnessed one of the most historic and inspiring events of our time. No longer simply an election, this moment in time slowly became a movement that would hear to the heart of the people and respond to the cry for change. "Things are changing, changing and changing. And I look for more change because this is something to be proud of," says Ann Nixon Cooper, 106.

As the 44th first family took their place it became evident that there are many dimensions to the man who holds the office of president. He possesses a strength that goes deeper than his educational or political background, but draws from the core of who he is.

As an affectionate husband and father, he openly displays his love for his wife and daughters, Malia and Sasha, and mother-in-law Marian Robinson. With genuine smiles of affection, family walks/runs in the garden with new family member Bo (the Portuguese water dog, his campaign promise to daughters), loving embraces and even the giving of his jacket for the warmth of Michelle, the world is seeing the true root of his success.

A family man, committed community activist, a man of faith with a true heart for the people and the man for change, he is our president, Barack Hussein Obama Jr.

Photos provided by: Monica Morgan, C. Sunny Martin

One day this nation will rise up and live out the true meaning of its creed. We hold this truth to be self evident that all men are created equal."- *Dr. Martin Luther King, Jr.*

A Sigma

Φ B Σ

**ESTABLISHED 1914
HOWARD UNIVERSITY
WASHINGTON, DC**

SIGMA MEN

for 95 years have provided

leadership worldwide and

we are proud to be a sponsor of

the Inaugural Edition of

Who's Who In Black

Washington, DC Metro Area.

We too Celebrate

African-American Achievement.

CORPORATE OFFICE
145 Kennedy Street, NW · Washington, DC 20011
202-726-5434 · www.pbs1914.org

FROM TOP: JAMES WELDON JOHNSON, A. PHILIP RANDOLPH, KWAMI NKRUMAH (Former President of Ghana, ROD PAIGE, CONGRESSMAN JOHN LEWIS, EMMITT SMITH, BLAIR UNDERWOOD, LES BROWN.

LaSans Ridgely wanted a career that made a difference. She didn't have to look far for inspiration.

CHOOSING A CAREER

When faced with big decisions, you turn to those you trust most for guidance

When it came time for LaSans Ridgely to choose a new career, she turned to someone she, and many others, have trusted for guidance — her father, New York Life agent Gil Ridgely.

"I wanted a stable career that would recognize my ability to excel, and one that would compensate me well for my hard work. I also wanted to educate and help people," she says. "While talking to my father about my goals, he suggested I consider becoming a New York Life agent, too."

"When I thought about it, he'd always been happy and excited about his career as a New York Life agent," LaSans recalls. "He worked with clients he wanted to work with, set his own schedule, and was well compensated. I liked the idea of being able to control my career in the same way — of being my own boss."

Making a Difference

An agent now for three years, LaSans has never regretted her decision to follow in her father's footsteps. "I'm making a real

difference in people's lives — helping them prepare for the retirement of their dreams, ensure their family's financial security, and create wealth to be passed to their children," she says. Gil and LaSans specialize in selling a variety of life insurance and retirement planning products from New York Life to employees of schools in predominantly African American communities.

A Career that Offers Balance and Stability

LaSans considers a career with New York Life ideal for young women. "It's a great opportunity to build your own business, set your own schedule, and have unlimited income potential," says LaSans. She adds, "And still have time for a family."

Millions of people have turned to a New York Life agent when faced with decisions impacting their financial security. Why? "It's a strong company that's been in business for more than 160 years," LaSans explains. "Everybody knows New York Life Insurance Company. It's The Company You Keep!"

WANT A CAREER THAT MAKES A DIFFERENCE?

To learn more about a career as a New York Life agent, please call 1-800-440-9414 or visit www.newyorklife.com/whoswho EOE M/F/V/D

New York Life Insurance Company, 51 Madison Avenue, New York, NY 10010

The Company You Keep®

Thank you 4 your Support :,)

1000 Books for 1000 Kids

Individuals

Cythia Miller
Bernard L Jackson
Earl W Stafford
Mark C Gaston
Charles G Young
Pastor Tim L Seay
Sinclair Harris
Julie S. Doar-Sinkfield
Donnie Simpson
Marco W McMillian
John Glover
Vercilla Brown

Organizations

The William E. Doar, Jr. Public Charter School for the Performing Arts
ODNI
US Navy
Crossover Church
Grady Young Foundation, Inc
The Wentworth Group, LLC
National Naval Association
Mark Gaston Consulting , LLC
Staff of WPGC Radio-95.5 FM
Phi Beta Sigma Fraternity

"Young people should embrace their youth and involve themselves in opportunities to expand their horizons." –Millicent D. Williams, President & CEO, DC Children and Youth Investment Trust.

Visit Us at
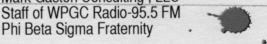
www.whoswhopublishing.com

A Real Times Media Company

"Dr. Height is a true legend, a tireless advocate for equality and justice."

-First Lady Michelle Obama

A TRIBUTE TO

Dr. Dorothy Irene Height

President Emerita
National Council of Negro Women

By Janis D. Hazel

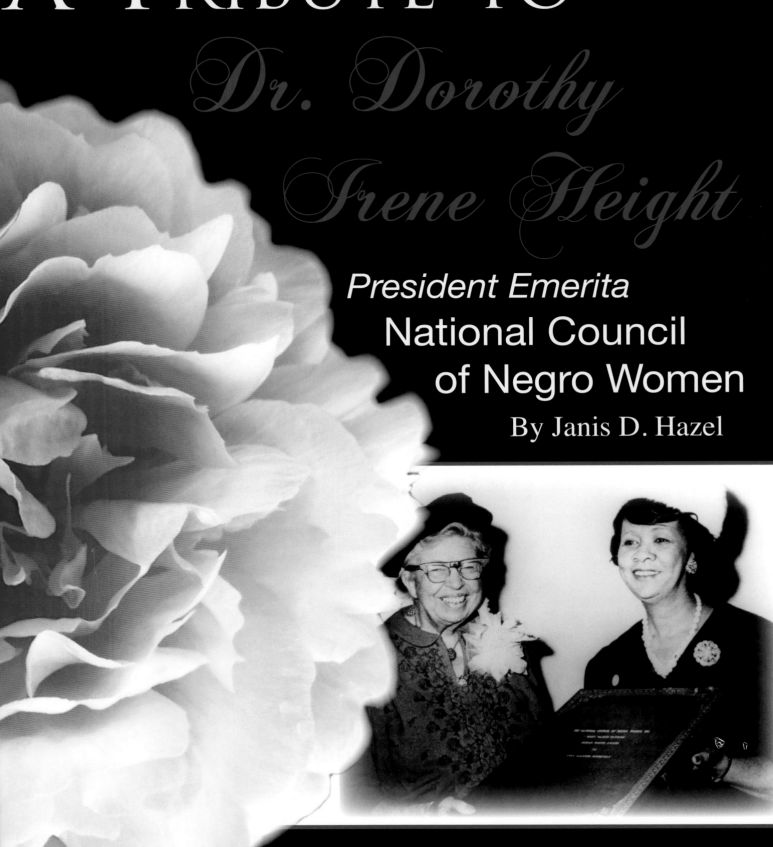

When we think of Dr. Dorothy Height, countless words come to mind: mother, visionary, hero, indefatigable, an indomitable spirit and the list goes on. But the single word she most associates with herself is "service." She has dedicated her life's work to be of service to others.

Born in Richmond, Virginia, in 1912 and raised in Rankin, Pennsylvania, she experienced racism firsthand as a child and later when she tried to enter New York's Barnard College. Although she had been accepted, they could not admit her due to a two-Negro-per-year quota policy, which was already filled. Undaunted, she went on to matriculate at New York University and came of age in the midst of the Harlem Renaissance. She was active with the Harlem Youth Council and organized the United Youth Committee Against Lynching. It was there that she met a young lawyer from the NAACP named Thurgood Marshall (who later became the first black Supreme Court justice of the United States). Marshall would meet with the Youth Council whenever he returned from a visit to the segregated South to discuss the anti-lynching work he was championing.

Height's career spans more than seven decades. Beginning as a civil rights advocate in the 1930s, she soon gained prominence through her tireless efforts to promote integration in education, to register and educate voters, and to increase the visibility and status of women in our society.

Height served as president of the National Council of Negro Women (NCNW) from 1957 to 1997 following in the footsteps of her mentor, Mary McLeod Bethune. In that capacity, she became a trusted advisor to U.S. presidents and civil rights leaders working to knock down barriers of both racism and sexism. NCNW, founded by Mary McLeod Bethune in 1935, is the umbrella organization for 250 local affiliates and 39 national groups engaged in economic development and other issues of special concern to women. NCNW has an outreach to more than 4 million women worldwide. Height has also been at the forefront of AIDS education, both nationally and internationally, and under her direction, NCNW opened offices in West Africa and South Africa, and has worked to improve the conditions of women throughout Africa and the world.

She was the only female member of the male dominated "Big Six" civil rights leaders, which included Whitney Young, A. Philip Randolph, the Reverend Dr. Martin Luther King Jr., James Farmer and Roy Wilkins. When the men sat down at the table, Height was with them developing strategies for the civil rights movement. She was a trusted consultant to First Lady Eleanor Roosevelt on human and civil rights issues and she successfully lobbied President Eisenhower to desegregate the nation's schools, and President Johnson to appoint black women to sub-Cabinet level positions.

Height has also been key to the success of other influential women's organizations, chiefly Delta Sigma Theta Sorority, Inc. and the Young Women's Christian

Association (YWCA). Her work with the YWCA led to its integration and more active participation in the civil rights movement. Height served as Delta Sigma Theta's tenth national president during a period of unparalleled growth in the organization's history. During her tenure (1947-56), the sorority purchased its national headquarters building, located in Washington, D.C., and hired its first executive director. Cynthia Butler-McIntyre, Delta's national president proudly declares, "I am grateful for the visionary leadership and committed service examples set by Dr. Dorothy I. Height. I was blessed with the honor of being installed into office as the 24th national president of Delta Sigma Theta by Dr. Height, so I am extremely honored to have the opportunity to continue her legacy and to expand it. Her contributions to humankind are known globally."

Working tirelessly for children and families living in poverty, Height is responsible for many of the advances made by women and black Americans throughout the 20th century and into the 21st century. Congresswoman Diane Watson (D-CA) proudly states, "Dr. Height epitomizes the woman of global stature who is a leader in the right place and time. Her grace, wisdom and leadership are examples for young woman all over the world. Her impact on the lives of women and families will be remembered for generations to come."

Another benchmark in Height's career was the 1986 launch of the Black Family Reunion. Height recalls that she conceptualized the reunion in response to the negative publicity regarding the vanishing black family. To counter it, she developed an idea for a positive, culturally-based event that would celebrate the enduring strengths and traditional values of the black family. She structured the event to be a connecting point for government agencies, corporations, community-based organizations and families of all ethnicities to come together to work on solutions to issues affecting families. The three-day festival held in Washington has become the most significant family event in the nation, attracting 500,000 people annually.

She has received countless awards for her efforts, including the Franklin Delano Roosevelt Freedom Medal, the Citizens Medal Award from President Ronald Reagan in 1989 and the Presidential Medal of Freedom presented by President William Jefferson Clinton in 1994. Topping the list of awards is the Congressional Gold Medal presented on her 92nd birthday in 2004 by President George W. Bush. The medal is inscribed with a quotation of hers that captures her spirit of service that simply states: "We African-American women seldom do just what we want to do, but always do what we have to do. I am grateful to have been in a time and place where I could be part of what was needed." The Congressional Gold Medal is the nation's highest civilian award given by Congress as an expression of national appreciation for distinguished

achievements and contributions. On that momentous occasion, Secretary of State Hillary Rodham Clinton (then senator from New York) said, "We are here today to honor a truly great American, someone who has long been an inspiration of mine." Secretary Clinton went on to say, "I have had few greater pleasures than the work I did on this resolution – going to my colleagues one-by-one to ask them to support this resolution and no one said 'no.'"

Height, still actively fighting for justice for all Americans at the age of 97, is recognized as one of the preeminent social and civil rights activists of our time, particularly in the struggle for equality, social justice and human rights for all people. Former Washington, D.C., Mayor Sharon Pratt shares, "Dorothy Height is a configuration of extraordinary intellect, determination, authority and grace. Her presence, especially her continuing presence, has been a gift to us all."

In 2003 Height penned her memoir, *Open Wide the Freedom Gates*, consisting of reflections on her life of service and leadership. It is a book to curl up with and take a journey through the eyes of a person who witnessed every significant struggle for racial equality in the 20th century. Cathy Hughes, founder of Radio One, TV One and 2006 recipient of the NCNW Uncommon Height award refers to Height as, "One of the most incredible human beings of our times...a true leader in the most serious definition... compassionate, warm, loving and brilliant. She is everyone's choice as our Queen Mother."

She has inspired legions of people to reach heights they never dreamed possible. One of those people is Alexis Herman, former U.S. Secretary of Labor (appointed by President Clinton). Herman was the first African American appointed to that post. She has considered Height as her mentor all of her adult life. "Dr. Height is both a doer and a dreamer. She has always expressed to me the importance of doing whatever has to be done to make a difference and a contribution," Herman reflects. "She is the epitome of what it means to serve."

When Height was asked what she would recommend to young people to help them be successful, she responded: "1) Get your education to be prepared; 2) Volunteer because you must learn how to be of service; 3) Learn your history so you know what the struggle has been; and 4) Find a goal and purpose for your life and don't let anyone deter you."

Even the acquisition of the current NCNW headquarters is a testament to the dedicated efforts of Height, and her continuance of a dream envisioned by the organization's founder. Mary McLeod Bethune told Height that she wanted black women to have a strong presence in the nation's capital, where materials pertaining to the history of black American women would be preserved. Bethune told Dr. Height how she initially found a beautiful, spacious stone building for sale on Dupont Circle, owned by Cissy Patterson, publisher of the *Washington Times-Herald*. Patterson learned that Negroes wanted to purchase her property and reacted by taking it off the market and then stated publicly, that "Negroes would never be on Dupont Circle." Bethune eventually found 1318 Vermont Avenue, and in 1943 received authorization from the NCNW board of directors to purchase it for $15,500. With a generous contribution of $10,000 from Chicago philanthropist Marshall Field, Height called upon women across the country to raise the additional $5,500. Through a series of bake sales, teas, fashion shows and dinners hosted by NCNW members, the organization raised the additional $5,500 to make the purchase. Built in 1874, the property became Bethune's private residence, the

first headquarters for NCNW, and later, The Bethune Museum and Archives. In 1991 it became a unit of the National Park Service, which maintains it for the public interest. The government paid $632,000 to acquire the property and the proceeds were used to launch the Fund for the Future aimed at acquiring a headquarters building.

Height often reflected on the racial injustices that went into purchasing property in certain areas of the nation's capital, injustices that continued into the 1990s when white bankers she approached to finance the current NCNW headquarters told her to "forget it and look for properties that were not on a main street, because NCNW didn't need to be on a main street." For six decades, she held the injustices in the back of her mind and set out to find a site that would be a complex to house a repository of black women's history and serve as the nerve center for the exchange of ideas and civic action. She found the grand, elegant building at 633 Pennsylvania Avenue, NW in 1994. Located midway between the White House and the Capitol on the corridor of U.S. power, Height affirms, "it is a strong presence for black women," harkening back to Bethune's dream. The property has added historic significance because it stands on the corner of the site of Washington's Center Slave Market, where enslaved men, women and children were bought and sold.

With an initial asking price of $20 million, negotiated down to $8 million in 1995 by a team of black U.S. automotive executives, this time the funds for the purchase of NCNW's headquarters were raised after Height summoned corporate black women and men across the country. The financing deal for the property was led by black vice presidents of Ford Motor Company, Chrysler and General Motors in what Height calls "a sterling example of corporate citizenship and partnership." The lead negotiator was Floyd Washington of Ford. Height explained to him the controversies and financial support that was threatened to be pulled from the NCNW Fund for the Future by her white and Jewish supporters when she decided to participate in the Million Man March. Height was a featured speaker at the historic 1995 event that brought one million black fathers and sons, brothers and uncles to the nation's Capitol for day of atonement.

Washington simply told her, "Dr. Height, you were there for us at the Million Man March, and so we decided to be there for you." In 2002 Oprah Winfrey donated $2.5 million to close the gap in the funds raised to retire the mortgage. NCNW's headquarters is the only property owned by a black American organization on the "corridor of power."

Oprah Winfrey, recipient of the 2009 NCNW Uncommon Height award and a longtime supporter of NCNW, credits her ascendance to the top of her field to Height's efforts to pave a way for her to enter the upper echelons of the business world. "I grew up understanding that Dorothy Height, Mary McLeod Bethune, Barbara Jordan, Fannie Lou Hamer, and so many other African-American women were a part of me and a bridge to where I was trying to get to, they were a bridge to this possibility of now that I live," Winfrey boasts. "I have carried Dr. Height and all of them in my heart. They were there for me to see and I have never forgotten that is where I come from and that is who I am."

Michelle Obama, first lady of the United States shares, "Dr. Height is a true legend, a tireless advocate for equality and justice. Always willing to stand up for what is right, even if it means standing alone. She exemplifies the best of the American spirit, displaying an uncommon combination of grace and dignity, tenacity and strength."

Thank you Dr. Height for being in a time and place where you were a part of what was needed and for doing that part selflessly with intelligence, grace, influence, passion and tenacity.

Photo Credits:

1. Dr. Height in her pink suit on her birthday, March 24, 2009. Courtesy NCNW Library.

2. First Lady Eleanor Roosevelt & Dr. Height. Courtesy Franklin D. Roosevelt Library.

3. Platform of March on Washington Dr. Height watches Martin Luther King, Jr. deliver "I Have a Dream" speech (1963).

4. President Barack Obama (then Illinois Senator) at Dr. Height's book signing (2005).

5. President Ronald Reagan presents Dr. Height the Citizens Medal Award (1989). Courtesy of the White House.

6. President George W. Bush at NCNW meeting with Dr. Height at the White House. Courtesy of the White House.

7. Dr. Height and Oprah Winfrey June, 4, 2009, Washington, D.C., at Uncommon Height Gala.

8. Dorothy Height surrounded by children at Black Family Reunion (1993). Courtesy of Betty Kleckley Stradford.

9. Dr. Height in her mink coat. Courtesy of Betty Kleckley Stradford.

10. Dr. Height, Betty Shabazz and Coretta Scott King. Courtesy of NCNW Library.

11. Secretary of State Condoleezza Rice, President William Clinton, President George W. Bush, Hillary Rodham Clinton and Dr. Height.

12. Dorothy Height and Mary McLeod Bethune (1942). Courtesy of Bethune Council House Museum, National Park Service.

13. Vernon Jordan, First Lady Rosalind Carter, Dr. Height, President Carter, Coretta Scott King. Courtesy of the White House.

14. Roy Wilkins (NAACP), Floyd McKissick (Congress of Racial Equality), Dr. Height, A. Philip Randolph (Brotherhood of Sleeping Car Porters), Whitney Young (National Urban League), Dr. Martin Luther King, Jr. (Southern Christian Leadership Conference). Courtesy of NAACP.

15. President Ronald Reagan hosts reception to honor NCNW's 50th Anniversary (Dr. Height behind Reagan) (1985) Courtesy of the White House.

16. Dr. Height & President Johnson in the Oval Office. Courtesy of the White House.

17. Dr. Height watches President Kennedy sign the Equal Pay Act (1963). Courtesy of the White House.

Sources:

1. Former D.C. Mayor Sharon Pratt – interview June 22, 2009, Washington, D.C.

2. Oprah Winfrey, June, 4, 2009, Washington, D.C., at Uncommon Height Gala.

3. Michelle Obama, First Lady – June, 4, 2009, Washington, D.C., at Uncommon Height Gala.

4. Dorothy Height, president emerita of NCNW – interview June, 10, 2009, Washington, D.C.

5. Alexis Herman, U.S. Secretary of Labor (1997-2001) – interview June, 22, 2009.

6. Congresswoman Diane Watson (D-CA) – interview June, 12, 2009, Washington, D.C.

7. Cathy Hughes, founder of Radio One/TV One — interview June, 23, 2009, Washington, D.C.

8. Cynthia Butler-McIntyre, national president of Delta Sigma Theta Sorority, Inc. interview June 12, 2009, Washington, D.C.

9. Secretary of State Hillary Rodham Clinton (then Senator D-NY) quotes extracted from her March 24, 2004, remarks upon the presentation of the Congressional Gold Medal to Dr. Height.

10. www.ncnw.org

11. *Open Wide the Freedom Gates: A Memoir by Dorothy Height* (2003).

12. Various NCNW staff interviews, June 2009.

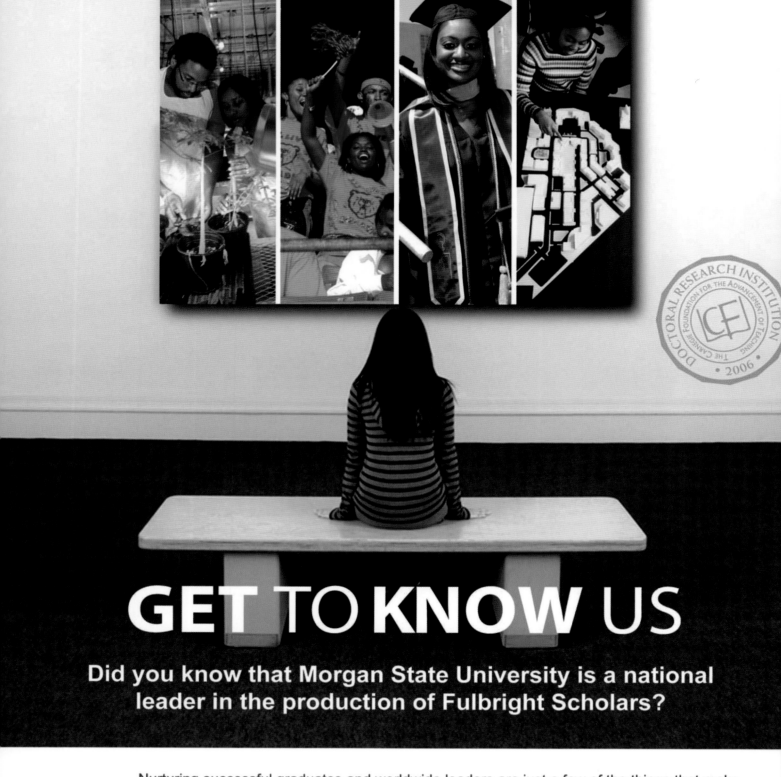

GET TO KNOW US

Did you know that Morgan State University is a national leader in the production of Fulbright Scholars?

Nurturing successful graduates and worldwide leaders are just a few of the things that make the Morgan *Experience* special. Our unwavering commitment to academics, excellence and a diverse culture allows us to make the dream of a better life an achievable reality for many.

With more than 75 undergraduate, master's degree and doctoral programs at your fingertips, you can create your very own successful experience.

Take some time and get to know Morgan State University. When you do, you'll discover so much more.

ΔΣΘ
Delta Sigma Theta

10th National President
Dorothy I. Height

Cynthia M. A. Butler-McIntyre
24th National President
Delta Sigma Theta Sorority, Inc.
2008 ~ Present

To serve as the 24th National President of Delta Sigma Theta Sorority, a global sisterhood approaching its centennial year of phenomenal achievements, is an exhilarating experience. Since 1913, Delta has been transforming lives and impacting communities – making a tremendous difference in the lives of countless people across the nation and around the globe. Songsters such as Dinah Washington and Esther Phillips sang about what a difference a day makes, 24 little hours. Just imagine what a difference a century has made – 36,525 days, 876,600 hours – not only in Delta Sigma Theta, but also in the lives of countless people who have been empowered by this organization. We have much to celebrate as we move toward 2013.

We celebrate our growth. The Delta membership has grown from 22 visionary young women to more than 250,000 initiated members, and has included a U.S. Presidential candidate, a Surgeon General, Cabinet Members, a U.S. Senator, Congresswomen, Ambassadors, an astronaut and Olympic gold medalists. Delta women consistently break new ground and have excelled in all professions: education, science, technology, law, theater, government, sports, arts and humanities.

We celebrate our effective service programs. Both individually and collectively, Delta women are recognized for the exceptional public service we render. Through the Sorority's Five Point Programmatic Thrust: *Educational Development, Economic Development, Physical and Mental Health, Political Awareness and Involvement, and International Awareness and Involvement*, we have educated, enriched and empowered individuals, families and communities.

Yes, a day and a century of days have made a difference. Although our nation is experiencing incredible economic tumult as financial institutions sink, unemployment soars and families struggle to survive, at the same time we are witnessing tremendous political triumphs and long worked-for change. We have elected the first African-American President, Barack Obama, a brilliant, honorable man with an appreciation for the dignity and worth of all human beings. His clarion call for change is reminiscent of the call for change our Founders answered when they marched for suffrage in 1913, less than two months after the Sorority's founding.

And so I feel both humbled and honored to lead Delta into its second century, validating daily the positive difference a day makes that is embraced by ***Delta Sigma Theta: A Sisterhood Called to Serve: Transforming Lives, Impacting Communities.***

Profiles in Delta Leadership
A Memorial to Past National Presidents

Sadie T.M. Alexander
1st National President
1919-1923

Dorothy Pelham Beckley
2nd National President
1923-1926

Ethel LaMay Calimese
3rd National President
1926-1929

Anna Johnson Julian
4th National President
1929-1931

Gladys Byram Shepperd
5th National Presidnt
1931-1933

Jeanette Triplett Jones
6th National President
1933-1935

Vivan Osborne Marsh
7th National President
1935-1939

Elsie Austin
8th National President
1939-1944

Mae W.D.P. Williams
9th National Preident
1944-1941

Jeanne L. Noble
12th National President
1958-1963

Geraldine P. Woods
13th National President
1963-1967

Lillian Pierce Benbow
15th National President
1971-1975

Dr. Dorothy Irene Height

10th National President
Delta Sigma Theta Sorority, Inc.
1947-1956

D r. Dorothy I. Height served ten years as national president during a period of enormous growth in the history of Delta Sigma Theta Sorority, Inc. The Sorority purchased a national headquarters building, streamlined and modernized its administrative structure and hired its first executive director. Additionally, the Sorority conceived and implemented the Delta Five Point project related to library service, job opportunities, community service, the international project and mental health.

Height encouraged the Sorority to work diligently for improved public housing, an impartial criminal justice system, better access to public accommodations, an adequate minimum wage, and the establishment of child labor laws as part of Delta's public service mission.

In 1965 Height received Delta's most prestigious honor, The Mary Church Terrell Award. She has received hundreds of other awards, including the Medal of Freedom presented by President Bill Clinton and the Congressional Gold Medal presented by President George W. Bush. Her memoir, *Open Wide the Freedom Gates*, was published in 2003.

Born in Richmond, Virginia, Height grew up in New York. She earned a Master of Arts degree in psychology from New York University.

Dorothy Penman Harrison

11th National President
Delta Sigma Theta Sorority, Inc.
1956-1958

H ighlights of Dorothy Harrison's administration include the burning of the mortgage on the first national headquarters building in 1957, the first publication of *The Delta Newsletter*, and the first Delta Christmas Party, a yearly event established to help relieve pain, oppression or need through the combined "gifts" from the chapters.

Currently in her 90s and still active in the community, Harrison was born in Portsmouth, Ohio. She earned a Bachelor of Arts degree in education from The Ohio State University, a Master of Science degree in education from Oklahoma State University, and was awarded an honorary doctorate degree from Langston University in 2003. She married educator Dr. Gerald Lamar Harrison who became president of Langston University. Their son, Gerald Lamar, passed away at age 13 in 1948, followed by the younger son, Richard, in 1950.

Harrison has traveled extensively to Europe, Africa, Asia, South America and the Caribbean. After spending 20 years at Langston University, the Harrisons relocated to Chicago where she continued her public service on the community and national levels, including being selected as co-chair of the federal Head Start program.

The Honorable Frankie Muse Freeman's administration focused on the elimination of discrimination based on race and sex and on fighting poverty, an unrelenting oppressor of black people. The Sorority supported programs designed to assist record-breaking numbers of black youth attend college. An American civil rights attorney, Freeman was appointed to the U.S. Commission on Civil Rights by President Lyndon Johnson. The first black female civil rights commissioner, she was subsequently re-appointed by presidents Richard Nixon, Gerald Ford and Jimmy Carter. She became inspector general for the Community Services Administration during Jimmy Carter's Administration in 1979.

Born in Danville, Virginia, Freeman attended the Hampton Institute and received a law degree from Howard University Law School in 1947. Inducted into the National Bar Association's Hall of Fame, she still practices law in St. Louis. She was elected trustee emeritus of the Howard University board of trustees following 16 years as a member of the board. She and her late husband, Shelby, had one daughter, Shelbe. Her published memoir is entitled *A Song of Faith and Hope: The Life of Frankie Muse Freeman.*

The Honorable Frankie Muse Freeman

14th National President
Delta Sigma Theta Sorority, Inc.
1967-1971

Under Dr. Thelma Daley's administration, Delta Sigma Theta Sorority's commitment to educational excellence was a major focus. The distinguished professor endowed chair was established to support quality instruction at Historically Black Colleges and Universities, which was especially significant because black colleges had suffered tremendously due to economic depression, withdrawal of federal support and shifting enrollment patterns. Another legacy of her presidency is the sculpture, *Fortitude*, on Howard University's campus.

Daley served as president of the American School Counselor Association, and was the first woman and first black person elected president of the American Counseling Association. By presidential appointment, she became the first woman to chair the National Advisory Council on Career Education. As the national director of the Women In the NAACP, she works to promote knowledge of sudden infant death syndrome and AIDS prevention within the African-American community.

A native of Annapolis, Maryland, Daley earned a Bachelor of Science degree from Bowie State University, a Master of Arts degree in counseling and personnel administration from New York University, and a Doctor of Education degree in counseling from The George Washington University.

Thelma Thomas Daley, Ed.D.

16th National President
Delta Sigma Theta Sorority, Inc.
1975-1979

Mona Humphries Bailey

17th National President
Delta Sigma Theta Sorority, Inc.
1979-1983

Under Mona Bailey's administration, Delta Sigma Theta Sorority focused on helping black youth and black women. The Sorority sponsored two conferences, Educating Black Youth for Survival and Advancement in the 80s and The Black Women's Summit, which addressed problems facing American women.

Delta participated in the First Annual March and Rally for Black Colleges Day; the gathering of the 1980 Census; the Operation Big Vote for the 1980 fall election; the White House Conference on Families; the Youth March for Jobs; efforts to establish a national holiday honoring Dr. Martin Luther King, Jr. and to alert mothers on infant formula controversy and toxic shock syndrome; and established an ongoing relationship with the Children's Defense Fund.

A senior associate with the Center for Educational Renewal at the University of Washington and the Institute for Educational Inquiry in Seattle, Bailey was born in Apalachicola, Florida. She received a Bachelor of Science degree in chemistry from Florida A&M University and a Master of Science degree in science education from Oregon State University. She and her husband, William, are the parents of Peter and Christopher Bailey.

Hortense Golden Canady

18th National President
Delta Sigma Theta Sorority, Inc.
1983-1988

Under Hortense Canady's administration, Delta Sigma Theta Sorority, Inc. focused on participating in national affairs. The Sorority's African Diaspora to study the dispersal of people from the African continent was established. A delegation of Deltas at the invitation of the official government of the Republic of China also traveled to Taipei, Taiwan, on a Goodwill tour.

Delta participated in the Global Aspects of Single Female Heads of Households seminar during the NGO Forum of the United Nation's International Decade for Women in Nairobi, Kenya. Additionally, Summit II: A Call to Action in Support of Black Single Mothers, Heads of Households was held in 30 cities where Delta chapters, government and private agency participants formulated recommendations to address the problems of single parenting. Noted author Paula Giddings was commissioned to write Delta's history, *In Search of Sisterhood*.

Canady earned a Bachelor of Arts degree from Fisk University and a Master of Arts degree from Michigan State University. Residents of Lansing, Michigan, she and her husband, Dr. Clinton Canady Jr., are the parents of three sons, all attorneys, and a daughter, a noted pediatric neurosurgeon.

During the Honorable Yvonne Kennedy's administration, much needed enhancements of the physical plant and office operations of the National Headquarters were made. A National Capital Improvement Fund was established for the renovation expense and the dedication of the newly renovated national headquarters was held on the 78th anniversary date of the Sorority founding. Reclamation was also emphasized, encouraging every Delta to become financial and active.

Delta launched School America to help children learn to read because illiteracy is a critical problem facing youth and produced a public service announcement in conjunction with "Just Say 'NO' to Drugs," which featured Delta member Natalie Cole. Delta's Commission on Arts and Letters re-issued *Roses and Revolutions* as a cassette in the 20th year since it was produced as a record album.

A native of Mobile, Alabama, Kennedy earned a Bachelor of Science degree from Alabama State University, a Master of Arts degree from Morgan State University, and a Doctor of Philosophy degree from The University of Alabama. Past president of the S.D. Bishop State Junior College, she is a representative for the Alabama House of Representatives.

The Honorable Yvonne Kennedy

19th National President
Delta Sigma Theta Sorority, Inc.
1988-1992

Under Bertha Roddey's administration, Delta Sigma Theta Sorority partnered with Habitat for Humanity to help eliminate poverty housing. As a tribute to the Sorority's 22 founders, Delta committed to building 22 solid and affordable homes, and the Delta Habitat Partnership extended to Africa when 30 volunteers traveled to Ghana and completed 40 houses, sponsored by the Sorority.

Delta participated in the Fourth World Conference on Women Non-Governmental Organizations Forum in Beijing and Huairou, China; conducted workshops during the Congressional Black Caucus Legislative Weekend; participated in the 75th Anniversary of Women's Suffrage celebration; and chartered a chapter in London, England, and Panama City, Panama. Project Cherish honored 83 Deltas for their exceptional contributions in civil rights, politics and governmental affairs with a sculpture by Elizabeth Catlett (one of the honorees).

Born in Seneca, South Carolina, Roddey earned a Bachelor of Arts degree from Johnson C. Smith University, a Master of Arts degree from The University of North Carolina – Greensboro, and a doctorate degree from the Union Graduate School in Cincinnati. Married to Theodore Roddey, she teaches African-American studies at the University of South Carolina.

Bertha M. Roddey

20th National President
Delta Sigma Theta Sorority, Inc.
1992-1996

The Honorable Marcia L. Fudge

21st National President
Delta Sigma Theta Sorority, Inc.
1996-2000

As national president, the Honorable Marcia Fudge increased the overall efficiency of the organization. The information system was upgraded, including a Delta homepage on the Internet. The Sorority became the first African-American organization to establish a perpetual archive to store, protect and catalog its history and artifacts, and registered and trademarked the crest and symbols commonly associated with Delta Sigma Theta Sorority. The Delta Research and Education Foundation and the Sorority launched its Research Center on African-American Women to study the diverse lifestyles of African-American women. Delta also convened Summit V: Health and Healing – Let it Begin Within to increase awareness of and to educate African-American communities about clinical depression and illness often mistaken as a personal weakness and shrouded in secrecy and shame.

A former mayor of Warrensville Heights, Ohio, Fudge was the first woman and first African-American elected. Currently, she is the Democratic congresswoman for Ohio's 11th District in the U.S. House of Representatives. Born in Cleveland, she received a Bachelor of Arts degree in business administration from The Ohio State University and a juris doctorate degree from Cleveland State University.

Gwendolyn E. Boyd

22nd National President
Delta Sigma Theta Sorority, Inc.
2000-2004

Gwendolyn E. Boyd utilized the latest communications technology in her administration. Highlights of her administration include launching Science and Everyday Experiences (SEE) to increase youth interest in science and mathematics; the Delta Homeownership partnership with GE Mortgage Insurance to increase homeownership by African Americans; presenting Howard University with a $1 million endowed scholarship (the first black Greek letter organization to endow a scholarship of this magnitude at any institution); publishing *Occasions to Savor*, the Delta stylebook; acquiring Non-Governmental Organization consultative status at the United Nations; establishing the General Electric-funded Leadership DELTA, a mentoring and leadership training program; taking a delegation to South Africa to conduct educational training workshops for teachers and principals; renovating Delta's national headquarters; and holding a National Day of Service to increase the awareness of HIV/AIDS.

Currently an engineer at The Johns Hopkins University, Boyd graduated, summa cum laude, from Alabama State University and was the first African American to earn a master's degree in mechanical engineering from the Yale University School of Engineering. She is a native of Montgomery, Alabama.

Dr. Louise Rice's administration, under the theme "One Mission, One Sisterhood: Empowering Communities through Committed Service," focused on providing effective programs in all areas of its national Five Point Programmatic Thrust. A health task force to develop a plan to reduce and prevent chronic diseases, which disproportionately affect African Americans, was established. The Sorority also held Summit VI: Health Issues that Impact Women of African Descent, in Montego Bay, Jamaica.

Additionally, Delta helped provide Hurricane Katrina relief assistance. More than $1.2 million was contributed to agencies, organizations and residents affected by the hurricane, including $700,000 collectively to three Historically Black Colleges and Universities: Dillard, Xavier and Southern universities. Delta also presented $1 million to the NAACP Legal Defense and Educational Fund in support of its exceptional work for civil rights.

A native of Augusta, Georgia, Rice earned a bachelor's degree from Tuskegee University, a Master of Arts degree from Columbia University, and a Doctor of Philosophy degree from The University of Georgia. She is the widow of Dr. Wilson L. Rice Sr. and the mother of two sons, Wilson Jr. and Christopher.

Louise A. Rice, Ph.D.

23rd National President
Delta Sigma Theta Sorority, Inc.
2004-2008

People Into Living

HIV Counseling and Testing

HIV Care Services

Workshops/ Weekend Retreats

Individual Counseling

Us Helping Us, People Into Living, Inc.
Specializing in HIV/AIDS
Prevention and Care services for
Black gay and bisexual men

Support/ Discussion Groups

3636 Georgia Avenue, N.W.
(@ Georgia Avenue - Petworth Metro)

202.446.1100

www.uhupil.org

Since 1985

UHU is a 501 (c) (3) organization funded by the D.C. HIV/AIDS Administration and the Centers for Disease Control and Prevention

GIVE YOUR BUSINESS
SOME SOUTHERN EXPOSURE.

MORE DESTINATIONS IN BRAZIL

NOW SERVING:

- Rio de Janeiro
- São Paulo
- Manaus
- Fortaleza
- Recife
- Brasília*

For the most destinations worldwide, visit delta.com today.

WASHINGTON, D.C.

LIVING LEGENDS

- WASHINGTON, D.C. LIVING LEGEND -

The Honorable Eleanor Holmes Norton

Congresswoman
U.S. House of Representatives, District of Columbia

Change is in the House

By Donald James

Congresswoman Eleanor Holmes Norton is one of the most revered members of the U.S. House of Representatives. Now in her ninth term, Norton represents the District of Columbia, which has limited status in Congress along with such U.S. territories as Puerto Rico, Guam, Northern Mariana Island, the U.S. Virgin Islands and American Samoa. This limited status allows Norton to serve on and vote with House committees, but prevents her from voting on final legislation.

Since taking office in 1991, however, the congresswoman has been on a mission to give the District of Columbia full voting status for the first time in about 200 years. In April of 2007, Norton introduced the House Voting Rights Act. Anticipation of passing the bill ran high, but is presently stymied by an amendment in the Senate to take D.C.'s government powers to regulate gun control laws. Undaunted, Norton continues to work with both House and Senate leaders, and is optimistic that the historic act will pass.

"Passage of the House Voting Rights Act is extremely important to me," says Norton. "For me it's personal, it's political and it's important to the people of the District of Columbia."

While it appears that Norton has limited power to help constituents in the District of Columbia, nothing could be further from the truth. Norton chairs the House Subcommittee on Economic Development, Emergency Management, and Public Buildings. She also serves on the Committee on Homeland Security; the Committee on Oversight and Government Reform; the Committee on Transportation and Infrastructure; and the Subcommittee on Information Policy, Census and National Archives. A reputable survey named her as one of the 100 most important women in America, while another called her one of D.C.'s most powerful women.

Norton's many victories for constituents in D.C. include the awarding of $10,000 per year to all Washington, D.C., high school graduates to attend any public college in America, and $2,500 for high school graduates who attend selected private colleges; the creation of the current $5,000 homebuyer tax credit that sharply increased home ownership in D.C.; and the creation of the significant business tax breaks for D.C. companies employing city residents.

Born and raised in Washington, D.C., Norton, a third generation Washingtonian, has always helped underserved people achieve social and economic status. After graduating from Antioch College with a bachelor's degree in history, Norton attended Yale University, where she earned a master's degree in American studies and a juris doctorate degree.

Perhaps a defining moment in shaping Norton's views on civil rights came in 1963 when she traveled to Mississippi to participate in the Mississippi Freedom Summer. She made the dangerous journey to help other freedom fighters register African Americans to vote. Norton also met civil rights legends Medgar Evers and Fannie Lou Hamer.

"Both Medgar Evers and Fannie Lou Hamer had a tremendous impact on how I viewed the civil rights movement," says Norton. "Fannie Lou Hamer became my lifelong mentor because I admired her courage and leadership."

Through the years, Norton has received dozens of awards and honors, including the Citation of Merit as Outstanding Alumna of Yale Law School. In addition to serving in the U.S. House of Representatives, this mother of two adult children is a tenured professor of law at Georgetown University.

Photo by: Donald L. Baker

The Honorable Rev. Walter E. Fauntroy

Retired U.S. Representative (D-D.C.)
Retired Pastor, New Bethel Baptist Church

Quiet Strength

By Misty Starks

To simply call the Honorable Reverend Walter E. Fauntroy an activist, preacher or politician does little justice to the man who is a strong thread in the fabric of the American civil rights movement. He has accepted as his mission in life the laborious task of setting at liberty those who are bound, physically and spiritually. Indeed, the very nature of Fauntroy's existence has been to help those who can't help themselves. Whether in his childhood neighborhood, the halls of Congress or the pews of his church, the power of this man's influence has resonated throughout the world.

Fauntroy grew up in a family of eight siblings in Northwest Washington, D.C., under the tutelage of his father and mother. He graduated from high school second in his class, and then went off to college at Virginia Union University, thanks to a community of caring adults, which included church members, neighbors and others who wanted to see him excel in life.

"I was at Virginia Union University because caring adults agreed to cook dinners every week and sell them to other caring adults in the neighborhood who wanted to get me out of what was called the 'wickedest precinct' in our nation's capital at that time and off to college," he recalls.

It was during Fauntroy's freshman year in 1951 when he met, by chance, Martin Luther King Jr. The two bonded over an all-night discussion of religion, government and the plight of black people.

Fauntroy says of King, "I was fascinated about his talk of how the nonviolent tactics of Mahatma Gandhi in India, when combined with the ethics of Jesus, could free our people from racial segregation and discrimination in America. Dr. King was impressed, in turn, with how much I knew about the workings of the federal government." The two became fast friends and kept in touch.

In 1959 Fauntroy became the pastor of New Bethel Baptist Church, a position he held for 50 years before retiring in 2009. He also served as King's personal representative to presidents John F. Kennedy and Lyndon B. Johnson, members of the U.S. House and Senate, and other government dignitaries and agencies. He became director of the Washington bureau of Dr. King's Southern Christian Leadership Conference, during which time he coordinated the historic March on Washington in 1963 and the Selma to Montgomery Voting Rights March in 1965.

In 1971 Fauntroy made history when he was elected the first delegate to serve the District of Columbia as a member of the U.S. House of Representatives. He held that post for the next 20 years, and became a founding member of the Congressional Black Caucus.

In recognition of his life's work as a humanitarian, Fauntroy received honorary Doctor of Laws degrees from Virginia Union University and Yale University. Although he is retired, he continues to work diligently on efforts to eliminate extreme poverty in Africa. He does this because he believes every person should have five fundamental elements in life: income, education, health care, housing and justice. Most of all, he is following in the footsteps of his Savior.

"I want to be more like Jesus every day. Jesus lived for the sake of others and I've learned to live for the sake of others," he shares.

He and his wife, Dorothy, have two children, Marvin and Melissa.

- WASHINGTON, D.C. LIVING LEGEND -

Marian Wright Edelman

Founder & President
Children's Defense Fund

An Advocate's Love for Children

By Karen Y. Perkins

Marian Wright Edelman was born June 6, 1939, in Bennettsville, South Carolina. The youngest of five children born to Maggie Leola Bowen Wright and Baptist minister Arthur Jerome Wright, Edelman was 14 years old when her father passed away after suffering a heart attack. His last words to her were, "Don't let anything get in the way of your education." These profound words provided direction and motivation for her during a time that was identified as the beginning of the civil rights movement.

In 1956 Edelman studied at Spelman College, where she won a Merrill scholarship to study abroad at the Sorbonne in Paris and the University of Geneva in Switzerland. She received a Lisle fellowship and traveled to Moscow prior to her senior year. After graduating from Spelman, she planned to pursue a career abroad, but became involved with the inequities faced by African Americans in the Deep South. These events inspired her to pursue a law degree from Yale Law School, which was to be her non-violent weapon of choice during the civil rights era.

After graduating from Yale Law School in 1963, Edelman traveled to New York and Mississippi to work with the NAACP Legal Defense Fund. She was the first African-American woman to practice law in Mississippi, and worked with the civil rights movement to outlaw racial discrimination, and restore freedom, respect and racial dignity to African Americans. When asked about her concerns during that turbulent time, she states, "Safety was always a concern during the civil rights movement, but it took a back seat to the thirst for justice."

Recalling events after the assassination of Dr. Martin Luther King, she shares, "The day after Dr. King was shot, I went into the riot-torn Washington, D.C., streets and into schools to talk to the children. I went to tell them not to loot and raid so that they would not get arrested and ruin their futures. A young black boy about 12 or 13 years old looked squarely at me and said, 'Lady, what future? I ain't got no future. I ain't got nothing to lose.' This young boy spoke the plain truth for himself and millions like him. Since then, I've spent my life trying to prove this boy wrong. I'm not going to stop until he and millions like him have a level playing field."

Edelman held true to those words. With strength, determination and her love for children, she founded the Children's Defense Fund in 1973. "Over the 36 years since the Children's Defense Fund was founded, we have been instrumental in making children's needs visible and led successful efforts to develop new laws, policies and programs that have improved the lives of millions of children," she explains.

When asked what she would recommend to young people today to help them stay focused and be successful, she expresses, "Hard work, discipline, perseverance and character are the substance of life. I hope young people will realize that intelligence is important but wisdom, common sense, compassion and effectiveness are of equal value, and that every single one of us has a part to play in leaving the world better than we found it."

Marion Barry Jr.

Council Member, Ward 8
Council of the District of Columbia

An Unwavering Will to Succeed

By Misty Starks

When Marion Barry Jr. was born in 1936, the chances of him becoming one of the most recognizable political figures in the nation were pretty slim. With his parents working as sharecroppers in a rural part of Mississippi, some would say the odds were indeed stacked against him. But with tenacity, hard work and an unwavering will to succeed, Barry has carved for himself a long and enviable career and a dedicated following in Washington, D.C., and beyond.

Although he describes his family as having been "dirt poor," Barry was the first to ever go to college. "We were so poor that I couldn't afford the 15-cent bus fare, so I had to walk 25 to 30 blocks to school, whether it was raining or not, in the snow or in sunshine," he recalls.

Through sheer determination and with a clear vision for his future, Barry earned a bachelor's degree from Le Moyne College. Thanks to a full scholarship, he later attended Fisk University, where he received a master's degree. Barry even completed three years of a Ph.D. program at the University of Tennessee before leaving to dedicate his time to the civil rights movement.

In the 1960s he moved to Washington, D.C., while working with the Student Nonviolent Coordinating Committee (SNCC), and from there he began a steady ascent in his career. During the next 40 years Barry would become the face of Washington. He was elected as the District's second mayor in 1978 and would hold that position for three consecutive terms, and for a fourth term in 1994. He also served for a number of years as a member of the city council, a post he currently holds, representing Ward 8.

Throughout the past four decades, Barry's work in the political arena has helped generations of Washington, D.C., residents. He is credited with completely transforming the District, making it the major metropolis it is today. His work helped build the black middle class and made D.C. government an institution for all people including other people of color, women and gays. Under his leadership, the District tremendously increased its contracts with minority businesses, created a construction boom and revitalized downtown. From economic empowerment to equality for all residents, Barry's work has made him one of the Washington's most influential public figures.

"I think God instilled in me a passion for people, faith in myself and faith in others. The tenacity, courage, persistence and resilience I have are strictly from God. I can't put it any other way," Barry explains.

In addition to his public service, Barry also has a heart for young people. He believes self-esteem is crucial to success, which is why his advice to today's generation is simple.

"Believe in yourself," he says. "A lot of young people don't see themselves being successful. They need to stop the negative thinking, stop associating themselves with negative people, have a vision for themselves and set some goals."

And when it comes to dealing with tough times in life, Barry sticks by one motto: "Never give up. If you get knocked down, fall down on your back so you can look up. If you can look up, you can get up. If you can get up, you can go up. Just be strong."

Photo by: Donald L. Baker

- WASHINGTON, D.C. LIVING LEGEND -

Alexis Herman

Former U.S. Secretary of Labor

Labor of Love

By Misty Starks

When Alexis Herman was born in 1947, women in America were struggling to gain equality in the workforce. It was just after World War II, unemployment was at 3.9 percent and there existed a great divide in the wage earnings of men and women. Herman would spend most of her career working to level the playing field for minorities and go on to affect the lives of many Americans through her dedication to equality.

Herman was raised in a Catholic home in Mobile, Alabama, by her mother, a teacher, and her father, a politician. In her household, public service was simply a way of life, and education was revered. Herman earned a bachelor's degree in sociology from Xavier University of Louisiana in New Orleans. Upon graduation, she got right to work in the community.

She began her career at Interfaith, an institution in Mobile, where she served as a community organizer. She then became a social worker at Catholic Social Services. In the years that followed, Herman held other positions at several organizations that advocated equal employment opportunities for minorities, particularly women, and helped break down barriers to economic advancement.

Herman eventually went to work for the government-funded Minority Women Employment Program (MWEP), an affirmative action program that placed minority women into white-collar jobs. While running for president of the United States, Jimmy Carter was so impressed with Herman's work at MWEP, he named her director of the Labor Department's Women's Bureau after he won the election. At 29 years old, she became the youngest person to ever hold that position.

Herman stayed in that position until 1981, when she started the consulting firm, A. M. Herman Associates.

Her company advised state and local governments on labor issues. Besides her consulting business, she remained active in politics and later held the titles of chief of staff and vice chair of the Democratic National Committee.

When Bill Clinton was elected president in 1992, Herman returned to the White House, taking on various positions during Clinton's first administration. When he won a second term, he named Herman to the secretary of labor post, making her the first African American to hold that position.

She faced challenges as labor secretary, but overcame them and earned a reputation for her great interpersonal skills and ability to handle tough political situations. Herman focused her efforts on establishing a secure workforce, which included developing aggressive job programs for youth and people in the welfare system. While at that post, the U.S. unemployment rate reached a 35-year low, and the country had the safest workplace record in the history of the Department of Labor. Under the Bush administration, Herman was replaced as secretary of labor, but she remains an active member of the Democratic Party.

Today, Alexis Herman is the chair and CEO of New Ventures, LLC and a sought-after public speaker. She serves on the boards of major corporations and participates in several organizations, including the National Urban League. Additionally, she has received numerous awards and is the recipient of more than 20 honorary doctorate degrees from colleges and universities across the country. She continues to dedicate her time and efforts to promoting the equality of minority women in the workforce.

Herman lives in Virginia with her husband, Dr. Charles Franklin.

- WASHINGTON, D.C. LIVING LEGEND -

Vernon E. Jordan Jr.

Senior Managing Director, Lazard Frères & Co. LLC
Senior Counsel, Akin Gump Strauss Hauer & Feld LLP

Still Hard at Work

By Nathan Wylder

A longtime fixture as one of Washington's most influential attorneys and powerbrokers, Vernon Jordan is the quintessential example of someone who refused to allow adverse circumstances to keep him down. Although he received a great deal of publicity while advising and golfing with his dear friend, President Clinton, during his two terms, Jordan did not set out to make a name for himself.

"I never spent much time thinking about when and if I had arrived," he reveals – his voice deep and throaty like low notes played on a baritone sax. "I was just very busy concentrating on a day-to-day basis to my stewardship at that particular time. I never gave thought to the next job."

Born in 1935 in segregated Atlanta, Jordan grew up in University Homes, the city's first public housing project, directly across from Atlanta University Center. Despite the systemic disadvantages he encountered growing up in the heart of the Jim Crow South, he made the most of every opportunity he was given. Attending every local NAACP meeting and civil rights function with his parents, who never missed, he was often inspired by the impassioned speeches of civil rights leaders and attorneys such as Col. A. T. Walden and Thurgood Marshall.

"I wanted to talk like Walden, walk like Walden, dress like Walden, be a civil rights lawyer like Walden, and that desire never left me," he recalls. Determined, he earned degrees from DePauw University and Howard University Law School, and almost immediately thereafter found himself on the legal team that won the landmark case desegregating The University of Georgia.

An incredibly hard worker, Jordan kept his nose to the proverbial grindstone, and the job offers came – primarily from people who had witnessed his assiduous work ethic in action. Some of these positions included serving as director of the Voter Education Project of the Southern Regional Council, executive director of the UNCF, and president and chief executive officer of the National Urban League.

Although he says he enjoyed every job along the way, Jordan encountered tremendous difficulty along the way. "The greatest challenge was just living," he admits. "Getting from University Homes to high school to college in the Midwest, Howard Law School...the challenge was living, hard work, sacrifice and trying to maintain some standard of excellence."

From transcending the segregated environment of his childhood to the prestigious job titles, numerous presidential appointments, board memberships for several of America's most successful businesses, to surviving an assassination attempt and frequenting the Oval Office, Jordan has met the greatest challenge in his life head on and triumphed. Given these experiences, most people would be content to sit back, relax and indulge the benefits of retirement.

Not Jordan. In fact, his schedule is as hectic as ever, and he shows no signs of slowing. "I don't want to sit around with nothing to do but worry about my tee time," he says confidently. "I like working, it's as simple as that."

He currently serves as senior managing director of Lazard Frères & Co. in New York City *and* maintains an office within the District of Columbia with Akin Gump Strauss Hauer & Feld LLP, where he is senior counsel.

"I'm an old guy, 74, with two jobs in two different cities, and I love it!" he boasts.

The book spines visible on the shelf:

CHRISTENSEN — THE INNOVATOR'S DILEMMA — Harper Business Essentials

BERNARD LEWIS — THE CRISIS OF ISLAM

...ainst All Enemies — Inside America's War on Terror — Richard A. Clarke

...OGUE REGIME — KIM JONG IL AND THE LOOMING THREAT OF NORTH KOREA

Who Says Elephants Can't Dance? — LOUIS V. GERSTNER, JR.

Finance — FOURTH EDITION — BARRON'S

THE WARREN BUFFETT WAY — Investment Strategies of the World's Greatest Investor

...RAZERMAN · NEALE — Negotiating Rationally

...Corporate Information Strategy and Management — APPLEGATE / AUSTIN / MCFARLAN — Irwin

...HEW — THE NEW CORPORATE FINANCE — Where Theory Meets Practice

MANKIW — MICROECONOMICS — SECOND EDITION

THE INNOVATOR'S SOLUTION

Corporate Governance — MONKS AND MINOW

STRATEGIES FOR THE 21st CENTURY — Fourth Edition — CONSTANCE E. BAGLEY

BARRON'S Dictionary of Finance

ENTREPRENEUR

- WASHINGTON, D.C. LIVING LEGEND -
Sharon Pratt
BI Solutions

"We will fight."

By Amanda Elizabeth Forbes

The 1960s in America gave history revolutionary icons – Dr. Martin Luther King Jr., Malcolm X, Medgar Evers – who were the first to discover an unbeaten path and make a way for those to come. Watching so many rise up in the name of African Americans, Sharon Pratt decided she would stand up next to these legends and do what these men could not – reveal a new path for African-American women.

Raised by her widowed lawyer father, Pratt says it was he who stimulated her interest in politics. "He made us keenly aware of the political shifts that were occurring in the country," she reminisces, "how that might portend for African Americans and as well as for women."

A native of Washington, D.C., Pratt graduated, with honors, from Howard University in 1968 with a juris doctorate degree.

"I was really introduced to innovative, out-of-the-box thinking," she says. "Stokely Carmichael was a classmate...you had Dr. King coming to the campus, there was activism throughout the campus. Toni Morrison was one of my introductory humanity teachers. It was just a very intellectually stimulating, politically pulsating environment."

Determined to be an agent of change, Pratt had to fight from the very beginning, including within the classrooms of law school, where she was one of 14 women in her class. She recalls that the professors rarely called on the female students, unless it was a domestic relations issue or a rape issue, and did not promote the women for recruitment to law firms.

From 1976 to 1989, Pratt climbed the ranks at Pepco to become vice president, where she battled to be paid equally as men. Regardless, Pratt believed in her ability to achieve anything, a belief that won her the title of Washington, D.C., mayor, where she served from 1991 to 1995.

As the first African-American woman to be popularly voted as mayor of a major American city, Pratt credits the youth who worked on her campaign. "These young people who had believed enough in me to continue that campaign...therefore [they] have beat the odds. To see that joy in their eyes that night, it just clicked – 'All things are possible. I *can* do this.'"

After her run as mayor, Pratt moved on to become principal and manager of Pratt Consulting and then on to BI Solutions, where she currently serves as executive vice president. A woman of many accomplishments, she has served on the boards of The Center for Creative Leadership and The Village Foundation, held positions with the District of Columbia Law Revision Commission and the National Democratic Committee, and was recognized by *Glamour*, *People* and *Ebony* magazines. Despite all of this, she insists her greatest achievement is her daughters.

"Of all things in life with which I've been involved and with which I've been associated, this is where I've had the greatest impact," she says. Pratt rose from the iconic 1960s to create her own legendary place in history and watch her daughters become the inhabiters of the change she helped create.

"[Today's youth] don't carry the same memory...the same scars. They don't feel the limits," she shares. "But you know, it fell to [my] generation to be agents of change. I think it's in our DNA now, that we will fight."

- WASHINGTON, D.C. LIVING LEGEND -

Donnie Simpson

Morning Show Host
WPGC – FM 95.5

The Smooth Media Giant

By Donald James

Donnie Simpson, WPGC-FM's longtime morning radio host heard in metropolitan Washington, D.C., has been called a trailblazer and a true media legend. Although such descriptions are flattering, Simpson, whose radio career spans 40 years, prefers to let others compliment, while he simply entertains his listening audience with electrifying music, a warm blend of humor and his unique perspective on current events.

Simpson's love for music and radio started as a young kid growing up in Detroit where his mother owned Simpson's Record Shop, a trendy music retail outlet started in 1967. He decided to become a disc jockey after WJLB, a popular Detroit radio station, broadcasted live one day from the shop. Simpson was asked to read live commercial spots by legendary disc jockey Al Perkins, who was greatly impressed by the little 15 year old with the big voice.

Within weeks, Simpson became a teen reporter for WJLB, followed by the station giving the high school student his own radio show. After eight years on the air, Simpson, one of Detroit's top DJs, headed to Washington, D.C., to host the morning show and serve as program director at WKYS. In 1993 he accepted a disc jockey position with WPGC-FM, but not before embarking on a television career.

In the early 1980s, Simpson was the backup sports anchor for WRC-TV, the NBC affiliate in D.C. He later paved his way into television history when he joined BET as host of the ultra popular *Video Soul*. Considered one of the nation's first video jockeys, Simpson stayed at BET for 14 years, racking up hundreds of memorable live interviews with many of the greatest recording artists of the era. "This guy carried us on his shoulders," Bob Johnson, founder of BET, once told a reporter. "You cannot write the history of BET without putting Donnie Simpson in the forefront as the major contributor to the creative and economic success of the company."

Moving from television to the silver screen, Simpson appeared in such classic films as *Krush Groove* and *The Five Heartbeats*. He also appeared on numerous popular sitcoms, such as *Martin* and *The Jamie Foxx Show*. While television and movies were gratifying, Simpson's love for radio gave him the freedom, creativity and spontaneity he craved.

Grateful for his loyal radio audience, Simpson, along with his wife, established the Donnie & Pam Scholarship Fund, created for minority students in need of assistance to pursue a college education. While adored by millions, perhaps Simpson's biggest fan is President Barack Obama, who, while on the presidential campaign trail in 2008, stopped to record and send a congratulatory video message to Simpson, citing the media giant for his great tenure in radio. Simpson, the father of two adult children, has also picked up dozens of national and local honors and awards saluting his career.

Throughout the years, he has turned down offers to nationally syndicate his morning radio show. While Simpson won't say "never," he does say, "I love the idea of local radio because I love this community. This community is one of my greatest blessings. I've always enjoyed high ratings for my morning radio shows. For me, it's simple...I can't wait for 6 a.m. every day to get back on the air."

Photo by: Donald L. Baker

Maudine R. Cooper

President & CEO
Greater Washington Urban League

In a League of Her Own

By Misty Starks

When Maudine R. Cooper was a young girl growing up in the town of Benoit, Mississippi, there weren't very many black role models for her to emulate. Her family lived in the poor part of the community and her parents did odd jobs to get by. In search of better opportunities, they moved to St. Paul, Minnesota.

As an only child, Cooper didn't have siblings with whom she could share life's experiences, so television was a regular source of entertainment. It was while watching a television show that she decided what her career would be: a secretary.

"Back in those days, my idea of a professional career was to be Della Street from *Perry Mason*," Cooper recalls. "We didn't have very many blacks on television back then. You had *Amos 'n Andy* of course, and *Julia* maybe, but for the notion of what you wanted to be, I thought Della Street was admirable. And at some point I had a revelation. I thought, 'Wait a minute. I can be Perry Mason.' So I went to law school."

Cooper graduated high school at age 16, and then earned both a bachelor's degree in business and a juris doctorate degree from Howard University. She admits it wasn't easy. "I was the first to go to college in my family, and I'm still the first to have a professional degree," Cooper shares. "I worked my way through school with work study, scholarships and everything else I could get. It wasn't a path filled with gold. I knew I had a goal, I just had to figure out how to get there."

After college, Cooper became a tax attorney and college lecturer. In 1973 she joined the National Urban League's Washington, D.C., bureau as the assistant director for federal programs. Later, she served as vice president of the national organization. In 1983 Mayor Marion Barry appointed her to the position of director of the Office of Human Rights. A few years later, he also named her to head the Office of Minority Business Opportunity. In 1989 she served as chief of staff in the executive office of Mayor Barry. In 1990 Cooper returned to the Urban League Movement as president and CEO of the Greater Washington affiliate, which provides services to more than 65,000 people each year.

"The most important part of my life that I'm proud of, besides being a source of pride for my parents, is my work with the Urban League," she says. "I love what I'm doing. I see the people we help, and they're in a better place and at a greater level of self sufficiency. That's the greatest pride. I go to bed at night knowing that today something good happened."

Cooper has served on the boards of various organizations and received numerous awards for her work. She considers it her responsibility to help others and pass on information, especially when it comes to young people.

"My advice to young people is to learn as much as you can and to become financially literate," she encourages. "Too many of them want to graduate on Friday and have a car on Monday. We need more economic self-sufficiency in our community."

Cooper, a devoted mother, grandmother and great-grandmother, looks forward to continuing her legacy of empowering others.

Joseph Yeldell

Godfather of D.C.

By Rachel Bobak

Joseph Yeldell is not a complex individual, yet he has worked with every mayor in the District of Columbia who was either appointed or elected. And, he was one of the first members of the Council of the District of Columbia.

Yeldell was born and raised in Washington, D.C., the tenth of 13 children. His parents raised their children insisting they receive an education. Yeldell describes his parents as hardworking and accomplished individuals, even though they had a 3rd grade education. Together, they founded a church in D.C. with seven other people, Springfield Baptist Church. "That's where they put their biggest energy," he recalls, "into the church itself."

One of three in his family to receive an advanced degree, Yeldell received a Bachelor of Science degree from what is now known as the D.C. Teacher's College and a master's degree in education from the University of Pittsburgh. Afterwards, Yeldell began teaching in Pittsburgh as a math teacher. Deciding it was time to move back to D.C., he taught at Coolidge High School before joining the federal government as a mathematical statistician.

Eventually, Yeldell left to join IBM as a marketing representative. While there, President Lyndon B. Johnson decided to re-invent the government of D.C. and appointed Yeldell to the first council in Washington. "There was little involvement, especially by minorities, in the government in the District of Columbia," he shares. "And when we took over, it was more than just a change in government; it was a revelation of a sort that minorities were now being involved in the process of government. It was an exciting time." While he served on the council, Yeldell was a member of many committees and boards, including serving as vice president of the Metropolitan Council of Governments and chairman of the Transportation Planning Board.

As he was serving on the Council of the District of Columbia, Walter Washington, mayor and commissioner of D.C., asked him to head the largest agency in the government, the Department of Human Services. Yeldell was appointed to serve as chairman of the Metropolitan Area Transit Authority board, during which time the subway system was built. Working positively to affect the residents of the District of Columbia, he served in several positions within the government, including head of human resources and managing the emergency unemployment services.

"I enjoy making things better for people," he says. "Being here in the nation's capital, we have a chance to meet those members of Congress who are African American, and get them involved in our community for our needs and our concerns. It made me realize that a civic-minded person who is educated can make a difference and that is what I impart to others."

Now retired, the dedicated Yeldell is still involved in the D.C. community. Remaining active in education organizations, he is a member of Phi Beta Sigma Fraternity, Inc. and a 33rd Degree mason. "I have a lot to keep me busy," he shares.

Yeldell remains close to his former wife, Gladys Johnson Yeldell, whom he describes as his best friend. They have two daughters, Gayle and Joi Lynn. Gayle has three daughters, Christina, Tiffany and Vanessa, who are students at the University of Michigan, Duke University and the University of Southern California, respectively. Joi Lynn has one son, Phillip, 10.

Photo by: Donald L. Baker

- WASHINGTON, D.C. LIVING LEGEND -

JC Hayward

Noon Anchor & Vice President, Media Outreach
WUSA 9

A Community Anchor

By Danielle Solomon

When reviewing JC Hayward's longstanding career with WUSA 9, it is difficult not to be impressed. As the first female anchor in Washington, D.C., she has commanded the news desk for nearly four decades, 35 of those years spent at the helm of the 5 p.m. newscast. She has garnered numerous local Emmy awards for her masterful work, and has had the opportunity to interview countless high-profile individuals and cover many memorable stories, most notably Nelson Mandela's visit to America. However, Hayward insists these accomplishments and accolades should only account for a fraction of her legacy.

"I've been blessed that I have a wonderful job, and it has been a grand experience, but I've always believed, more importantly, that it is what I do with this opportunity," she shares. "The emphasis should not be that I'm on television or that people know my name and my face. That to me is not what I should be remembered for."

Instead, Hayward wants to be remembered for her service to the community.

From the start, Hayward had a desire to work with people, which she achieved in her role as a counselor. In the early 1970s, as television stations began opening their doors to minorities, she was offered a fellowship at the Columbia University Graduate School of Journalism. Hayward then began her new career path at a CBS affiliate in Atlanta, Georgia, for two years before accepting a position at WUSA 9, then WTOP-TV.

Though she had the backing of her news director and the endorsement of Katharine Graham, *The Washington Post*'s then-president, she had to face the criticism of those who did not believe women should deliver the news. Unfazed, Hayward only used those complaints as motivation to be stronger.

What ultimately shaped her life, though, were the ordinary people engaging in extraordinary things she covered in feature stories, or as she calls it, "the good news." Hayward found incredible inspiration in such people as the retired man who handcrafted beautiful wooden toys for needy children or the woman with multiple sclerosis who began a knitting club to make caps, scarves and mittens for thousands of inner-city youth. She also fondly recalls a particularly blustery Sunday afternoon following a woman who, with donations from supermarkets, fed the homeless soup and sandwiches from the back of her station wagon. These stories touched Hayward's heart, strengthening her commitment to community service.

Besides maintaining her role as anchor of the noon newscast, Hayward took on another position in April of 2006 that is a seemingly perfect fit: vice president for media outreach. A liaison between the station and the community, she links WUSA 9 to nonprofit organizations and fundraisers, and ensures its presence at special activities. Personally, she mentors teenage girls and serves on the boards of such organizations as Luke C. Moore Academy Senior High School, the United Black Fund and Hospice Caring. Hayward strongly encourages youth to look beyond their personal comfort zones and volunteer to help the less fortunate.

"I've tried to be active, I've tried to be involved, and I've tried to leave a legacy for other young people to follow because it's my belief that we must care about our community, our young people, our seniors, and try to make a difference," she says.

THE PARK
AT FOURTEENTH

The Park has established itself among DC's savvy as the most sophisticated destination for after work cocktail hours, corporate events, and late night fêtes.

Located in the heart of downtown Washington, The Park at Fourteenth is loaded with eye-appeal – polished wood, gorgeous blown-glass chandeliers and floor to ceiling vistas of Franklin Square. Our exhibition kitchen turns out delectable American Classics on the first two floors, while the top two floors are devoted to a lounge (DJ's Thursday - Saturday) and private event space.

Featuring:

Stuffed Salmon
Prime Rib
Catfish
Waffles

Welcome to our OLDE TOWNE INN

Prince George's County legal district's hottest new meeting spot!

We offer a full selection menu to include breakfast, lunch and dinner. We are **ope**
7 days a week. In addition we have a **Happy Hour Monday – Friday from**
4:00pm – 7:00pm and a **weekend brunch til 2:00pm**.

Just across the street from the Prince George
County Administration building and around t
corner from the County Courthouse, we a
conveniently located to serve our patrons.

Mention this ad and receive a *20% Discount*

We accept Visa, Mastercard, American Express,
Diner's Club & Discover. No personal checks.

14745 Main Street
Upper Marlboro, MD 207
Tel: 301.627.1400

Remember Everyone Meets At The OTI.....

WASHINGTON, D.C.
INTERESTING PERSONALITIES

PROFOUND

CAPTIVATING

DISTINCT

IMPASSIONED

ORIGINAL

INSPIRING

REMARKABLE

INDIVIDUAL

PRODIGIOUS

GOING THE DISTANCE

THE HONORABLE ADRIAN M. FENTY

Mayor
Washington, D.C.

By Karen Y. Perkins

Adrian M. Fenty was elected the fifth mayor of Washington, D.C., and began his term January 2, 2007. Elected at age 35, he is the youngest person to win the mayoral seat in the District of Columbia. During his run for office, Fenty launched an unprecedented door-to-door campaign where he and his volunteers visited every block in the city. He ran on a platform of bringing a more energetic, hands-on approach to city government.

Improving education is the cornerstone of Fenty's public schools restructuring agenda, with special attention paid to improving graduation rates and reducing truancy. He has become a national leader in the area of urban education reform after changing the city's public schools governance structure during his first months in office. With his newly restructured school system, working with the city's school chief allows Fenty the flexibility to make changes to improve teacher qualification requirements, and to focus on stronger academic programs. As a direct result of the restructuring program in 2008, both elementary and secondary schools achieved significant gains in reading and math proficiency.

When asked what he would recommend to young people today to remain focused and successful through grade school and into college, Fenty states, "As mayor of the District of Columbia, education has been and continues to be the top priority of my administration. I believe that a quality education is key to ensuring a successful future for young people, for our communities and for our economy. As young people grow into adulthood, they will face many challenges just as I have as mayor of the nation's capital city, but education is key to successfully rise to meet those challenges."

Fenty is an advocate of Marion Barry's famous D.C. Summer Youth Job Program, which helps teens with part-time summer employment. The Summer Youth Employment Program has approximately 22,000 registrants who are ready to embark on a positive, productive summer work experience that provides career exposure, academic enrichment and opportunities for young people between the ages of 14 and 21.

Fenty has also added police officers to the streets of Washington, D.C., expanded health care coverage for the uninsured, and established thousands of units of affordable housing, while creating the Housing First program to provide permanent supportive housing for the District's homeless. He is committed to creating new jobs, and spurring neighborhood economic development in an effort to stimulate the economy.

Even though Fenty has a hectic work schedule, he feels that exercise is important to stay physically fit. He was a long distance runner in high school and regularly competes in triathlons and other races in the Washington, D.C., area. *Men's Fitness* magazine named him as one of its 25 fittest men, ranking him alongside a major league baseball player, basketball great LeBron James, and *X-Men* and *Wolverine* star Hugh Jackman.

Born in the District of Columbia on December 6, 1970, Fenty attended Oberlin College, earning a bachelor's degree in English and economics before earning a juris doctorate degree from the Howard University School of Law.

After a hard day and a job well done, Fenty likes to spend quiet time with his wife, Michelle, twin sons Matthew and Andrew, and daughter Aerin.

This piece was commissioned and placed on a permanent loan to the Recreation Wish List Committee for the Southeast Tennis and Learning Center and the Department of Parks and Recreation by the employees of Hensel Phelps Construction Co. Dedicated April 27, 2001

Photo by: Donald L. Baker

IMPACTING THROUGH PARTNERSHIPS

CORA MASTERS BARRY
Founder & CEO
Recreation Wish List Committee

By Donald James

As founder and chief executive officer of the Recreation Wish List Committee (RWLC) in Washington, D.C., Cora Masters Barry simply knows how to get things done. In a town where ideas and initiatives are often stymied by red tape and political party affiliations, Barry, the former first lady of the District of Columbia, doesn't take "no" for an answer.

Masters Barry heads an organization comprised of business, government and community leaders who work together to ensure that every youth in the city has safe and viable recreation programs, facilities and equipment in their neighborhoods. Throughout the 14 years of RWLC's existence, Barry has secured millions of private and public dollars to renovate playgrounds, resurface tennis and basketball courts, purchase gym sets and acquire computers for after-school programs.

While Masters Barry can point to numerous successful projects and programs that she has spearheaded for children, perhaps her greatest accomplishment is the Southeast Tennis and Learning Center (SETLC), erected in Ward 8's Washington Highlands, one of the city's most underserved areas. Built in 2001, the $5.1 million facility provides children with a positive environment where tennis and life skills are bolstered by academic and tutoring programs. SETLC and Barry have been touted by ESPN, CBS, CSPAN, the *Washington Post*, the United States Tennis Association, and many other local and national media outlets and organizations.

"I'm extremely proud of the Learning Center [SETLC] and what it provides to help so many underserved children," says Masters Barry. "The Learning Center is a shining example for other major cities as to what can happen when serious public-private partnerships are formed."

Masters Barry's triumph in building this "first of its kind in the nation" facility should have been expected as this mover and shaker has a proven track record of success throughout the city. Her track record includes serving, and eventually chairing, the D.C. Boxing Commission from 1979– 1987, which at the time was uncharted waters for women. The dynamo also served on the Executive Committee for the World Boxing Council (WBC) and the International Boxing Federation (IBF).

If one thinks that Masters Barry's strong suit is reserved for sports initiatives only, consider that while on the D.C. Boxing Commission, she was also a professor of political science at the University of the District of Columbia. The former 21-year tenured professor taught classes in black politics, the presidency and the Constitution.

It is Masters Barry's strong political mind and her "think outside the box" mentality that have positively affected numerous local and national initiatives. She is widely credited with facilitating the return of her then-husband, Marion Barry Jr., to political life in Washington, D.C. He was re-elected as D.C.'s mayor in 1994 for an unprecedented fourth term.

Born in Oklahoma City, Oklahoma, and raised in Pasadena, California, Masters Barry developed a strong social and political conscience. She went on to earn an undergraduate degree in sociology from Texas Southern University, before picking up a master's degree in government from Howard University.

After 35 years as a proud Washingtonian, Masters Barry, the mother of two adult daughters, continues to impact the social and political landscape of the nation's capital. She sits on several influential boards and committees that address social, voter registration, educational and political issues.

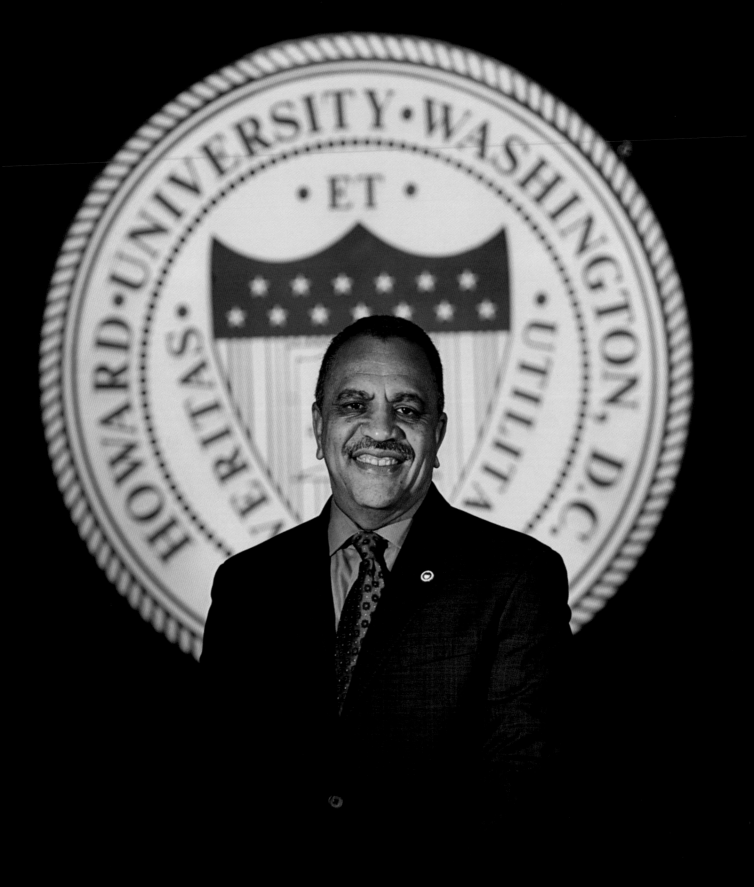

DEVELOPING CHAMPIONS

DR. SIDNEY RIBEAU
President
Howard University

By Karen Y. Perkins

Dr. Sidney Ribeau began his teaching career in 1976 as a professor of communication studies at California State University, Los Angeles. He was named dean of undergraduate studies for California State University, San Bernardino, and then went on to become dean of liberal arts for California Polytechnic State University in San Luis Obispo. He served as vice president of academic affairs for California Polytechnic in Pomona, California, until he accepted the position of president at Bowling Green State University in Bowling Green, Ohio. In May of 2008, the Howard University board of trustees announced him as their unanimous choice to become the 16th president to lead the university. Howard University is known for excellence in the fields of math, science, engineering and technology, and is one of the nation's leading HBCUs.

Ribeau's profound commitment to education was evident during his tenure at Bowling Green State University. A major fundraising effort had a five-year goal of reaching $120 million for scholarships, endowed chairs, capital improvements and academic program enhancements. With hard work, determination and gusto, Ribeau raised $115 of their $120 million goal in just three years. Additionally, while at Bowling Green, he also worked with the GED program, where he was able to help a record number of men and women who had been disregarded in society by helping them get a new opportunity in life.

As the 16th president of Howard University, he is most proud of the Howard University Middle School of Mathematics and Sciences. The middle school was the first charter school established by a university in Washington, D.C. "When we see our middle school students graduate, we know they will return to Howard University for another journey in their preparation to positively impact the world," says Ribeau.

When asked what he would recommend to young people today to help them be focused and successful, he states, "Every challenge in life serves as a building block to developing a champion. No matter the obstacles, it is imperative to use every effort to overcome the struggle and reach an optimal outcome. You cannot cut your way to excellence. You have to pursue education and delay gratification. Most importantly, you need to build a level of confidence and skills which will benefit you in many ways, now and in the future."

Ribeau lives a life filled with commitments to education, faculty, research projects and fundraisers, but at the end of the day, spending quality time with his wife and family are among the most important things to him. "There is nothing more relaxing than enjoying the blessings of life and the fruits of your labor with your family," he shares.

Ribeau finds spiritual motivation in his daily reading of the Bible, which serves as the guiding direction in his life. What resonates most in his day-to-day life are the sacrifices his parents made that provided opportunities that shaped his path. "Through their expressions of faith, hope and unconditional love, I know there is someone greater than me who has divinely created my purpose on this earth," he shares. His dad's philosophy, "You do not always have to be the best, but you always need to do your best," are words he lives by.

Photo by: Donald L. Baker

BORN TO LEAD

ELSIE L. SCOTT, PH.D.
President & Chief Executive Officer
Congressional Black Caucus Foundation, Inc.

By Donald James

Scholars and academicians have long debated whether some people are natural born leaders, or are people taught to lead based on life's vast experiences and education. While such debates make for great conjecture, for Dr. Elsie L. Scott, president and chief executive officer of the powerful Congressional Black Caucus Foundation (CBCF) in Washington, D.C., leadership is simply her natural calling.

Since taking the reigns of the CBCF in July of 2006, Scott oversees an $11 million annual budget while effectively addressing and implementing public policy, research projects, educational issues and fundraising initiatives that help advance the socioeconomic circumstances of African Americans. Founded in 1976, the nonpartisan, nonprofit foundation's mission is to advance the global black community by developing leaders, informing policy and educating the public. Under the leadership of Scott, the CBCF has launched numerous projects aimed at influencing and uplifting African Americans in political, legislative, social and public policy arenas. Such hallmark events and projects include presenting the CBCF's Annual Legislative Conference held each September in D.C. Additionally, Scott and the CBCF are proud of the launch of Avoice: African American Voices in Congress, an innovative Web site designed by the organization to encapsulate and preserve the political and legislative contributions and history of black lawmakers for the education of future generations.

Scott's passion for addressing social, political, public policy and civil rights issues comes naturally. Growing up in Lake Providence, Louisiana, she witnessed the injustices that black people faced at the hands of segregation. In addition, she observed a champion who courageously fought so that black people in Lake Providence could vote and breathe the fresh air of equality. This champion was Scott's father, the late John H. Scott, a legendary civil rights advocate, minister and president of the local NAACP. Born in 1901, his lifetime crusade for justice is chronicled in the book, *Witness to the Truth...My Struggle for Human Rights in Louisiana*, written by the elder Scott, along with his daughter, Cleo Scott Brown. "My parents taught the eight of us that we had to get an education, and that we had to serve and help advance our community," recalls Scott. "That's just how we were raised."

After earning an undergraduate degree in political science from Southern University, a master's degree in political science from The University of Iowa, and a Doctor of Philosophy degree in political science from Atlanta University, Scott was a much sought-after consultant to mayors, police departments and community groups on an array of social, race and community issues. She also taught criminal justice, urban studies and political science at Howard, Rutgers and North Carolina Central universities. Prior to joining the CBCF, she served as deputy commissioner for training for the New York City Police Department, and executive director of the National Organization of Black Law Enforcement Executives.

As the old saying goes, "You can't teach what you don't know, and you can't lead where you don't go." For Scott, the lessons have been well taught, and the clarity of leadership is crystal clear as she continues to empower and improve the quality of life for African Americans. "I love what I do here at CBCF," says Scott. "It's gratifying to help shape the next generation of leaders, while helping to educate and inform on public policy issues."

INTERESTING PERSONALITIES

Photo provided by: The Republican National Committee

HEEDING THE CALL TO SERVICE

MICHAEL S. STEELE
Chairman
Republican National Committee

By Nathan Wylder

Long before he would become a household name in the American political discourse, Michael Steele, the new chairman of the Republican National Committee, was drawn to the idea of service. As a boy, two factors influenced his decision to become a politician: friends of his parents who were heavily involved in city politics and the Catholic Church. "I saw politics as a unique form of public service with positive outcomes," he recalls. "Pair that with wanting to become a priest and the real question was, would [my service] be religious or political?"

A first generation Catholic, Steele was born on Andrews Air Force Base in 1958, and grew up in Washington, D.C., the epicenter of American politics. Steele's involvement at St. Gabriel Parish as a boy provided him a category for appreciating and valuing service. In fact, he was so enamored with making a difference in people's lives, specifically on a broader stage, that in the third grade he decided to become a priest, which he came very close to doing.

Steele earned a bachelor's degree in international relations from The Johns Hopkins University in 1981 and enrolled at the Augustinian Friars Seminary of Villanova University, where he began completing the prerequisite training for priesthood. As time passed, Steele began to wrestle with his childhood ambition. "Several of my priest friends encouraged me to go enjoy college; know what you're walking away from," he shares. After three years in the monastery and finding "a great deal of comfort in prayer and speaking to friends about it," Steele decided to go in a different direction, taking what he had learned from the experience and applying it to vocational endeavors outside of the church.

A mere footnote in the narrative of his political ascension, Steele's transition into the secular realm included receiving a law degree from Georgetown University Law Center in 1991 and practicing complex financial and corporate securities law internationally for several years. A self-described Lincoln Republican with the firm resolve that "government should work for the people, not against them," he engaged in political activism with ease and fervor.

From his initial affiliation with the GOP on the local level to his current role on the national level, Steele's passion, intensity and rhetorical savvy have long been trademarks of his leadership, serving as chairman or an executive committee member of numerous councils, task forces and organizations. The Maryland Republican Party's Man of the Year in 1995, Steele made history in 2000 when he was elected chairman of the Maryland Republican Party – the first African American elected to head a state Republican party nationwide – and again in 2003, when he took office as lieutenant governor of Maryland, another first.

Despite the level of success he has enjoyed with political conservatives, he addresses the partisan opposition with grace. "I may stand out like a sore thumb in a Democratic environment, but we have more in common than it appears," he points out. "Not every battle is as ugly as it seems in the press or on TV."

Steele's advice for today's young people is provocative: "Don't wait for permission to get involved," he says resolutely. "Especially now, you have a voice and an opportunity to express where the country should go. Don't wait until you're 40 to get involved...engage in all levels of the government."

INTERESTING PERSONALITIES

Photo by: Mike Styles

LOOKING OUT FOR OTHERS

MILLICENT D. WILLIAMS
President & CEO
DC Children and Youth Investment Trust

By Danielle Solomon

While some children dream of being an athlete or a movie star, Millicent Williams knew from a young age that her life's work would involve helping others. "My mother tells me I was always looking out for someone else," she laughs. "I have a younger brother, and whenever he would wander off in the neighborhood, I would always be the one that would go find him."

It is of little surprise, then, that Williams would find herself as an adult in roles that influence positive change in the lives of many, particularly young people, for whom she holds a great affinity. Currently, she is president and chief executive officer of the DC Children and Youth Investment Trust, an organization that focuses on fostering key partnerships between public and private entities to develop and improve programs for the benefit of Washington, D.C.'s youth. Prior to this opportunity, she served as executive director of Serve DC – the DC Commission on National and Community Service, and as general secretary of the African Methodist Episcopal (A.M.E.) Zion Church's Youth Missionary Society, where she was the youngest person elected to serve on the international domination's executive board in its 200-year history. In each of these opportunities, she was able to impact widespread involvement of children, youth and families locally, nationally and internationally.

An alumna of the Florida A&M University School of Business, Williams cites her parents as sparking her interest in service. Her father, a bishop in the A.M.E. Zion Church, and her mother, an educator, made a strong impression on Williams through their passion for their professions. "Every memory I have from childhood on through adulthood has been one that has shown dedication to service and interest in people," she says.

Besides her resolve to look out for others, Williams, a native of Buffalo, New York, is incredibly well suited for a career that breeds hope in younger generations because she has witnessed firsthand the byproducts of tenacity. "I didn't feel the option of giving up," she recalls of her upbringing. Her mother, born into a family of sharecroppers, was forced to balance school with work at an early age but was able to graduate valedictorian of her high school class, salutatorian of her college class, and with honors from graduate school while married to a busy pastor and sharing the responsibility of raising three children at that time.

When considering how youth can exercise their potential for success, she thinks, "young people should embrace their youth and involve themselves in opportunities to expand their horizons." Hard work is an absolute necessity, and she encourages youth to consider that the path to achieving their goals may not always be predictable or aligned with their expectations, but that determination will bear the fruit of accomplishment. She knows this as a fact because she has lived it.

"When I was in college, I decided then that I was going to provide senior leadership to a Fortune 500 corporation by the time that I turned 40," Williams reflects. "I had no idea that my opportunity would come through service in the nonprofit sector nor did I realize that Washington, D.C., would be the community in which I would ultimately have the opportunity to serve. However, I certainly couldn't imagine being in a better place to do

THE PARK

AT FOURTEEN

Photo by: Donald L. Baker

D.C.'s KING OF ENTERTAINMENT

MARC BARNES
Entertainment Entrepreneur

By Donald James

If you want to know about politics in Washington, D.C., ask a politician. If you want to know about entertainment and having a good time, ask Marc Barnes. As an entrepreneur and owner of three of D.C.'s most exclusive venues, Republic Gardens, LOVE (formerly Dream) and The Park at 14th, Barnes is the master of promoting exclusive events, hosting world-class parties and operating upscale nightclubs in the nation's capital and beyond.

In 1995 Barnes began his quest into nightlife entertainment with the purchase of Republic Gardens, a popular meeting spot in D.C.'s historic U Street neighborhood. The club quickly earned premier status as the place to see and be seen by D.C.'s sexiest party crowd. Featuring outstanding food, an inviting atmosphere, nonstop music and dancing, Republic Gardens established Barnes as the go-to guy for having a good time in Washington, D.C. On the verge of something bigger, he closed Republic Gardens in 2001.

Shortly after closing the venue, Barnes launched Dream, a grand, four-story destination nightclub in Northeast D.C., which featured stunning VIP rooms, multiple dance floors and bars, and a breath-taking rooftop deck. Dream, which underwent an extravagant renovation and name change to LOVE in 2005, routinely sees crowds of up to 3,000, and similar to Republic Gardens, has become a "must" nightclub destination for both local residents and visitors from around the world.

Not one to sit back and marvel at his successes, in October of 2007, Barnes opened The Park at 14th, a chic restaurant and lounge located near historic Franklin Square in the K Street corridor.

Like his other entertainment diamonds, The Park at 14th offers patrons an upscale and exciting atmosphere tempered with elegance, exquisite design and amazing cuisine.

Barnes' success as an entrepreneur is not surprising. While in high school, the native Washingtonian dreamed of becoming a successful businessman in charge of his own destiny. At age 19, he started his first business, Personal Courier, a delivery and messenger venture that he operated for ten years. After a bit of friendly banter between music moguls Russell Simmons and Andre Harrell on who could throw the best party, Barnes took the challenge and organized a blowout event at his own home that mesmerized more than 1,200 people. He realized that his next business venture had been born. Barnes sold Personal Courier, and as the old saying goes, the rest is history. "My success at any venture starts with a clear vision, perpetuated by hard work, and is rounded out with many strokes of good luck," says Barnes.

Although Barnes has achieved a high level of prosperity, he always gives back by contributing to and supporting numerous community organizations and worthy causes. Among his many charitable outreaches are turkey giveaways at Thanksgiving, providing coats and toys for underserved children and families at Christmas, and sponsoring kids to attend summer camp. "It's important for me to give back to the community," says Barnes. "Our venues are made available for the community to meet and enjoy, and we take the lead in addressing numerous issues that negatively impact our city."

A HIGHER CALLING

SHAYNA RUDD
Miss Black USA

By Donald James

Take one look at Shayna Rudd, and it's easy to see why she wears the 2009 Miss Black USA crown. Take one minute to listen to Shayna Rudd, and it's easy to realize why she is much more than just a pretty face.

Although Rudd wowed pageant judges with her beauty, the 23-year-old also dazzled them with her intellect, grace, talent and genuine passion for helping inner-city youth. When her name was called as the new Miss Black USA in August of 2009, Rudd was in disbelief. "I was humbled and couldn't believe it because all the contestants were worthy," says Rudd. "However, I felt I was well-prepared, and I felt that I was walking in a higher calling to what God had in store for me."

As Miss Black USA, Rudd is looking forward to the one-year media tour that will take her across America, as well as to Ghana. In addition, she is ecstatic to have a national platform to champion the Heart Truth Campaign, which will help raise awareness that heart disease is a major killer among African-American women. Rudd will also bring awareness to her own Lady Diva Corp., a nonprofit organization she started in 2005 to cultivate, encourage and empower young African-American women between the ages of 14 and 20. Lady Diva Corp. presently has chapters in Washington, D.C., and Philadelphia, with others ready to launch in New Orleans and Baton Rouge, Louisiana.

Rudd's victory as Miss Black USA was not the first time she had been crowned in pageant competition. As a matter of fact, she has won seven of the eight pageants she has entered. Some of her crowns include Miss District of Columbia, Miss Black Pennsylvania USA, Miss Howard University and Miss Black and Gold at Howard. In 2008 Rudd was a contestant in the Miss America pageant held in Las Vegas. While unsuccessful in her bid to capture the crown, she won the pageant's talent competition and placed in the top five in the interview segment.

Born in a tough neighborhood in west Philadelphia, Rudd is a product of a single-parent home. She was raised by what she calls "a strong stock of black women," which included her mother, grandmother and great aunt. Rudd's father was not a major part of her life because of his affinity for drugs. Yet, she was determined to be somebody, and the three black women in her life were determined to give her the strong foundation and encouragement to succeed.

After earning a bachelor's degree in journalism and African-American studies from Howard University, Rudd entered Trinity Washington University in D.C., where she is currently pursuing an MBA. In addition, she teaches English and creative writing at Maya Angelou Public Charter High School, which is located in Southeast Washington, D.C., one of the city's most impoverished and underserved areas. Even with a full plate, she remains committed to reaching out to help empower young African-American women in the inner city. "While I am still young and still learning, I tell other young women that they owe it to themselves to complete whatever they start," says Rudd. "They owe it to themselves to be the best and to see what God has for them."

CB

A BRIEFCASE AND A THREE-PIECE SUIT

CARL BROOKS
President & Chief Executive Officer
The Executive Leadership Council

By Amanda Elizabeth Forbes

Growing up in south Philadelphia, Carl Brooks had atypical aspirations compared to his classmates. A Golden Gloves boxing champion, an offer to play professional baseball and multiple college scholarships were opportunities Brooks considered at the dawn of his professional career. However, he wanted something a little more substantial, something that required carrying a briefcase and wearing a three-piece suit. Brooks wanted to be an African-American businessman.

Born in 1949, Brooks' parents were nurturing and supportive, yet encouraged strong academics. "I was raised in a way that I was very focused on success," he recalls. A proficient student and athlete, he was an early achiever who won awards in both the academic and athletic arenas, and graduated first in his junior and senior high school classes.

In 1967 Brooks entered Hampton Institute, where he earned a bachelor's degree, cum laude, and Southern Illinois University awarded him an MBA in 1976. Brooks began to climb the ranks of corporate America, a feat he knew would be especially difficult for an African American. However, the dream of the briefcase and a three-piece suit never escaped him.

"I had to prove myself...I had to demonstrate my competence and confidence every step along the way. I had to compete against everybody," he remembers. "With a great academic preparation and the supportive environment that I grew up in, I was able to achieve and thrive in very competitive environments."

Achieve he did, as Brooks served in several executive positions such as chief financial officer of GENCO, vice president of human and technical resources at GPU, and president and CEO of The Executive Leadership Council (ELC), where he has served since 2001. Representing the most senior African-American corporate executives in Fortune 500 companies, the ELC is an organization Brooks believes African Americans need to know and emulate.

"I think African Americans and other young people need to have heroes that go beyond those that sing and shoot a ball," he says. "They also need to have as their heroes those who have risen to the very top in a most competitive corporate world and are having a positive impact on our community."

Brooks has seen the ELC grow from 100 to more than 500 members under his leadership, and is fulfilled by the more than 12,000 young professionals who have been touched by the ELC's Pipeline, Next Generation and mid-level manager programs, and its work with HBCUs. He takes satisfaction in knowing that young professionals will fill the pipeline of more African Americans moving into executive positions.

"I think we have to set our standards high," he insists. "We should set our sights on real success."

Brooks also enjoys the success of his children. He and his wife of 36 years, Drena, have watched their son, Tarik, graduate at the top of his class from Howard University and Harvard Business School; he is currently a senior vice president at Urban Trust Bank. Their daughter, Karima, is happily married to a doctor and earning a doctorate degree in pharmacy.

By all accounts, Brooks' dream of becoming a businessman who could have an impact in his community has come true, made possible by his parents, brother Nathaniel and sister Barbara, all of whom have been a source of inspiration, and helped Brooks wear his three-piece suit and carry his briefcase throughout a lifetime of achievement.

THE OBAMAS' MUTUAL ADVISER

VALERIE JARRETT

Senior Adviser & Assistant to the President for
Intergovernmental Affairs
Office of Public Engagement

By George E. Curry

Valerie Jarrett, senior adviser to the president, has been called the first friend, President Obama's "big sister," "Barack's rock," "Barack's secret weapon," and even "the other half of Obama's brain." Regardless of what she is called, she is undeniably one of his most influential advisers.

Jarrett, who joined the administration of Mayor Harold Washington and stayed on as deputy chief of staff to Chicago Mayor Richard Daley, was introduced to Obama after she interviewed Michelle LaVaughn Robinson in 1991 for a job as assistant to the mayor. Jarrett was immediately impressed with the future first lady, but before the candidate would accept the job offer, she wanted Jarrett to meet her fiancé and future husband.

Over dinner, Jarrett and Barack Obama discovered that both had lived unusual childhoods. Obama, the son of a white woman from Kansas and a black man from Kenya, had lived in Indonesia and Hawaii.

Jarrett was born November 14, 1956, in Shiraz, Iran. Her father, Dr. James E. Bowman, a highly respected pathologist and geneticist, operated a hospital for children there as part of a U.S. effort to improve health care in developing countries. Her summers were spent traveling with her parents to such places as Egypt, Ghana and Nigeria. After five years in Iran, James and Barbara Bowman, moved with their only child to London for a year before returning to Chicago.

Obama has spoken and written about his struggle to establish his racial identity. Jarrett said that when her family lived in Iran, they were viewed as Americans, not African Americans. Consequently, she said she was not aware of race until her family moved back to the United States.

From a distinguished family, her grandfather was the first black to graduate from the Massachusetts Institute of Technology. Jarrett attended Northfield Mount Hermon School, an elite New England boarding school, before graduating from Stanford and the University of Michigan Law School. She was briefly married to Dr. William Robert Jarrett, a childhood friend and the son of famed journalist Vernon Jarrett. The couple has one child, Laura, who graduated from Harvard Law School.

Both Obamas graduated from Harvard Law School after the president finished Columbia University and the first lady graduated from Princeton.

Jarrett's friendship with Michelle Obama, then 27 years old, was immediate. "I was just unbelievably bowled over by how impressive she was," Jarrett said in an interview with *Vogue*. "Michelle was so impressive beyond her years, so thoughtful and perceptive. She really prodded me about what the job would be like because she had so many choices. I offered it to her on the spot, which was totally inappropriate because I should have talked to the mayor first. But I just knew she was really special."

Evidently, the Obama family has concluded that Jarrett is special. She is the person the president turns to when he wants the unvarnished truth. He has said, "I trust her completely."

After serving as co-chair of the president's transition team, the politically and socially connected Jarrett was touted as a possible replacement for Obama in the U.S. Senate and as secretary of housing. But she chose to work in the White House, advising President Obama on major issues, directing his Office of Public Engagement, and operating the other side of his brain.

Photo by: Donald L. Baker

SERVICE THROUGH LEADERSHIP EXCELLENCE

MARCO WATSON MCMILLIAN & J. DAVID REEVES

Executive Director & COO, Phi Beta Sigma Fraternity, Inc.
National President, Blacks In Government

By Donald James

As frat brothers of Phi Beta Sigma, Marco Watson McMillian and J. David Reeves stand on the shoulders of the fraternity's founding fathers, who deeply believed that members should not gain skills just for themselves, but should also acquire skills to benefit the community. Therefore, both men exemplify their fraternity's motto, "Culture for Service and Service for Humanity."

McMillian, executive director and chief operations officer of Phi Beta Sigma Fraternity, Inc., based in Washington, D.C., oversees the daily operations of the 95-year-old predominantly African-American men's organization. Appointed to the post in 2007, McMillian, then 27, became the youngest person to ever lead Phi Beta Sigma, an international organization that currently boasts 125,000 members in 47 states, with chapters in Africa, Europe, Japan and South Korea.

McMillian's leadership abilities are not a surprise. *Ebony*, in its February 2004 issue, included him in the publication's list of 30 Leaders Under 30 to Watch. McMillian was 24 at the time. Additionally, the *Mississippi Business Journal* included him in its Top 40 Leaders Under 40, a major honor considering the publication's perennial propensity to exclude African Americans.

Prior to his current position, McMillian, a Clarksdale, Mississippi, native, was executive assistant to the president at Alabama A&M University, and assistant to the vice president of institutional advancement and associate director for development at Jackson State University.

Placing a great value on education, McMillian holds an undergraduate degree in elementary education from Jackson State University, a master's degree in philanthropy and development from Saint Mary's University of Minnesota, and a certificate in fundraising management from Indiana University. "Education is the great equalizer," says McMillian. "Once you have it, you can do just about anything that you want to do."

J. David Reeves agrees. With a bachelor's degree in secondary education and a master's degree in public administration, both from Bowling Green State University, the Columbus, Ohio, native has built an extraordinary career in service to humanity through leadership excellence. He is the national president of the powerful Blacks In Government (BIG), a service organization that advocates for equitable treatment for 3.5 million African-American civilians and military employees who work in local, state and federal government workforces. According to sources, BIG is the nation's largest African-American organization that addresses issues in the government workplace.

In addition, Reeves is an executive with the U.S. Department of Housing and Urban Development (HUD), where he has enjoyed a 24-year career. As deputy assistant secretary for the Real Estate Assessment Center, Reeves oversees nationwide inspections and evaluations of federal properties for the purpose of determining habitability. His reach also includes U.S. territories such as Guam, Puerto Rico and the Virgin Islands. With HUD, Reeves has functioned in a number of executive and management capacities while based in Washington, D.C., and Los Angeles.

While extremely busy, Reeves finds time to host a federal news radio program heard throughout Metro D.C. called *The BIG Experience*. The program tackles broad issues that critically impact African Americans across the country.

Committed to community issues, Reeves, a father of two sons, is a regular speaker on forums that impact adults and youth. Sharing his philosophy with others, Reeves says, "Whatever God gives to us, we have an obligation to give back to others. Because giving back to others is when we receive our greatest gift in return."

Photo by: Donald L. Baker

A Passion for Education, Civil Rights and the Law

JUNE WHITE DILLARD, ESQ.

President
Prince George's County NAACP,
Maryland Branch

By Donald James

If one attempted to define the long, prominent career of June White Dillard, words of praise would describe her love for education, her tenacious fights for civil rights and her time-tested zeal for practicing law. Although the aforementioned accolades speak volumes to depict this mover and shaker, for Dillard, action always speaks louder than words.

For the last 25 years, Dillard has been an intricate part of the Prince George's County NAACP, Maryland Branch. She served as second president of the branch for 20 years before taking over as president in 2004. In both capacities, Dillard has stood at the forefront of resolving critical issues facing more than 500,000 African Americans living in Prince George's County.

Earlier this year, Dillard convinced the U.S. Department of Justice to investigate the death of a 19-year-old African American killed last year while detained in Prince George's County Jail. Dillard has also spearheaded numerous rallies against police brutality and harassment, developed and implemented a unique voter education and registration empowerment program, and established strong candidate forums to better inform local voters.

In addition, Dillard is a strong advocate for meaningful education reform throughout Prince George's County. "We have to continue to actively tackle educational issues to reduce the achievement gap for African American students and, of course, to stop the violence in our schools," says Dillard. "If we don't correct our education system, our children won't have a chance for a bright future."

It's not surprising that Dillard has a strong passion for educating children. Growing up in Cleveland, Ohio, she always wanted to teach. After earning a bachelor's degree in education from The University of Chicago, and a master's degree in special education and guidance counseling from Chicago State University, Dillard taught in the Chicago Public Schools and District of Columbia Public Schools systems.

Dillard, however, made a career transition from education to law in 1972, when at age 35 and with three children (6, 8 and 10), she entered the Howard University School of Law. After receiving a juris doctorate degree, graduating cum laude, she began a new career.

In addition to her NAACP presidency, Dillard heads Dillard and Associates, a Fort Washington, Maryland, law firm that specializes in small business and family law and mediation. She also serves as a mediator for the Maryland Human Relations Commission. With teaching and education always tugging at her heart, Dillard is a former adjunct professor at the Howard University School of Law, where she taught small business law for ten years.

Although proud of her many past and present affiliations and accomplishments, Dillard is extremely honored to oversee the Cora Rice-Annual Police Community Christmas Party for Deserving Children, a special holiday initiative started by the late Cora Rice 25 years ago.

"Cora L. Rice was my mentor," says Dillard. "She served for a long time as president of the Prince George's County NAACP, and was a great community activist who fought discrimination and segregation throughout this area. After she passed many years ago, it has been my honor to give leadership to her annual tradition of making Christmas special for over 500 underserved children."

ORCHESTRATING BLACK LEADERSHIP

GARY L. FLOWERS

Executive Director & Chief Executive Officer
Black Leadership Forum, Inc.

By Donald James

Gary L. Flowers was just 5 years old when he heard the shocking news that civil rights leader Dr. Martin Luther King Jr. had been murdered. Flowers was deeply moved because his parents constantly talked about King's valiant work as a "drum major for justice" that brought people together, regardless of race, religion or resources. "The little Flowers boy," as he was referred to in his hometown of Richmond, Virginia, vowed to one day connect people around civil and human rights, much like King had done.

Today, 41 years following King's death, Flowers is executive director and CEO of Black Leadership Forum, Incorporated (BLF), an alliance of more than 50 of the nation's premier and proactive African-American organizations that includes the National Urban League, the Congressional Black Caucus Foundation, Inc., the National Council of Negro Women, the Conference of Minority Transportation Officials, the NAACP, the National Newspaper Publishers Association, the National Coalition on Black Civic Participation, the RainbowPUSH Coalition, and 100 Black Men of America. Collectively, member organizations advocate the policy interests of black people at the federal, state, county and municipal level.

For more than four decades, Flowers' career has been a natural progression of passion and preparation, coming together for the opportunity to serve and help people. After studying anthropology, black history and economics at the University of Virginia, Flowers was trained in civil rights law at the historic law firm of Hill, Tucker & Marsh in Richmond. Following an executive directorship of the Old Dominion Bar Association in Virginia, he served as a special assistant to Virginia Governor Lawrence Douglas Wilder, and later as a policy analyst on the Lawyers' Committee for Civil Rights Under Law in Washington, D.C.

In 1997 Flowers joined the national staff of Jesse Jackson's RainbowPUSH Coalition in Chicago, where he directed policy analysis, message development, program development, historical research and protest logistics. As a writer, he penned the *Jacks Fax,* a weekly public policy publication. While on sabbatical in 2004, Flowers accepted a fellowship to teach a course on coalition politics at Harvard University's Kennedy School of Government.

Since 2007, Flowers views his role much like that of a jazz orchestra leader who develops each section separately and later aggregates them harmoniously. Under his directorship, Flowers masterfully connects BLF member organizations, one to another, while simultaneously coupling them to help people in need. In essence, when the capability of each organization is exposed, the power of the entire organization is enhanced.

Additionally, in February of 2009, Flowers was instrumental in launching BLF's first-of-its-kind Internet television network, Black Leadership Forum Television (BLF.tv). BLF.tv features the video content of national black organizations that are BLF members. Using a new media platform, BLF.tv exposes archival content and video streams live events, while digitizing to a new demographic globally. In short, BLF.tv is a 24-hour, seven-day-a-week Internet television network, functioning as a "black C-SPAN" to change the perception of how the world views black organizations in America.

For Flowers, the "drum beat for justice" goes on. "Although I never met Dr. King, I have studied and been heavily influenced by his philosophy and practices," says Flowers. "And now, I have the honor and privilege to do what I really love to do-advance the interests of black people by linking leadership to legislation."

Photo by: Donald L. Baker

THE TRUTH LIVES ON

TIERRA HOLLOWAY
Little Ms. Sojourner Truth

By Donald James

It has been 126 years since the demise of Sojourner Truth, the bold black woman who valiantly battled for women's rights and courageously fought against slavery in America. However, through the spirited actions of 13-year-old Tierra Holloway, "the truth" lives on.

An 8th grader at K.I.P.P. AIM Academy in Southeast Washington, D.C., Holloway has portrayed Truth on numerous occasions. Her amazing depiction of the abolitionist, complete with authentic attire, dialogue and grit, was first showcased during the annual "Blacks in Wax" event in February of 2009. Sponsored by the Recreation Wish List Committee (RWLC), located in the nation's capital, the event featured young people realistically portraying prominent African-American figures. Since then, Holloway has received great reviews for her depictions of Truth. The recognition, however, reached a higher level in April of this year when she gave a brilliant performance at a ceremony unveiling a bust of Truth. This historic event, held at the U.S. Capitol, marked the first time that an African-American woman had been memorialized with a bust at the famed Washington, D.C., landmark. Accolades for Holloway's performance were in abundance, and emanated from such guests as First Lady Michelle Obama, Secretary of State Hillary Clinton and Speaker of the House Nancy Pelosi.

"Sojourner Truth was a brave woman who was not afraid to stand up and speak up for what she believed in," explains Holloway of her admiration for Truth. "She was passionate about helping people gain freedom."

Holloway thanks Cora Masters Barry, former first lady of Washington, D.C., and founder and chief executive officer of RWLC, for helping prepare and develop the script for the tributes to Truth. She calls Masters Barry a great mentor and coach.

Holloway's mother, Tamika, introduced her daughter to Masters Barry several years ago, while working as an administrative assistant for the Washington, D.C., powerbroker. Through mentoring and opportunities offered by RWLC, Holloway has participated in an array of academic, cultural, life-building and sports programs, the latter of which introduced her to playing competitive tennis.

Holloway also credits Masters Barry with introducing her to numerous prominent women who include Maya Angelou, Dr. Dorothy Height, Susan Taylor, Cicely Tyson and Cathy Hughes. Holloway has also met Dr. Julianne Malveaux, president of Bennett College for Women in Greensboro, North Carolina. Holloway was so inspired by Malveaux that the young lady formed the Junior Bennett Belles, a club for girls age 10 to 15 that combines team step dancing with community service and college preparatory activities. Malveaux was so impressed with Holloway's ambition that she invited the youth, along with two other Junior Bennett Belles, to attend and speak at her presidential inauguration at Bennett College for Women in March of 2008.

While college is several years away, Holloway, who carries a 3.65 GPA, has Bennett College for Women at the top of her list of institutions to consider after high school. With a great love for math and science, she wants to become a neurosurgeon.

Even at 12, Holloway, a proud Christian, offers this advice to youth: "Have goals in life and don't let people stop you from reaching your goals. It's not always about having fun; it's about being serious and working hard to reach life's goals."

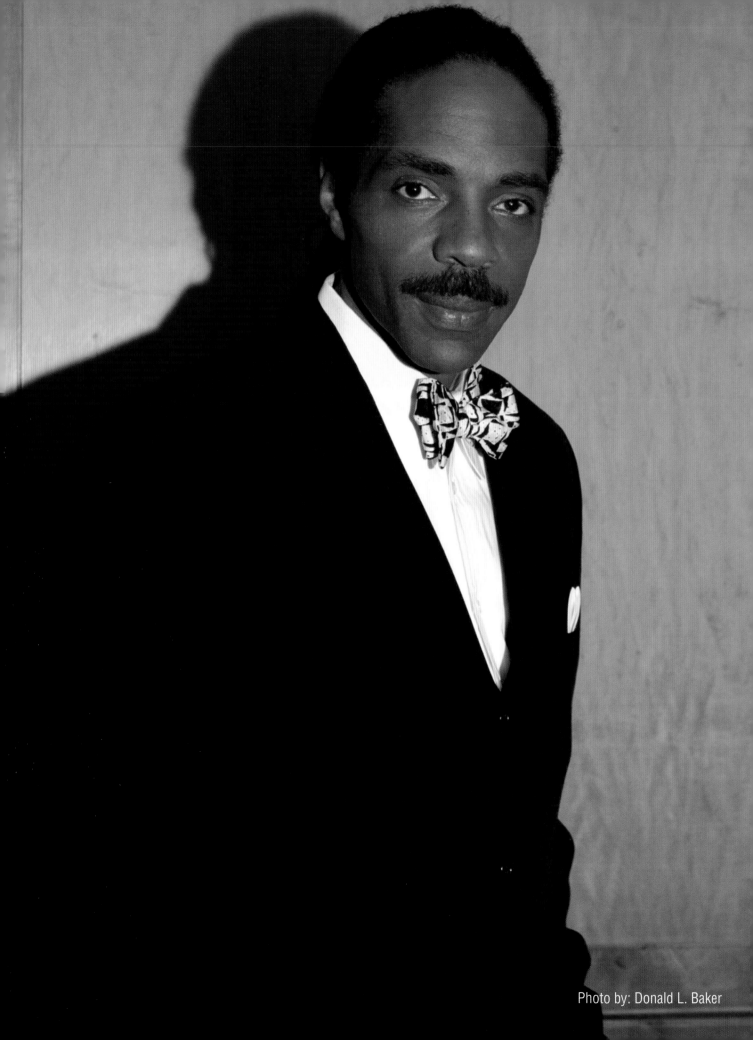

Photo by: Donald L. Baker

A MAJOR INSPIRATION

JEFF MAJORS
Gospel Composer, Harpist & Television Host

By Donald James

As one of the world's premier gospel composers, singers, harpists and recording artists, Jeff Majors has touched the souls of music lovers with his incredible and unique style of inspirational songs and vocalizations. One music critic boldly describes Majors as "a stunning composer, singer and musician, who has the inspirational vehicle to musically transport audiences to the essence of God."

After releasing his debut CD in 1998 entitled *Sacred*, Majors has recorded seven other spirit-stirring recordings. His latest CD, *Sacred 8*, released in August of 2009, represents his efforts to fulfill his planned series of 12 faith-affirming, soul-touching recordings. *Sacred 8* includes such guest artists as Shirley Murdock, Ali Woodson, Chuck Brown and the legendary 1970s powerhouse band Mandrill.

Born and raised in Washington, D.C., Majors began playing the harp after dreaming about the instrument while in his mid-teens. Determined to master the instrument, he moved to Los Angeles in the early 1980s, where he met and studied with two of the world's greatest harpists and pianists, Dorothy Ashby and Alice Coltrane, the latter of whom was the wife of the late John Coltrane, an iconic jazz saxophonist.

"Dorothy Ashby and Alice Coltrane were both incredible harpists," says Majors. "Alice Coltrane was also a great inspiration and influence on me, not just musically, but also from a spiritual point of view. She helped me to become more disciplined, and helped me to gear up for my spiritually travels."

While Majors has taken his ministry of music to places near and far, he continues to host *The Gospel of Music with Jeff Majors*, a daily TV One flagship program that appears in more than 44 million homes. The program is now in its sixth season. Many of the top recording artists in gospel and secular music have appeared on his television shows, including Yolanda Adams, Shirley Caesar, Gerald Levert, James Ingram, Mavis Staples and more.

In an effort to focus more on his music and humanitarian projects, Majors is presently on hiatus from his position as vice president of gospel programming for Radio One, Inc., a network of 13 gospel radio stations. Founded and owned by entertainment mogul Cathy L. Hughes, Radio One is the largest radio broadcasting company that primarily targets African-American and urban listeners.

As a humanitarian, Majors, through his nonprofit organization, The Network of Doves, works hand-in-hand with churches, charitable organizations and social agencies across America to address the issues of homelessness. In conjunction with his organization, he continues to perform on his annual multicity tour of free concerts called Jeff Majors Blankets for the Homeless. Now in its fourth year, the concerts give Majors the national platform to distribute needed blankets and street survival kits to the homeless, while giving a voice of advocacy to the voiceless. Through The Network of Doves, he has helped more than 60,000 homeless people and families.

"We live in perhaps the greatest country in the world, yet we have people and entire families that are homeless and are sleeping on the streets," says Majors. "It's not a cash issue; however, it's a resource issue. Through my organization and my music, I'm working to connect the dots that are bridging churches, corporations, social agencies and community groups to help the homeless."

KUSTOM LOOKS
CLOTHIER

clothes for YOUR body . . .
not ANY body

8737 Colesville Road . Silver Spring MD 20910 . (877) 371-2161

Washington, D.C.
CORPORATE SPOTLIGHT

INTEREST

LIMELIGHT

ATTENTION

PROMINENCE

NEW
YORK
LIFE

The Company You Keep®

HIGHLIGHT

CELEBRATE

HEADLINE

FOCUS

RECOGNITION

CORPORATE SPOTLIGHT

Myra Abdullah

Financial Services Professional
Northern Virginia General Office
New York Life

Moses Eric Cobb II

Financial Services Professional
Northern Virginia General Office
New York Life

Myra Abdullah joined New York Life Insurance Company in June of 2007. Myra has parlayed her business management skills and education into a growing financial services practice as a registered representative with New York Life. She has achieved the prestigious Executive Council status with New York Life in both 2008 and 2009.

Myra serves the residents and small businesses of Prince George's County, Maryland, and its surrounding area. She specializes in helping families understand and select their appropriate amount of life insurance coverage; she conducts seminars for women's groups that focus on helping women build strong financial foundations; and she assists numerous young professionals in attaining personal assets for future use.

Myra earned a Bachelor of Science degree in health care administration with a minor in business administration from Penn State University in 1989. She then pursued a Master of Business Administration degree from Baruch College/Mount Sinai School of Medicine in 1991.

Myra and her business continue to flourish with the support of her husband, Ameer, who also helps her raise their two school-aged children in Bowie, Maryland.

Moses Cobb is an agent and registered representative for NYLIFE Securities in the Greater Washington, D.C., metropolitan area.

He has garnered several company awards and achievements including being a yearly qualifying member of New York Life's internal producing clubs, which measure commitment to service as well as outright production. Moses served in the capacity as a partner and recruiter for the company for three years. During his tenure in management, he assisted in growing his general office's number of agents as well as servants to the community.

Moses believes in spreading the basic to more complex elements of insurance and investment planning to everyone he is blessed to come in contact with. Moses understands that people wish not to be sold products but do wish to have the information they need to get to the next level.

A lifetime member of Alpha Phi Alpha Fraternity, Inc., Moses sits on the board of directors for Winner's Lacrosse in D.C., which seeks to expose inner-city youth to the game of lacrosse. Moses is a lucky husband along with being a very proud father.

CORPORATE SPOTLIGHT

Robert Gregory, Ph.D.

Agent, Manager &
Registered Representative
Greater Washington General Office
New York Life

Dr. Robert Gregory is a trusted financial adviser, management associate and recruiter for the Greater Washington General Office of the New York Life Insurance Company.

With more than 30 years of financial services industry experience, Gregory's "service above self" commitment is anchored by his involvement as vice chair of the Baltimore County Planning Board, trustee of the Maryland Historical Society, board member of the National Association of Independent Financial Advisors, president of the Owings Mills/Reisterstown Rotary Club, and advisory board member of the National Association of Black Accountants.

Gregory remains active in the prestigious Million Dollar Round Table, a premier association of financial professionals. He is also a member of The Maryland 10th Calvary Gun Club, the Fraternal Order of Police Lodge No. 3, and Iota Phi Theta Fraternity, Inc.

Gregory received bachelor's and Master of Business Administration degrees from Loyola College and a Doctor of Philosophy degree from LaSalle University. He also holds a seventh degree master black belt. When he is not working for his clients and the community, he enjoys hunting, fishing and spending time with his family.

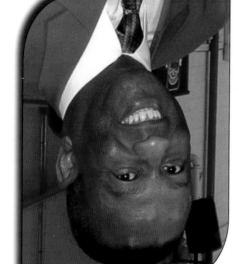

Richard "Sonny" Hill

Financial Services Professional
Northern Virginia General Office
New York Life

Richard "Sonny" Hill joined New York Life Insurance Company 28 years ago. He has been a consistent producer throughout his career. He focuses his professional practice in the area of long-term care planning and executive benefits for large and small businesses. He has mentored many new agents as a way of giving back to the career he has long enjoyed.

Sonny is an active member of the Prince Hall Masons and Prentice-Hall Shrine organizations through which he provides information on financial literacy to the members and the African-American community at large. He is highly respected as a financial professional through his many social activities as well, which include ballroom and salsa dancing. Additionally, he is a private pilot and an avid scuba diver and snowboarder.

A native of New York City, Sonny is a veteran of the U.S. Army during which time he served as the first African American to be accepted into the prestigious Army Golden Knights Parachute Demonstration Team. He was also invited and participated in the parachute jump commemorating the 75th birthday of President George H.W. Bush.

CORPORATE SPOTLIGHT

George Nichols III
Senior Vice President
Office of Governmental Affairs
New York Life

George Nichols III serves as the senior vice president in charge of the Office of Governmental Affairs, which includes federal, state and international and NYLPAC. He is a member of New York Life's Executive Management Committee.

In his previous role, Nichols was senior vice president and Profit Center head for New York Life's AARP Tampa Operations, the No. 1 direct marketer of life insurance for people more than 50 years old. From October of 2001 until April of 2003, he was senior vice president of agency, working with the company's 10,000 licensed U.S. agents in the areas of compliance, standards, communications and technology.

Before joining New York Life as senior vice president and assistant to the chairman in January of 2001, Nichols was commissioner of the Kentucky Department of Insurance.

Nichols received an Associate of Arts degree from Alice Lloyd College, a Bachelor of Arts degree from Western Kentucky University, and a Master of Arts degree from the University of Louisville. He currently resides in Potomac, Maryland, with his wife, Cynthia, and their three children, Courtney, Jessica and George IV.

Melanie V. White
Agent/Registered Representative
Greater Washington General Office
New York Life

Melanie V. White is a member of Harbor Financial Group, which specializes in protection, retirement, wealth accumulation and preservation planning for individuals and small businesses. She is a Series 66 licensed registered investment advisor and a Series 7 licensed registered representative with NYLIFE Securities, LLC, and earned the certified in long term care designation.

Currently, Melanie serves as a board member of the National Association of Insurance and Financial Advisors, Baltimore Chapter, and is a member of the National African American Insurance Association.

Melanie has received the First Year Top Achiever Award, the Presidents Award and the Professional Experienced Agent of the Month. As a consistent council agent, she regularly receives the Annuity Champion Award and the Long Term Care Circle of Champions Award.

Melanie graduated from the University of Virginia as an economics major and a sociology minor. She has also earned an executive certificate in financial planning from Georgetown University. She is a member of the Women's Ministry and secretary of the usher board at her church. Melanie also enjoys running, traveling, watching football and spending time with family and friends.

Broderick L. Young is a director of development in the Greater Washington General Office, a Tier I general office in the New York Life agency system. Some of his responsibilities include retention, marketing, increasing sales, case development and new agent development.

Broderick joined New York Life Insurance Company in 2000 as an agent and registered representative in the South Florida General Office. Before deciding to transition into management, he received awards as the Leading New Sales Associate in the South Florida General Office in 2001 and 2002. He has held positions in Valley Forge, Pennsylvania, and Orlando, Florida.

Broderick is a graduate of the University of Florida and while working with New York Life, he has obtained the designations of certified financial planner, chartered life underwriter, chartered financial consultant and chartered advisor for senior living. He is dedicated to helping individuals obtain financial stability.

Broderick and his wife, Nicolette, live in Columbia, Maryland.

Broderick Young

Director of Development
Greater Washington General Office
New York Life

Washington, D.C.
CORPORATE SPOTLIGHT

INTEREST

LIMELIGHT

ATTENTION

PROMINENCE

Pepco Holdings, Inc

HIGHLIGHT

CELEBRATE

HEADLINE

FOCUS

RECOGNITION

Joy J. Dorsey

Director of Diversity &
Supplier Diversity
Pepco Holdings, Inc.

Thomas H. Graham

Region President
Potomac Electric Power Company
Pepco

Joy J. Dorsey is director of diversity and supplier diversity for Pepco Holdings, Inc. (PHI). In this position, Joy is responsible for corporatewide coordination and execution of PHI's internal and external diversity strategies, particularly the promotion of fair and consistent talent management practices, and the maximization of contracting opportunities for diverse suppliers and vendors.

Joy joined Pepco in 1988 as a lawyer and has held various positions of increasing responsibility within the company, including vice president/general counsel for Pepco Energy Services and vice president/deputy general counsel for Potomac Capital Investment.

Joy received a Bachelor of Arts degree in economics from Howard University and a juris doctorate degree from Hofstra University. She is a member of the New York State and Maryland State bar associations, The District of Columbia Bar, The Conference Board's Council of Diversity Executives, Jobs for America's Graduates – D.C. board of directors and the North Carolina State University College of Management diversity advisory board.

Joy lives in the District of Columbia with her children, Gabriel and Dakota.

Thomas H. Graham is the region president for Pepco, a power delivery company that provides electricity to more than 750,000 customers. Graham is the key spokesman for the company, responsible for developing public policy and reconciling government and civic issues throughout the company's service territory.

Graham created Pepco's Community Partnership Program that received two industry excellence awards from the Edison Electric Institute and the Southeastern Electric Exchange.

Graham graduated from St. John's College High School and received a Bachelor of Science degree from The University of Tampa. He was a member of their first national championship soccer team and played professionally for the Jacksonville Tea Men. He recently completed the Senior Executive Leadership Certificate Program at Georgetown University.

Graham is a native Washingtonian and has two sons, Jordan, 19, and Jeffrey, 14. He serves on numerous boards including the D.C. and Maryland chambers of commerce, Strathmore, Mentors, Inc., HEROES, Inc., and Leadership Prince George's County.

Debbi Jarvis

Vice President of
Corporate Communications
Pepco Holdings, Inc.

Beverly L. Perry

Senior Vice President
Government Affairs & Public Policy
Pepco Holdings, Inc.

Debbi Jarvis is vice president of corporate communications for Pepco Holdings, Inc., the parent company of utilities Atlantic City Electric, Delmarva Power and Pepco. She is responsible for external and internal communications and serves as the "face and voice" of the company in radio and television commercials. Before joining Pepco, she co-anchored the weekend morning news for NBC4.

Debbi graduated from Hope College in Holland, Michigan, with a degree in international business. She has also pursued MBA studies at Southeastern University and completed the utility executive course at the University of Idaho. Additionally, she is a member of Leadership Greater Washington.

Debbi believes in giving back to the community and is proud to serve on the advisory councils of the Capital Breast Care Center and the Washington Mystics. She also serves on the board of the D.C. Police Foundation and the United Way of the National Capital Area. For the second consecutive year, Debbi is chair for the United Way National Capital Area's charitable campaign.

Debbi is married to real estate executive Ernest Drew Jarvis, and is the mother of two sons.

Beverly L. Perry is senior vice president for government affairs and public policy for Pepco Holdings, Inc. (PHI), a regional energy holding company that provides utility service to approximately 1.9 million customers. PHI is the parent company of Potomac Electric Power Company, an electric utility serving Washington, D.C., and suburban Maryland; Delmarva Power, an electric and gas utility serving Delaware and the rest of the Delmarva Peninsula; and Atlantic City Electric, an electric utility serving southern New Jersey.

Perry is a native of Franklinton, North Carolina, and a former tobacco farmer. She received a law degree from Georgetown University and an undergraduate degree from The George Washington University.

Perry developed her career in public policy through civic leadership and her commitment to community activities. She currently serves on numerous boards and commissions, including chair of the board of the Washington Convention Center Authority and The African American Civil War Memorial. Additionally, she is an active member of the Greater Washington Urban League, Arena Stage, the Congressional Black Caucus Political Education & Leadership Committee, and the Capital City Chapter of The Links, Inc.

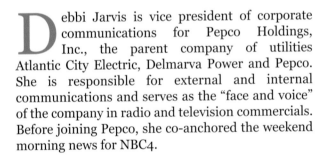

CORPORATE SPOTLIGHT

Pepco Holdings Inc

Pepco Holdings Inc

Deborah M. Royster

Deputy General Counsel
Pepco Holdings, Inc.

Deborah Royster serves as deputy general counsel for Pepco Holdings, Inc. (PHI). In this role, she manages PHI's diverse range of issues before the public service commissions of Maryland, Delaware and the District of Columbia, the New Jersey Board of Public Utilities, and the Federal Energy Regulatory Commission.

Royster is a magna cum laude graduate of the University of Maryland, College Park, with a Bachelor of Science degree in journalism. A graduate of the University of Virginia School of Law, she is a member of The District of Columbia Bar.

Her active record of community service includes chairman of the board of directors of the Providence Health Foundation; vice chair of DC Appleseed; parliamentarian of the Capital City Chapter of The Links, Inc; a commissioner on the D.C. Arts and Humanities Commission; and a member of the D.C. Public Access Corporation board of directors and the Washington, D.C. Alumnae Chapter of Delta Sigma Theta Sorority, Inc.

Royster is a native of Washington, D.C., where she resides with her husband, Robert A. Malson.

Pepco Holdings, Inc

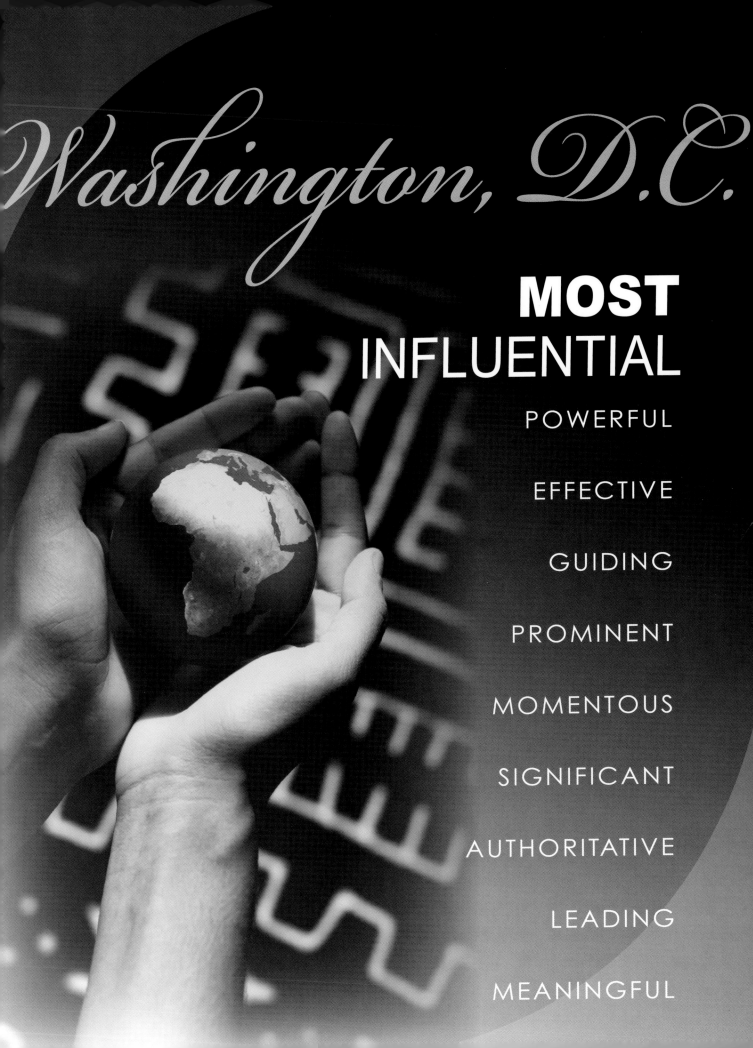

Washington, D.C.

MOST
INFLUENTIAL

POWERFUL

EFFECTIVE

GUIDING

PROMINENT

MOMENTOUS

SIGNIFICANT

AUTHORITATIVE

LEADING

MEANINGFUL

Abe Abraham

President & Chief Executive Officer
CMI Management, Inc.

Abe Abraham is president and chief executive officer of CMI Management, Inc. Through his executive, strategic and operational direction, he has fostered the company's growth from an 8(a) program graduate to a thriving corporation, securing a $400 million records management contract. Founded in 1989 by Abe, CMI's corporate revenue for 2008 was $62 million.

Abe and CMI have been recognized across the industry. They have been featured in the *Washington Business Journal*, ranked as the 11th fastest-growing company in *Washington Technology*'s Fast 50, named to *Washington SmartCEO*'s Future 50, named one of the nation's 50 Most Influential Minorities in Business by the Minority Business and Professional Network Inc., and featured in the *Black Enterprise* Top 100 list for four consecutive years. Additionally, he recently received CMI's third Northern Virginia Business Success Award.

Abe received a Bachelor of Arts degree from Baldwin-Wallace College and a Master of Business Administration degree from Northwest Missouri State University. Natives of Ethiopia and now United States citizens, Abe and his wife, Azzi, are the proud parents of daughter Jiitu and son Yohannes.

Marcellus W. Alexander Jr.

Executive Vice President of Television
National Association of Broadcasters

Marcellus Alexander was named executive vice president of television for the National Association of Broadcasters (NAB) in October of 2002. He is responsible for providing a broadcast operator's perspective on legislative and regulatory issues, as well as oversight of television membership, and other key events and sessions.

Effective April 1, 2004, he was also named president of the NAB Education Foundation. His focus is providing broadcast training programs that strengthen the industry's workforce, community service and philanthropy.

Previously, Marcellus was station manager and acting general manager of KYW-TV Philadelphia from 1987 to 1989, and then served as vice president and general manager from 1999 until 2002. Before KYW, Marcellus was vice president and general manager of WJZ-TV Baltimore. Earlier on, he spent ten years in radio at the then-ABC-owned station WRIF-FM Detroit, advancing to become vice president and general manager.

A native of Austin, Texas, Marcellus holds a Bachelor of Science degree from Texas State University. In 1994 his alma mater presented him with its Distinguished Alumni Award. The following year, he received an honorary doctorate degree from Western Maryland College.

The Honorable Yvette Alexander was born, raised and educated in Washington, D.C., and advocates for long-term progressive change for all Ward 7 citizens and the District of Columbia.

In her first term, she introduced 11 pieces of legislation, and co-introduced and co-sponsored numerous others. Alexander chairs the Committee on Aging and Community Affairs and is a member of the committees on Public Safety and the Judiciary; Health; Economic Development; and Libraries, Parks and Recreation. The only female representative of the D.C. Democratic State Committee at the Democratic Convention in 2004, she lobbied for support of D.C. voting rights. Additionally, she was elected as a District of Columbia super delegate in 2008.

Alexander has received several prestigious awards, including the Paula Nickens Grassroots Award from the District of Columbia Democratic State Committee and the Lorraine H. Whitlock Democrat of the Year from the Ward 7 Democrats, among others.

Alexander received a Bachelor of Business Administration degree from Howard University and studied graduate work at Trinity College. She is a member of Holy Redeemer Catholic Church, where she serves on the Parish Council.

The Honorable Yvette M. Alexander

Council Member, Ward 7
Council of the District of Columbia

The Honorable Marilynn M. Bland is currently serving her second term of office representing District 9 on the Prince George's County Council. First elected to the county council in 2002, she was chosen by her colleagues to serve as council chairperson for the legislative year of 2009.

Committed to enhancing the quality of life for young people, and a longtime education advocate, Bland was elected to the Prince George's County Board of Education in 1996 and re-elected in 2000. She successfully introduced legislation adopted by the council establishing the County Youth Commission and giving youth a voice in policy decisions.

Bland earned a Bachelor of Science degree from The University of Southern Mississippi, and a Doctor of Humane Letters degree from Springfield Christian College and Theological Seminary. A registered nurse, she has served the country as a commissioned officer in the U.S. Air Force Nurse Corps.

Bland was recognized in *Cambridge Who's Who*. In addition, she is the proud mother of college students Justin, a master's candidate, and Tonya, an undergraduate student.

The Honorable Marilynn M. Bland

Representative, District 9
Prince George's County Council

The Honorable
Muriel Bowser

Council Member, Ward 4
Council of the District of Columbia

The Honorable Muriel Bowser is a fourth-generation Washingtonian with a long-standing record of active participation in local and regional government. She is currently serving her second term on the Council of the District of Columbia, and is focused on bringing programs and services closer to the communities and neighborhoods that need them.

Bowser is chair of the Committee on Public Services and Consumer Affairs and is also a member of the committees on Economic Development, Human Services, Public Works and Transportation, and Public Safety and the Judiciary.

In the past, she served as an advisory neighborhood commissioner with an executive committee post, as well as vice president of the Ward 4 Democrats. She has been an active participant in her local civic association, rising to the rank of second vice president of the Lamond-Riggs Citizens Association.

Bowser has a Bachelor of Arts degree from Chatham College in Pittsburgh, Pennsylvania, and a master's degree in public policy from American University in Washington, D.C.

Pamela K. Brady, D.D.S.

Dentist
Pamela K. Brady, D.D.S., P.C.

Dr. Pamela Brady is a general dentist in Washington, D.C., where she has been in private practice since 1993. Her practice offers comprehensive general dentistry, with a gentle touch and an eye for detail.

Brady received a Bachelor of Science degree from Clark College in Atlanta, Georgia, and a Doctor of Dental Surgery degree from Howard University in Washington, D.C.

Additionally, Brady is a member of the American Dental Association, the District of Columbia Dental Society, the American Association of Dental Examiners, the District of Columbia Board of Dentistry and the North East Regional Board.

Clayola Brown is the first and only female president of the A. Philip Randolph Institute (APRI). Additionally, she serves as international vice president and civil rights director for Workers United, and national director of Amalgamated Bank.

Clayola's board service includes positions with the NAACP's Image Awards and Labor Ad-Hoc committees, the Congressional Black Caucus Foundation, Inc. and the United Nations Advisory Council. She was appointed by President Bill Clinton as commissioner of the National Commission on Employment Policy and by Governor George Pataki as a member of the New York State Workforce Investment Board.

The RainbowPUSH Coalition awarded Clayola the Jackie Vaughn Award. In addition, she received the NAACP's Freedom Leadership Award, the Coalition of Black Trade Unionists' Bill Lucy Award and the YWCA Academy of Women Achievers Award. Additionally, the Southern Christian Leadership Conference awarded her the Drum Major for Justice Award and the APRI honored her with the Rosina Tucker Award.

A graduate of Florida A&M University, Clayola completed postgraduate work at American University, Queens College and York University. Presently, she is a lecturer at Cornell University.

Clayola Brown

President
A. Philip Randolph Institute

The Honorable Kwame R. Brown has spent a lifetime working for the things that matter most to Washington, D.C.'s families. In a short time, he has emerged as a national leader, and currently serves as chair of the council's Committee on Economic Development and vice chair of the Metropolitan Washington Council of Governments. He is the first D.C. council member to serve on the Congressional Award Foundation board of directors, a national organization that promotes youth volunteerism, public service and physical fitness.

His first term in office led to the construction of Phelps Architecture, Construction & Engineering High School, passage of the School Modernization Act, a reform of the district's domestic violence laws, and an unprecedented focus on neighborhood revitalization, job training and local small businesses.

Kwame was recently named one of the Top 10 People to Watch in 2009 by the *Washington Business Journal* and was featured as The Watchdog in a summer of 2009 *OnSite Magazine* cover story.

The Honorable
Kwame R. Brown

At-Large Council Member
Council of the District of Columbia

William Burrus

President
American Postal Workers Union

William Burrus is president of the American Postal Workers Union, which represents more than 280,000 employees of the U.S. Postal Service. Elected president of the world's largest postal union in 2001, he had served as executive vice president since 1980. In 2001 Burrus was also elected to the Executive Council of the AFL-CIO, where he serves as a vice president. He began his employment with the U.S. Post Office in 1958 as a distribution clerk in Cleveland and participated in the Great Postal Strike of 1970.

Burrus is a member of the Executive Committee of Union Network International, a global federation of unions representing postal and other service workers, and serves on the Federal Advisory Council on Occupational Safety and Health. Each year since 2002, *Ebony* has named him one of their 100 Most Influential Black Americans.

A native of Wheeling, West Virginia, Burrus and his wife, Ethelda, reside in southern Maryland. He has four daughters, Valerie, Doni, Kimberly and Kristy, one stepson, Antwon, seven grandchildren and seven great-grandchildren.

LaVarne A. Burton

President & Chief Executive Officer
American Kidney Fund

LaVarne A. Burton is president and chief executive officer of the American Kidney Fund, the nation's No. 1 source of direct financial assistance to kidney patients.

Prior to joining the American Kidney Fund in 2005, LaVarne served as president of the Pharmaceutical Care Management Association. From 1997 to 2001, she served as executive secretary to the U.S. Department of Health and Human Services (HHS), where she managed policy development and regulations, and was an advisor to the secretary of the largest domestic agency within the federal government. Previously, she served as deputy assistant secretary of budget policy at HHS, and worked on Capitol Hill as a senior analyst for Medicare, Medicaid and health policy on the U.S. House of Representative's Budget Committee.

LaVarne received a bachelor's degree from Howard University and a master's degree from The George Washington University. She sits on the board of advisors for Women Business Leaders in the U.S. Health Care Industry Foundation, of which she is a founding member. Additionally, LaVarne is a National Academy of Public Administration fellow.

J ohn B. Catoe Jr. has more than 30 years of experience in public transportation. As general manager of the Washington Metropolitan Area Transit Authority (Metro), he leads the second-largest rail transit system and the seventh-largest bus network in the United States, which includes more than 10,000 employees, a $1.3 billion operating budget and a $3.1 billion five-year Capital Improvement Program.

Upon joining Metro in 2007, John immediately focused on a complete overhaul of the transit system with the goal of operating Metro in the most efficient and cost-effective manner without sacrificing safety or service for customers.

In 2009 the American Public Transportation Association named him the nation's top public transportation manager and he oversaw the exceptional, record-breaking service that Metro provided during the inauguration of President Barack Obama. That day, Metro transported more than 1.5 million people and operated rush-hour service for 17 straight hours.

Originally from Washington, D.C., John graduated from Cardozo High School. He earned a Bachelor of Science degree in business administration from the University of Redlands in Redlands, California.

John B. Catoe Jr.

General Manager
Washington Metropolitan Area
Transit Authority

J ohn Crump has served as executive director of the National Bar Association (NBA) for more than 30 years. He has led the NBA to define itself as an institution committed to the preservation of jurisprudence. His leadership has allowed him to manage and coordinate policies and procedures that impact legal professionals of color.

A Carnegie Urban fellow, Crump has served on several executive committees and as vice chairman for the American Society of Association Executives and the Convention Liasion Council. He received the Distinguished Service Award from the Council of Black Judges in America, the Washington, D.C. Bar Association's 2009 President's Recognition Award, and was named one of the most influential African Americans in the meeting and tourism industry.

His legacy and commitment to service is extended though his annual Crump Law Camp, which provides students grades 9 through 11 the opportunity to diversify the legal profession and acquire the skills to become effective lawyers.

Crump received bachelor's and juris doctorate degrees from Texas Southern University. A native of La Grange, Texas, he is the husband of Edythe. They have one son, Jason.

John Crump

Executive Director
National Bar Association

Ralph B. Everett

President & Chief Executive Officer
Joint Center for Political and
Economic Studies

Ralph B. Everett is president and chief executive officer of the Joint Center for Political and Economic Studies, a think tank focused on African-American issues. Prior to this position, he spent 18 years with the law firm of Paul, Hastings, Janofsky & Walker LLP, where he became its first African-American partner. Previously, Everett worked in the U.S. Senate for more than a decade, including service as staff director and chief counsel of the Committee on Commerce, Science and Transportation. He is on the boards of Cumulus Media, Inc.; Connected Nation; the National Coalition on Black Civic Participation, Independent Sector; and the Black Leadership Forum.

President Clinton appointed Everett as U.S. ambassador to the International Telecommunications Union Plenipotentiary Conference in 1998. That year, he also led the U.S. delegation to the Second World Telecommunication Development Conference.

Most recently, Everett was team lead for the Obama-Biden Transition Project Agency Review Working Group. One of *Ebony*'s 150 Most Influential African Americans, he is a Phi Beta Kappa graduate of Morehouse College and holds a Doctor of Jurisprudence degree from the Duke University School of Law.

Elliott Ferguson II

President & Chief Executive Officer
Destination DC

Elliott Ferguson serves as president and chief executive officer of Destination DC. Starting his tenure with the organization as vice president of convention sales and services back in December of 2001, he led the organization's efforts to promote Washington, D.C., as a premier meeting and convention destination. In his new role, he will lead the sales and marketing organization, and manage the finance and business development operations.

A 20-year veteran of the convention and visitors bureau (CVB) industry, Elliot previously served as vice president of sales at the Atlanta, Georgia, CVB. Additionally, he has served as director of sales for the Atlanta and Savannah, Georgia, CVBs.

Elliot received a Bachelor of Arts degree in marketing and business administration from Savannah State University. He is a member of the American Society of Association Executives, the National Coalition of Black Meeting Planners, the Religious Conference Management Association and the Professional Convention Management Association. In addition, he also serves as a board member for the March of Dimes Maryland-National Capital Area Chapter.

Angie M. Gates, a New Orleans native via Mississippi, made history in 2006 when she was appointed as the first African-American general manager of Washington, D.C.'s Warner Theatre. Throughout her career, she has worked with BET, Jamie Foxx, Jay-Z, Lil Wayne, Patti LaBelle, Tyler Perry, General Colin Powell, Julia Roberts, Chris Rock, Paul Simon, Sting, Stevie Wonder, Broadway productions and President Barack Obama.

Gates received a Bachelor of Arts degree in communication and a Master of Arts degree with a concentration in sports management, graduating summa cum laude, from The University of New Orleans.

Departing New Orleans as director of entertainment at the Saenger Theatre, Gates joined Live Nation, the world's largest entertainment promoter, in New York City as director of engagement relations and marketing before coming to the Warner Theatre.

Gates, former Miss University of New Orleans, serves as a mentor in the Powerful Beyond Measure Program, and is a board member of the Negro League Hall of Fame and the Recording Academy. Gates is also a charter member of Alpha Kappa Alpha Sorority, Inc.

Angie M. Gates

General Manager
Warner Theatre

Michael Grant serves as president of the National Bankers Association and its foundation. Additionally, he serves as board secretary for the Minbanc Foundation, Inc., an organization that provides opportunities to promote banking careers within the country's minority communities.

A co-founder of the Greater Nashville Black Chamber of Commerce, Grant is a 1983 graduate of the Howard University School of Law. The author of two books, *Beyond Blame: Race Relations for the 21st Century* (1994) and *Your Marvelous Mind* (2000), he also served as president of the NAACP Nashville Branch. In addition, he taught political science at Morgan State University in Baltimore, Maryland.

A dynamic motivational and inspirational speaker, Grant has spoken to audiences across America, in the Virgin Islands, Puerto Rico, Jamaica and Canada. A recognized leader in community economic development for the past 20 years, he has worked with national organizations to advance and promote minority economic development.

Michael A. Grant

President
National Bankers Association

The Honorable Vincent C. Gray

Chairman
Council of the District of Columbia

A native Washingtonian, the Honorable Vincent C. Gray is a proud graduate of the District of Columbia Public Schools and The George Washington University. In 2009 he received the Distinguished Alumni Achievement Award from the university.

Gray has been the chairman of the Council of the District of Columbia since January 2, 2007. Previously, he was the Ward 7 council member for two years.

Gray began his career with the Association for Retarded Citizens where he successfully advocated for innovative public policy initiatives on behalf of people with developmental disabilities. He also held leadership roles with the Special Olympics. In 1990 Gray was appointed director of the D.C. Department of Human Services under Mayor Sharon Pratt. He founded the Covenant House Washington in 1995, a faith-based organization dedicated to serving homeless and at-risk youth.

His late wife, Loretta, who was an outstanding educator in the D.C. Public Schools, passed away in 1998. He has two children, Jonice and Carlos, and two grandchildren, Austin and Jillian. He is a lifelong baseball player and lives in the Hillcrest neighborhood of Washington, D.C.

Ernest G. Green

Managing Director, Public Finance
Barclays Capital

Ernest Green is managing director of public finance for Barclays Capital in Washington, D.C., and has served as a senior investment banker on transactions around the country. Previously, he was assistant secretary of labor under President Jimmy Carter and executive director of the Recruitment and Training Program.

Born in Little Rock, Arkansas, Green earned a high school diploma from Central High School. He and eight other black students, who would later become known as the Little Rock Nine, were the first to integrate Central High School following *Brown v. Board of Education* in 1954. Green received a Bachelor of Science degree in social science and a master's degree in sociology from Michigan State University. Additionally, he received honorary doctorate degrees from Michigan State University, Tougaloo College, Central State University and Spelman College.

Green has been the recipient of the Urban League Frederick Douglass Freedom Medal, the John D. Rockefeller Public Service Award, the NAACP Spingarn Medal and a Congressional Gold Medal of Honor, to name a few.

Married to Phyllis Caudle, he is the proud father of Adam, Jessica and MacKenzie Anne.

Chief Judge William P. Greene Jr. was appointed by President Clinton to the U.S. Court of Appeals for Veterans Claims on November 7, 1997. The court provides judicial appellate review of adverse decisions on veterans benefit claims. As chief judge, he is the principal spokesman and head of the seven-judge court.

At the time of his appointment, Greene was serving as a U.S. immigration judge, presiding over immigration cases in Maryland and Pennsylvania. A retired U.S. Army colonel from the Army Judge Advocate General's Corps, his distinguished legal career spans more than 40 years.

Greene is the recipient of many awards and decorations. A graduate of West Virginia State College and Howard University School of Law, he is married and has two sons and six grandchildren.

The Honorable
William P. Greene Jr.

Chief Judge
U.S. Court of Appeals for Veterans Claims

Norman Hill has a lifelong commitment to the struggle for racial equality, and economic and social justice. He was mentored by and worked with A. Philip Randolph, father of the modern civil rights movement, and Bayard Rustin, a civil rights activist and key advisor to Dr. Martin Luther King Jr.

Hill has served in positions with the Congress of Racial Equality and the AFL-CIO. In 1965 he co-founded the A. Philip Randolph Institute (A.P.R.I.) to promote an alliance between blacks and organized labor. Hill turned the A.P.R.I. into a grassroots-based organization with 200 national affiliates and was elected president of the institute in 1980.

Hill has published articles in such journals as *The New Leader, Social Policy, Dissent* and the *AFL-CIO News*. Additionally, he has addressed audiences throughout the world, including France, Israel, Germany, South Africa and Brazil.

In 2004 Hill retired from the A.P.R.I., but as president emeritus, he remains a tireless and dedicated activist, and stays involved in the institute's activities. He continues to promote the vision of Randolph and Rustin through his work as a writer and speaker.

Norman Hill

President Emeritus
A. Philip Randolph Institute

Eric H. Holder Jr.

U.S. Attorney General
U.S. Department of Justice

President Barack Obama announced his intention to nominate Eric H. Holder Jr. to the position of U.S. attorney general on December 1, 2008. Vice President Joe Biden swore him in as the 82nd attorney general of the United States of America on February 3, 2009.

Holder became the first African-American deputy attorney general upon appointment by President Clinton in 1997. In addition, he served as a U.S. attorney for the District of Columbia and was nominated to become associate judge of the Superior Court of the District of Columbia by President Reagan in 1988.

A native of New York City, Holder graduated from Stuyvesant High School, where he earned a Regents scholarship. He graduated from Columbia College in 1973 and majored in American history. He also graduated from Columbia Law School in 1976, where he clerked at the NAACP Legal Defense Fund and the Department of Justice's Criminal Division.

Prior to becoming attorney general, Holder was a litigation partner at Covington & Burling LLP. He lives in Washington, D.C., with his wife, Dr. Sharon Malone, a physician, and their three children.

The Honorable
Carolyn J.B. Howard

Deputy Speaker Pro Tempore
Maryland General Assembly

Delegate Carolyn J.B. Howard is a well-respected legislator with a solid record of public service, experience and high integrity. Working to preserve families and communities, secure funding for education, receive support for children and schools, fight crime and injustices, and provide affordable health care for all are among her major priorities. Her voting record has won her a 100 percent approval rating from the Maryland State Teacher's Association and a 100 percent record from the League of Conservation Voters for the environment.

Howard is currently serving in the Maryland General Assembly as speaker pro tempore and chair of the transportation subcommittee of ways and means. She is an active member of the Joint Audit, Legislative Policy, Joint Committee on the Management of Public Funds, and the Rules and Executive Nomination committees. Previously, she has chaired the Prince George's County House Delegation, the House Democratic Caucus and the Maryland Legislative Black Caucus.

Howard received a Bachelor of Science degree from Florida A&M University and a Master of Science degree from Bowie State University.

Cathy Hughes is founder and chair of Radio One, Inc., the largest African-American-owned and -operated broadcast company in the nation. Radio One is the first African-American company in radio history to dominate several major markets simultaneously, and possesses the first woman-owned radio station to rank No. 1.

Born in Omaha, Nebraska, Hughes entered radio in 1973 as general sales manager at WHUR, Howard University radio, increasing station revenue from $250,000 to $3 million her first year. In 1975 Hughes became the first female vice president and general manager of a station in D.C. and created the "quiet storm" format. Purchasing her first station in 1980, WOL-AM in D.C., Hughes pioneered another innovative format – "24-hour talk from a black perspective." With the theme, "Information is Power," WOL is the most listened to talk radio in the nation's capital.

Radio One's newest ventures includes TV One, Inc., in partnership with Comcast, *Giant* magazine, REACH Media Inc. and Interactive One.

Hughes was honored with the Lifetime Achievement Award from the Washington Area Broadcasters Association and the Seventh Congressional District Humanitarian Award.

Catherine Liggins Hughes

Founder & Chair
Radio One, Inc.

Michael Jack is president and general manager of WRC-TV NBC4's owned and operated station in Washington, D.C. Branded NBC4, the station is the news, information and community outreach leader in the market.

Michael previously served as president and general manager of WCMH-TV NBC4 in Columbus, Ohio, where the station led the market in prime time, early morning news, and the late news audience. Michael also served as vice president of sales for KNBC in Los Angeles, as well as vice president of diversity for NBC Universal from 2002 to 2006.

In addition to career achievements, Michael serves on the boards of the Greater Washington Urban League, the Boys & Girls Clubs of Greater Washington metropolitan board of directors, The Emma Bowen Foundation, the DC Chamber of Commerce, the Greater Washington Board of Trade, the Greater Washington Sports Alliance, and Destination DC. He is also a member of the 100 Black Men of Greater Washington, D.C.

Michael graduated from Haverford College in Pennsylvania with a Bachelor of Arts degree in political science. He resides in Maryland with his wife, Mary, and daughter, Truce.

Michael Jack

President & General Manager
WRC-TV NBC4

Debra L. Lee

Chairman & Chief Executive Officer
BET Networks

D ebra Lee is chairman and chief executive officer of BET Networks, a unit of Viacom Inc., and the nation's leading provider of quality entertainment for the African-American audience and consumers of black culture.

Her achievements in a 20-plus-year career at BET Networks have earned her numerous accolades from across the cable industry. Lee serves on the corporate boards of directors for Revlon, Marriott, Eastman Kodak and Washington Gas Light Co. She is also a member of the National Cable & Telecommunications Association national board of directors, the Alvin Ailey American Dance Theater, Girls Inc., the National Symphony Orchestra, the Center for Communication and the Kennedy Center's Community & Friends Board. Recently, she was appointed to the Federal Communications Commission's Advisory Committee on Diversity for Communications in the Digital Age.

Lee earned a juris doctorate degree from Harvard Law School, while earning a master's degree in public policy from the John F. Kennedy School of Government. She also graduated from Brown University with a bachelor's degree in political science, with an emphasis in Asian politics. Lee resides in Washington, D.C., with her two children.

David Baker Lewis

Chairman & Chief Executive Officer
Lewis & Munday, P.C.

D avid Baker Lewis serves as chairman and chief executive officer of Lewis & Munday, P.C., and chair of the Corporate Services Practice Group, comprising the firm's public law and corporate law groups. He has specialized in municipal finance since 1974, and has served as the firm's lead attorney on many municipal bond offerings.

Previously, Lewis served as a board of directors member of the National Association of Bond Lawyers and chairman of the National Association of Securities Professionals. He was a director of Comerica, Inc., TRW Inc., LG&E Energy Corp., M.A. Hanna Company and Consolidated Rail Corporation (Conrail). Lewis was an assistant professor of law at the Detroit College of Law, and a former member and board of trustees chairman of Oakland University. Currently, he is a board of directors member of The Kroger Co. and H & R Block.

Lewis received a bachelor's degree from Oakland University in Rochester, Michigan, majoring in business administration. He earned an MBA degree from The University of Chicago Graduate School of Business and was awarded a juris doctorate degree from the University of Michigan Law School.

Fred Douglas Mason Jr., a member of the American Federation of Teachers Local 8018, holds a record of labor and social activism that spans more than four decades. He is president of the Maryland State and District of Columbia AFL-CIO, a federation of more than 500 local unions with a combined membership of 350,000. He is also a co-convener of United States Labor Against the War, a national organization of labor organizations and individuals opposed to the war in Iraq.

His activism began as a student at Morgan State University. Fred spent more than a decade employed at Bethlehem Steel and General Motors, then later worked as an organizer and served as executive vice president of SEIU 1199E-DC, a 8,000-member health care workers union.

Fred is committed to enhancing democratic institutions while bettering the lives of working families. He frequently asks, "Why is it that the majority of the people are workers, the majority of the voters are workers, yet economic development and governmental policies do not emanate from that perspective?" He answers, "It is a question of power."

Fred Douglas Mason Jr.

President
Maryland & District of Columbia
AFL-CIO

The Honorable Kendrick B. Meek is chairman of the board of directors for the Congressional Black Caucus Foundation, Inc., a nonpartisan, nonprofit, public policy, research and educational institute founded by members of the Congressional Black Caucus in 1976. Additionally, Meek is serving his fourth term in the U.S. House of Representatives, and is a member of the powerful House Ways and Means Committee. In January of 2007, he was appointed to the NATO Parliamentary Assembly, where he is one of 12 members of Congress to represent the United States.

An experienced legislator, Meek served in the Florida House of Representatives and Senate for a total of eight years. Before his service in elected office, he was a captain in the Florida Highway Patrol and the first African American to hold that rank.

A native of Miami, Florida, Meek received a Bachelor of Science degree in criminal justice from Florida A&M University in 1989. The son of former Congresswoman Carrie P. Meek, he is married to the former Leslie Dixon of Brooklyn, New York, and they have two children, Lauren and Kendrick Jr.

The Honorable Kendrick B. Meek

Chairman, Board of Directors
Congressional Black
Caucus Foundation, Inc.

The Honorable Thomas J. Motley

Associate Judge
Superior Court of the
District of Columbia

Judge Thomas Motley was appointed to the Superior Court of the District of Columbia in 2000 by President William J. Clinton.

Born in Washington, D.C., Motley received a Bachelor of Arts degree in philosophy from Columbia College in 1976, and a law degree in 1979 from Harvard Law School, where he was a staff editor for the *Harvard Civil Rights – Civil Liberties Law Review.*

Motley served, with distinction, in nearly every section of the U.S. Attorney's Office, trying more than 60 cases in both local and federal court. He received numerous awards throughout his tenure at the U.S. Attorney's Office. In 1996 then-U.S. Attorney Eric H. Holder Jr. presented him with the Harold J. Sullivan Award, annually awarded by the Assistant United States Attorneys Association. In 1999 U.S. Attorney Lewis presented him with the STAR (Special Thanks for Achieving Results) Award, in recognition of his contributions as principal assistant.

An active member of the Thurgood Marshall Inn of Court since its founding in 1990, Motley was a member of Big Brothers Big Sisters of the National Capital Area for ten years.

John J. Oliver Jr.

Chief Executive Officer,
Publisher & Chairman
The AFRO-American Newspapers

John J. Oliver Jr. (Jake) has served as chairman of the board, chief executive officer and publisher of *The AFRO-American Newspapers* since 1986, where he oversees the company's business and editorial operations, founded in 1892 by his great-grandfather, John H. Murphy Sr. Through his leadership and innovation, he has expanded the *AFRO* from a historic print publication that serves more than 100,000 readers to a media enterprise that delivers information through its print, Web and electronic delivery products.

Oliver holds a Bachelor of Arts degree from Fisk University in Nashville and a juris doctorate degree from Columbia University School of Law in New York. A member of both the New York and Maryland bars associations, he is also a member of the board of directors of First Mariner Bank, The President's Roundtable, Inc., The Guardsmen, Kennedy Krieger Institute and Kappa Alpha Psi Fraternity, Inc.

In addition, Oliver served two terms as chairman of the National Newspaper Publishers Association, the trade organization for publishers of black-owned and -operated newspapers, and as president of the Maryland – Delaware – DC Press Association.

D r. Edward Anthony Rankin is senior partner in the Rankin Orthopaedic & Sports Medicine Center. Practicing in Washington, D.C., since 1973, he specializes in hip, knee and hand surgery. Rankin is a clinical professor of orthopaedic surgery at Howard University, and an associate professor in community health and family medicine at Georgetown University. Additionally, he is chief of orthopaedic surgery at Providence Hospital.

Elected as the 76th president of the American Academy of Orthopaedic Surgeons, Rankin was the first African American to serve in this position. He received the Medical Society of the District of Columbia Community Service and Meritorious Service awards. In addition, he was inducted into the Historically Black Colleges and Universities Hall of Fame and was recognized as one of the Best Doctors in America.

Rankin received a bachelor's degree from Lincoln University and a doctorate degree from Meharry Medical College. He completed an internship and orthopaedic residency at the Walter Reed Army Medical Center. Rankin is married to Dr. Frances Espy Rankin, and is in practice with their son, Dr. Marc Espy Rankin, an orthopaedic surgeon and sports medicine specialist.

Edward Anthony Rankin, M.D.

Senior Partner
Rankin Orthopaedic &
Sports Medicine Center

T he Honorable Richard W. Roberts was sworn in on July 31, 1998, as a U.S. District judge for the District of Columbia. Before his appointment to the bench, he served as chief of the Criminal Section in the Civil Rights Division of the U.S. Department of Justice. In prior posts, Roberts served as the principal assistant U.S. attorney for the District of Columbia; an assistant U.S. attorney for the District of Columbia and for the Southern District of New York; an associate with the Washington, D.C., law firm of Covington & Burling LLP; and a civil rights prosecutor in the Justice Department where he was hired in the Attorney General's Honors Program.

Roberts earned an Artium Baccalaureus degree, cum laude, from Vassar College in 1974, a Master of International Affairs degree from the School for International Training in 1978, and a juris doctorate degree from Columbia Law School. A founding member and past deputy general counsel of the Washington, D.C., chapter of Concerned Black Men, he has been a visiting faculty member of the Harvard Law School Trial Advocacy Workshop since 1984.

The Honorable Richard W. Roberts

Judge
U.S. District Court

Jamal Simmons

Principal
The Raben Group

Democratic strategist and political commentator Jamal Simmons emerged from the 2008 election as one of the new young voices in the world of political analysis. With an extensive background in democratic politics and international affairs, he was a strong supporter of Barack Obama's campaign and became a fixture on CNN's political coverage, where his entertaining and pithy opinions distinguished him as one of the freshest commentators in the media.

Since traveling with then-presidential candidate Bill Clinton in 1992, Simmons has been an advisor to presidential candidates, a cabinet secretary, U.S. senators and members of Congress. Committed to engaging more people of color in the political process, he regularly volunteers his time to mentor and speak to young people interested in politics.

Simmons is a 2009-2010 French-American Foundation young leader and former term member of the Council on Foreign Relations. A graduate of Morehouse College, he received a Master of Public Policy degree in public policy from Harvard University. He is currently a principal with The Raben Group, a Washington, D.C.-based public affairs consulting firm, where he advises corporations and nonprofit clients.

Jarvis C. Stewart

Chairman & Managing Partner
Ian Reid, LLC

Jarvis C. Stewart is chairman and managing partner of Ian Reid, LLC. He provides corporate and business development strategy for a wide range of companies in sectors such as homeland security, banking and financial services, energy, and emerging markets.

Jarvis' clients include Fortune 100 companies, mid-sized firms and small businesses poised for domestic and international growth. He has been profiled in *The Wall Street Journal*, *Forbes* and *Black Enterprise* magazines. Additionally, Jarvis is a founding partner of the Washington Nationals, a major league baseball franchise.

Louis Stokes played a pivotal role in the quest for civil rights, equality, and social and economic justice throughout his tenure in the U.S. Congress.

Stokes was educated in the Cleveland Metropolitan School District, graduating from Central High School. Following three years of service in the U.S. Army, he returned to Cleveland and attended Case Western Reserve University. He earned a Doctor of Laws degree from Cleveland-Marshall College of Law in 1953.

Prior to serving in Congress, Stokes practiced law for 14 years and was one of the founders of Stokes, Character, Terry, Perry, Whitehead, Young and Davidson law firm. As a practicing lawyer, he participated in three cases in the U.S. Supreme Court, including arguing the landmark stop and frisk case of *Terry v. Ohio*. On November 6, 1968, Stokes was elected to the U.S. Congress and became the first African-American member of Congress from the state of Ohio. Additionally, he has served 15 consecutive terms in the U.S. House of Representatives.

Louis Stokes

Senior Counsel
Squire, Sanders & Dempsey L.L.P.

Dr. Duane J. Taylor is medical director of Le Visage ENT & Facial Plastic Surgery, one of Washington, D.C.'s premier facilities for cosmetic and reconstructive procedures of the face and neck. He has been in the area since 1991 and is trained in two specialties – facial, plastic and reconstructive surgery and otolaryngology (ear, nose and throat).

A member of the Alpha Omega Alpha Medical Honor Society, Taylor received the National Role Model Mentor Award and the American Red Cross Real Heroes Award. He has been featured on national television for his work with at-risk youth, and has been involved with international medical missions.

Taylor completed a Bachelor of Science/Doctor of Medicine degree program at the Northeastern Ohio Universities College of Medicine after serving as a congressional page. He completed training through The University of Texas and UCLA-affiliated hospitals and the American Academy of Facial, Plastic and Reconstructive Surgery.

Taylor grew up in Shaker Heights, Ohio, and is in the Shaker Heights Hall of Fame. He resides in the Maryland area with his wife and daughter, and enjoys golf and listening to jazz.

Duane J. Taylor, M.D.

Medical Director
Le Visage ENT &
Facial Plastic Surgery

The Honorable Herman Taylor

Delegate, District 14
Maryland House of Delegates

The Honorable Herman Taylor was first elected to the Maryland House of Delegates in 2002. He serves on the House Economic Matters Committee and is chairman of the subcommittee on unemployment insurance.

Taylor has received several prominent awards. In 2004 he was named Legislator of the Month by the Center for Policy Alternatives for his work on the living wage bill, and in 2006 he was given the Clean Energy Partnership Award.

Recently, Taylor was awarded the Bethune-DuBois Institute Award and The Arc of Montgomery County Community Builder Award. He also received the 2008 Public Service Award from Alpha Phi Alpha Fraternity, Inc. for his work on securing funding for the Martin Luther King Jr. National Memorial. Additionally, the Washington, D.C. Building and Construction Trades Council named him Legislator of the Year in 2008.

Taylor's community service has included involvement with the RainbowPUSH Coalition's Wall Street Project, the National Coalition of Minority Businesses, the American Council of Young Political Leaders, the Olney Theatre Center, the Boys & Girls Club of Greater Washington, The Arc of Montgomery County, and Youth Leaders International.

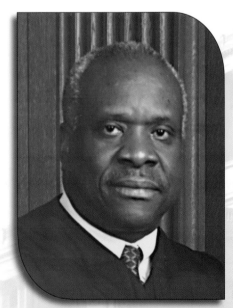

The Honorable Clarence Thomas

Justice
U.S. Supreme Court

The Honorable Clarence Thomas entered Immaculate Conception Seminary in northwestern Missouri to prepare for the priesthood. However, the prejudice he encountered there convinced him to resign. He enrolled at Holy Cross in Worcester, Massachusetts, where he helped found the Black Student Union and graduated with an English honors degree.

Thomas graduated from Yale Law School in 1974 and joined the staff of Missouri Attorney General John Danforth, who would become his political mentor. In 1981 the Reagan administration appointed Thomas assistant secretary for civil rights in the Education Department. After ten months, Reagan promoted him to director of the Equal Employment Opportunity Commission.

In 1990 Thomas was appointed to the U.S. Court of Appeals for the District of Columbia. President George Bush nominated him to replace Thurgood Marshall on the U.S. Supreme Court and the Senate confirmed Thomas on October 15, 1991. Upon his appointment at age 43, he was the youngest member of the court.

A Georgia native, Thomas is married to Virginia Lamp Thomas, director of executive branch relations at The Heritage Foundation, and has one son, Jamal, from a previous marriage.

The Honorable Harry "Tommy" Thomas Jr. represents Ward 5 for the Council of the District of Columbia and chairs the council's Committee on Libraries, Parks and Recreation. He sits on four additional committees, which include Workforce Development and the Environment, Aging and Community Affairs, Housing and Workforce Development, and Public Services and Consumer Affairs.

Raised in a family with a strong commitment to public service, he is the son of the late, three-term Ward 5 Council Member Harry Thomas Sr. and a former District of Columbia public school principal, Romaine B. Thomas. Tommy has been actively involved in a wide range of community matters for the past two decades. He is co-founder of DCTC-Team Thomas, a nonprofit organization for social change, citizen empowerment, community development, and youth and senior citizens program development.

Tommy attended District of Columbia Public Schools and graduated from Woodrow Wilson High School. He holds a degree in public relations/marketing from Bowie State University. Tommy is married to Diane Romo Thomas. They are active sports enthusiasts and their children share their spirit of competition and sportsmanship.

The Honorable Harry "Tommy" Thomas Jr.

Council Member, Ward 5
Council of the District of Columbia

As national chair of the National Congress of Black Women, Inc. (NCBW), Dr. E. Faye Williams manages the nonprofit organization, conducts its activities and serves as the chief spokesperson.

Williams has received hundreds of awards for her community service, as well as for her international peace and human rights work throughout the world. The projects of the NCBW of which she is most proud are College for Kids, a project for teaching 9- to 12-year olds about various vocations, and Young Ambassadors, a project for teaching the value of diplomacy to individuals ages 13 to young adulthood. Additionally, she has been named one of *Ebony*'s Most Influential and Power 150 for three consecutive years.

Grambling State University awarded Williams a Bachelor of Arts degree, and she received a master's degree from the University of Southern California. In addition to a law degree from Howard University, she has also earned a Doctor of Philosophy degree and a Doctor of Ministry degree. A native of Alexandria, Louisiana, she is a member of Delta Sigma Theta Sorority, Inc., and many other professional and community organizations.

E. Faye Williams, Ph.D.

National Chair
National Congress of
Black Women, Inc.

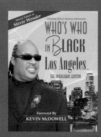

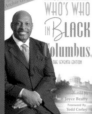

Washington, D.C.

CORPORATE BRASS

PROFICIENT

EXCEL

OUTSHINE

SURPASS

TRANSCEND

ENHANCE

SURMOUNT

MASTER

TRIUMPH

Kenneth D. Baker

General Manager
The Blvd at the Capital Centre

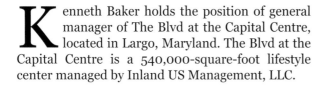

Kalonniee K. Barker

Assistant Vice President &
Banking Center Manager II
Bank of America

Kenneth Baker holds the position of general manager of The Blvd at the Capital Centre, located in Largo, Maryland. The Blvd at the Capital Centre is a 540,000-square-foot lifestyle center managed by Inland US Management, LLC.

From 1998 to 2006, Baker held the position of senior property manager for First Washington Realty, Inc., a national real estate firm headquartered in Bethesda, Maryland. In this capacity, he was directly responsible for the oversight and management of assets valued at more than $400 million, totaling in excess of 1.5 million square feet. Formerly, he was the principal broker of Kenneth Baker Realty, Inc., a full-service real estate advisory firm.

Baker completed real estate course work at the University of Maryland, College Park. In addition, he is a 1997 graduate of the Real Estate Associate Program (REAP), a commercial real estate pilot program for professional minorities.

Baker and his wife, Teryl, co-pastor Abundant Life Family Church in Fairfax, Virginia. They have three children, Kimberly, 18; Kelley, 16; and Kenneth II, 13.

Kalonniee K. Barker is an assistant vice president at Bank of America. Holding the position of banking center manager II, she is responsible for community relations, maintaining profitability, team coaching and executing key sales initiatives.

Prior to joining Bank of America, Kalonniee began her career in management at Enterprise Rent-A-Car, where she was frequently recognized as one of the region's top performing managers. She was also a member of Enterprise's Team Diversity, a program that promotes diversification of the company's local business efforts. Additionally, she was an active participant in a company mentoring program designed to coach and develop new employees.

In 2004 Kalonniee received the prestigious YWCA Women of Achievement Award in Cleveland, Ohio. This award is presented to local businesswomen who demonstrate outstanding leadership and serve as mentors to other women who desire direction in achieving their goals. A graduate of Kent State University, Kalonniee received a degree in psychology. In addition, she is an alumni member of Alpha Kappa Alpha Sorority, Inc.

Willard M. Bracey Jr.

Medical Technologist
Kaiser Permanente Medical Center

Alpheaus Campbell

Chief Quality Officer
The Specialty Hospital of Washington

Willard Bracey Jr. is a medical technologist, formerly of the Hematology Department of Walter Reed Army Medical Center. He presently works with Kaiser Permanente Medical Center, serves part-time with Largo Medical Center and is on-call at the North Capitol Medical Center laboratory facilities. His duties include all phases of medical technology work and are performed as assigned.

Willard recently won second place in the AMT Feature Writing Awards contest in the category of lab efficiency through organizing with reusable containers. He is a graduate of Barbizon Model and Acting School and has enjoyed many male runway assignments. His outreach entails visiting the sick and sending cards of encouragement.

Willard received a bachelor's degree in pre-med biology from Jackson State University in Mississippi. He is a member of Ebenezer AME Church and sings baritone in the Kings Men Choir, as well as the Fort Washington Community Chorus. Willard resides in Fort Washington, Maryland, with his wife, Bessie, and is an active member of Phi Beta Sigma Fraternity, Inc.

Alpheaus Campbell is chief quality officer for The Specialty Hospital of Washington, a comprehensive health system comprised of 500-plus licensed beds, three acute care hospitals and three long-term care nursing centers. In this position, he manages the quality, risk management, patient safety performance improvement and regulatory affairs efforts for the hospital.

Alpheaus has extensive clinical and administrative experience, including expertise in nursing, data analysis, benchmarking and process improvement. He is a member of several professional organizations, including the American Assembly for Men in Nursing and the Maryland Organization of Nurse Executives. He is an associate member of the American Society for Quality and an American College of Healthcare Executives fellow.

Northern Virginia Community College awarded Alpheaus a diploma in nursing. He received a Bachelor of Arts degree from Norfolk State University and master's degrees in business administration and health care administration from the University of Maryland.

Sabrina Campbell

Director, Federal Relations
American Electric Power Co., Inc.

Harriett Edwards-White

Vice President
Retail Leasing
Forest City Washington, Inc.

Sabrina Campbell is director of federal relations for the Washington office of American Electric Power Co., Inc. (AEP), where she lobbies Congress on tax, finance and energy issues. She also advocates AEP public policy positions at the FERC, the administration, DOE, the Treasury and the IRS.

Campbell began her career in the Fuels Department at Central and South West Corporation (CSW) in 1993. In June of 2000, following the merger of CSW with AEP, she was promoted to her current position.

She served several years as chair of the Edison Electric Institute (EEI) Tax Subject Area Committee and on the EEI Power Political Action Committee board. She is president of the D.C. Chapter of the American Association of Blacks in Energy and a member of the Tax Coalition and National Energy Resources Organization.

A graduate of St. Paul's College in Lawrenceville, Virginia, with a Bachelor of Science degree in business administration, Campbell also earned a master's degree in business and public administration from Southeastern University in Washington, D.C. Additionally, she is a certified public accountant, licensed in Texas.

Harriett Edwards-White is currently Forest City Washington's vice president of retail leasing. She directed the leasing for The Mall at Stonecrest, a $200 million, 1.3 million square foot super-regional shopping center in suburban Atlanta, and is presently involved with Forest City's Washington, D.C.-area retail properties and a one million square foot mega development in South Florida.

Previously, Harriett spent 17 years with The Taubman Company and two years with General Growth Properties as vice president of leasing. She has leased numerous multimillion-dollar projects throughout the United States.

Harriett is an active member of the International Council of Shopping Centers and a board of directors member of both the Real Estate Associate Program and the Washington, D.C. Economic Partnership. Additionally, she is founder of a diversity networking event held annually in Las Vegas and is a tutor and mentor to inner-city children in southeast Washington, D.C.

Her affiliations extend internationally, with her development and involvement in European markets. Harriett is married to Ret. Command Sergeant Major AJ White and they have two daughters, Ragin and Sonja, and one son, AJ Jr.

Jean-Galvanis M. Gassiyombo

Chief Enterprise Architect
Spectrum IT, Inc.

Marion O. "Duke" Greene Jr.

President & Chief Executive Officer
American Development Corporation

Jean-Galvanis Gassiyombo is the chief enterprise architect for Spectrum IT, a technology firm focused on business intelligence and decision support systems for clients in the banking, finance and health care industries. He is the developer of the Spectrum Methodology, a framework for developing technology blueprints. Additionally, he works collaboratively with leaders across the United States to craft and execute a comprehensive strategy called Spectrum Vision, designed to help the firm become recognized as one of the best professional services organization.

Jean-Galvanis' leadership by example is noteworthy for both a commitment to client and community services. He has distinguished himself on numerous client engagements, including PricewaterhouseCoopers, Blue Cross Blue Shield, Merrill Lynch, Alcoa, Fleet Bank, Kaiser Permanente and Waste Management. He also has a strong interest in the understanding of human consciousness evolution and political philosophy, and their impacts on human conditions.

Western Illinois University awarded Jean-Galvanis a master's degree in economic and quantitative analysis, and he received an executive master's degree in software engineering from The George Washington University.

Marion O. "Duke" Greene Jr. is president and chief executive officer of the American Development Corporation (ADC). ADC has more than 40 years of experience in problem solving professional support services to publicly traded companies, federal government agencies, and state and municipal governments.

As former executive vice president of McKissack & McKissack, a black-owned engineering firm, Greene designed the necessary systems, procedures and marketing plans that resulted in the firm's successful $800 million-plus contract to manage the construction of the new Washington, D.C. Convention Center. The firm is currently managing projects valued in excess of $1.3 billion.

Greene founded International Business Services, which grew from a $500 investment in his home basement to a $95 million corporation with such clients as the U.S. Coast Guard, Dulles Airport, the Washington National Airport, the U.S. Department of Labor and the U.S. Department of Transportation. His achievements have been reported in a number of media sources, including *The Washington Post*, *The Washington Times*, *U.S. News & World Report*, *BusinessWeek*, *Forbes* and *Black Enterprise*. Additionally, Greene was honored with the Reginald F. Lewis Achievement Award.

Harlan E. Hall

Account Executive
Alliance Financial, Inc.

Jason Harvey

Architectural Engineer
Devrouax & Purnell Architects

Harlan Hall is an account executive for Alliance Financial, Inc., based in Olney, Maryland. In this position, he markets Alliance's purchasing and refinancing services to Realtors and consumers throughout the Washington, D.C., metropolitan area.

Harlan is also a marketing representative for Cheeky Sasso Entertainment & Marketing Group, LLC, marketing events in the Washington, D.C. area and abroad. In addition, he leads client development for Genese Music & Entertainment Group, LLC, based in Baltimore. He co-hosted Genese's talent auditions at the Black Heritage Arts Show in Baltimore.

Harlan is currently enrolled in the University of Phoenix seeking a bachelor's degree in business finance. During his leisure time, he volunteers as a coach for the 6 and under Jr. NBA Wizards basketball team.

A native of Washington, D.C., Harlan is the proud parent of two daughters, Khortni and Tiara, and a son, Jalen.

Born and raised in Brooklyn, New York, Jason Harvey began his career in architecture six years ago with the Washington, D.C., architectural firm Devrouax & Purnell. Since then, he has been instrumentally involved in key projects, including the new Washington Nationals baseball stadium, the Department of Employment Services, the broadcast center for Radio/TV One, the Marlow Heights Community Center and many more.

Striving to achieve yet another long-term personal goal, Jason is currently working to establish and operate his own architecture firm. From his experience and expertise, he plans to excel in the study of entrepreneurship and eventually position himself to explore the opportunities in franchising.

Jason has earned a Bachelor of Science degree in architecture from Alfred State College and a Master of Architecture degree from The Catholic University of America.

Blair H. Hayes, Ph.D.

Associate & Human Capital Specialist
Booz Allen Hamilton

Dawn Hicks-Roy

Institutional Review Board Administrator
Holy Cross Hospital

Dr. Blair Hayes, associate for Booz Allen Hamilton, has turned his commitment and passion for diversity into a career by working with organizations as they strive to enhance their strategic approach to diversity and inclusion. After completing courses at Morehouse College, Hayes received a doctorate degree in organizational psychology from Temple University. Upon completing his thesis on sexual harassment in the workplace and dissertation on diversity and group dynamics, he began his work for Booz Allen Hamilton.

After managing internal diversity initiatives, Hayes began working with external clients to improve their human capital processes. He is currently working to further the diversity offering, while working on projects across the talent management landscape. He has combined an academic rigor with professional curiosity to ensure diverse and inclusive practices are ingrained into strategic approaches for clients across the professional landscape. Hayes says that working with people who approach work and life from varied perspectives makes life interesting, as well as helping clients realize the benefits of having an inclusive workforce is rewarding.

When not working, Hayes enjoys writing, working out and watching 'his' Washington Redskins.

Dawn Hicks-Roy is the institutional review board administrator for Holy Cross Hospital. In this position, she not only provides leadership and direction on all federal, state and institutional regulatory compliance issues related to the protection of human subjects, she also oversees a portfolio of approximately 90 research clinical trials, of which 85 percent are cancer-related research clinical trials for Holy Cross Hospital.

In addition to her role with Holy Cross Hospital, Dawn serves on the Perinatal Loss Committee and the No One Dies Alone Committee at the hospital, and is president of the Holy Cross "Words" Toastmasters Club.

Dawn received a Bachelor of Arts degree in political science from Winston-Salem State University. In April of 2009, the National Association of IRB Managers certified her as an institutional review manager. A native of Washington, D.C., Dawn is the wife of Steven Timothy Roy Sr., and the proud mother of two sons, Steve Jr. and Malik.

Julius W. Hobson Jr.

Senior Policy Advisor
Bryan Cave LLP

Carl Jordan

Senior Defense Analyst
Zel Technologies, LLC

Julius Hobson Jr. is senior policy advisor at Bryan Cave LLP, lobbying on behalf of clients in the areas of appropriations, budget, financial services, defense, health care, foreign relations and tax policy. Additionally, he is a professorial lecturer at The George Washington University Graduate School of Political Management.

Previously, Hobson served as director of congressional affairs for the American Medical Association, worked in the U.S. House of Representatives and U.S. Senate, and handled congressional affairs for Howard University and the District of Columbia. A former elected member of the D.C. Board of Education, he served as a board member and chair of the D.C. Health and Hospital Public Benefit Corporation.

Hobson was profiled in *Lobbying in Washington, London, and Brussels: The Persuasive Communication of Political Issues*, and his family was profiled in *The Washington Century: Three Families and the Shaping of the Nation's Capital*.

A native Washingtonian, Hobson received a bachelor's degree from Howard University and a master's degree in legislative affairs from The George Washington University. Married to Diane Lewis, he is the proud father of two adult daughters and two granddaughters.

Carl Jordan is a senior defense analyst for the Department of Defense in the Pentagon. In support of the chairman of the Joint Chiefs of Staff's Protection Functional Capabilities Board (FCB), he oversees the Warfighting Mission Area IT portfolio management process, which identifies and recommends balanced and prioritized IT investments to the FCB to enable the joint warfighter to accomplish their assigned missions. The Protection FCB IT portfolio is comprised of more than 140 IT investments with a budget of more than $66.9 million.

An active member of Omega Psi Phi Fraternity, Inc., Carl is also a member of The Most Worshipful Prince Hall Grand Lodge of Maryland and Jurisdiction, Inc., and the National Black MBA Association, Inc., Washington, D.C. Chapter.

Carl received a bachelor's degree from Park University and an MBA degree from Golden Gate University. A native of Washington, D.C., he is a retired U.S. Air Force veteran with 24 years of leadership and management experience. An avid photographer, he also plays tennis and golf, and loves to travel. Carl is father to a stepson, Damon, and two daughters, Rhonda and Shanice.

Jeannette Jordan

Financial Services Representative
MetLife

Nicolle McCarty

Regional Manager
Island Def Jam Records

Jeannette Jordan is a financial services representative with Ambassador Financial Group, an affiliate of MetLife. In this position, she provides families and business owners with assistance in building their financial freedom. Her goal is to be a lifetime resource for each client.

As a top producer with her company, Jeannette has received awards of recognition. She is vice president for the National Association of Insurance and Financial Advisors – Prince George's County. Additionally, she is a member of the Ambassadors for Economic Independence, a giving circle devoted to creating pathways to economic independence for low-income families, and headed by women in the Washington, D.C., region through spiritual, personal and career enrichment services.

Jeannette is creator of the WomenOnTheMove blog, "Red Carpet Interviews," a social blog that highlights the accomplishments of women business owners in the Washington, D.C., region, and also functions as a networking platform.

Jeannette received a Bachelor of Arts degree from Towson University, Towson, Maryland, in 1985. A native of Washington, D.C., she is the wife of Barry Jordan and the stepmother of Kelli.

Nicolle McCarty represents her label's artists to urban radio programmers, disc jockeys, clubs and retail entities. She is responsible for creating awareness of Island Def Jam's current releases, as well as developing and executing events within her region. Nicolle has worked with such artists as Rihanna, Kanye West, LL Cool J and Lionel Richie, and was a part of the team that brought Ne Yo, Chrisette Michele and The Dream national success. Additionally, she was nominated as the 2006 Regional of the Year in *R&R* magazine.

A graduate of Michigan State University, with a Bachelor of Arts degree in marketing, she began her career as a college intern for General Mills. After graduating, Nicolle eventually landed a regional promotions job with a jazz label, GRP, and later with RCA Records. After holding various positions, she returned to her passion and joined Island Def Jam Records.

Born in Flint, Michigan, but raised in Muskegon, Michigan, Nicolle is the eldest of three, born to Ossie and Carol McCarty. Her sister, Nashawn, lives in Nashville, Tennessee, and her brother, Tory, lives in Phoenix, Arizona.

Craig M. Muckle

Manager, Public Affairs &
Government Relations
Eastern Division
Safeway Inc.

Nikia J. Okoye

Director, Government Relations
American Kidney Fund

Craig M. Muckle is manager of public affairs and government relations for Safeway Inc.'s Eastern Division. In this position, he assists with the daily management of consumer, media, community and government affairs activities, serves as a primary spokesperson, coordinates grand openings and other special events, seeks out and creates community programs through partnerships with community-based organizations, and is the editor of the division newsletter CheckOut. Additionally, he is a member of the division's diversity advisory board, which provides recommendations to management on a myriad of cultural matters.

Muckle represents Safeway on the boards of several organizations, including the Prince George's Chamber of Commerce, where he is completing a term as chairman; the Greater Washington Urban League, where he is second vice president; and the March of Dimes.

The University of Dayton awarded Muckle with a bachelor's degree in communications. A 2001 graduate of Leadership Prince George's, he is also a certified basketball referee, officiating collegiate and high school games. An avid competitive bowler, the West Haven, Connecticut, native lives in Bowie, Maryland, with his wife and three children.

As director of government relations, Nikia J. Okoye manages the advocacy and public policy initiatives of the American Kidney Fund, the nation's No. 1 source of direct financial assistance to kidney patients. In this role, Nikia interacts daily with congressional leaders and members of the administration to communicate issues of importance to Americans living with kidney disease.

Before joining the American Kidney Fund in 2009, Nikia served as senior project manager for the Congressional Black Caucus Foundation, Inc. From 2003 to 2008, she served on Capitol Hill as a senior policy advisor to the late Representative Stephanie Tubbs Jones of Ohio. In this capacity, she managed the federal appropriations process, and advised the representative on issues related to women's health, transportation, defense and labor.

Nikia received a bachelor's degree in political science from Wright State University and a master's degree in business administration from Trinity University. She is a founding member of the Congressional Black Caucus Foundation, Inc.'s Leadership Network and a member of Blacks in Government. Nikia enjoys swimming, roller-skating and spending time with her husband, Billy, and children, Noah and Noel.

Endi Piper

Vice President
Business & Legal Affairs
TV One, LLC

Monique Kendinique Rolle

Executive Chef
ARAMARK

Endi Piper is vice president of business and legal affairs for TV One, LLC, a cable network targeting African-American adults. As vice president of business and legal affairs, she brokers network deals related to original programming and production, acquisitions, and new media distribution including video on-demand and the Internet. Prior to TV One, she worked in the Business and Legal Affairs departments of Scripps Networks and Black Entertainment Television.

Through the International Senior Lawyers Project, Endi teaches commercial law to practicing black lawyers in South Africa each summer. She has also been an active court appointed special advocate for foster children in Prince George's County since 2006.

Endi received Bachelor of Arts and juris doctorate degrees from the University of Virginia in Charlottesville, Virginia. She is originally from Richmond, Virginia, and is a member of Delta Sigma Theta Sorority, Inc.

Monique Rolle is an executive chef for the business division in ARAMARK. She manages all kitchen staff, food preparation and cooking activities in its dining facilities, and incorporates her culinary creativity as a chef manager and food production manager to produce captivating and nutritional cuisine responding to trends in the food industry.

Monique received the president's scholarship at The Culinary Institute of America and has received many accolades and culinary medals. Additionally, she will be featured in *Cambridge Who's Who*. She is an active member of Zeta Phi Beta Sorority, Inc. and is also a member of the Golden Key International Honour Society.

Formally trained at the Bahamas Hotel Training College (now The College of the Bahamas), Monique received a Bachelor of Professional Studies degree, with honors, from the Culinary Institute of America in Hyde Park, New York. In 2008 she was awarded a Master of Science degree in nutritional science from Howard University in Washington, D.C. She resided in Nassau, Bahamas, and is the daughter of attorney Norwood A. Rolle and Roselyn M. Rolle.

Helen G. Rountree

Deputy Director
Networx Program
Qwest Communications

Kim D. Sawyer

Program Manager
Northrop Grumman Corp.

Helen Rountree is deputy director of the Networx Program for Qwest Communications, where she manages the $60 billion Networx contracts administered by the U.S. General Services Administration (GSA). Helen leads cross-functional teams in the planning and execution of contracts, and serves as a subject matter expert in many of the function program activities.

She has received the GSA Commissioner's Most Valuable Person, the Fairfax County Outstanding Volunteerism and the Outstanding Member of the Prince William County's Consumer Advisory Board awards. Additionally, Helen received the Outstanding Young Women of America Award and was included in the *International Who's Who of Professionals.*

A magna cum laude graduate of Park University with a bachelor's degree in management and human resources, Helen received a master's degree in business administration from Strayer University, and a doctorate degree in business administration and management from Nova Southeastern University. She is a senior executive fellow of the John F. Kennedy School of Government at Harvard University.

Helen is a member of Sigma Beta Delta, Women In Community Action, the Academy of Management and the Armed Forces Communications and Electronics Association.

Kim D. Sawyer is a program manager for Northrop Grumman Corporation. She joined the company in 2005 and currently oversees a multi-year, multimillion-dollar Human Capital Program for the Department of the Treasury, Office of the Chief Information Officer. She is responsible for the program's execution, management of cost and schedule and contract compliance, and for providing leadership and vision in achieving business goals and objectives.

Kim holds a Bachelor of Science degree in business information systems from Virginia State University and a Master of Business Administration degree from the University of Maryland University College. She also holds a graduate certificate from the University of Virginia Darden School of Business Leadership Program.

Certified in project management, Kim holds memberships in the Project Management Institute and the National Black MBA Association, and is a Golden life member of Zeta Phi Beta Sorority, Inc., where she has held major leadership roles. She also serves on the board of directors for Operation Reach, Inc., a community-based organization in New Orleans. Additionally, Kim is the owner and designer of Bolina Elegant Jewelry.

Efrem Z. Stringfellow

Regional General Manager
Small & Mid-market
Solutions & Partners Group
Microsoft Corporation

Sylvie Tannhäuser

Director of Special Events
The Galleria at Lafayette Centre

Efrem Z. Stringfellow is the east region general manager of sales of Microsoft's small and mid-market Solutions and Partners Group. He is responsible for solution sales, marketing, client satisfaction and working closely with solution providers throughout the eastern region of the United States.

Prior to Microsoft, he served as vice president of sales and marketing of the Solutions Platform Group for the NEC Corporation of America, and as senior director of sales, channels and marketing for Silicon Graphics International. In addition, he served as regional vice president of sales and services for the IBM Corporation, where he led a team of executives and salespersons in the creation and sale of IBM enterprise hardware, software and solutions across multiple industries.

Stringfellow holds a master's degree in business administration, with a concentration in management, from the J.L. Kellogg Graduate School of Management at Northwestern University. He received a bachelor's degree in business, with a concentration in marketing, from the University of Illinois at Champaign-Urbana. Stringfellow lives in Malvern, Pennsylvania, with his wife, Crystine. He is the father of four children.

Sylvie Tannhäuser has an intriguing blend of creativity and international flair. Her passionate approach to event planning leads her to create successful events worldwide. As event director at The Galleria at Lafayette Centre, which is one of Washington, D.C.'s most distinctive event venues, she oversees every event, meeting and wedding with grace and professionalism. Sylvie began her career 12 years ago in the hospitality industry as director of public relations for the French Convention and Visitors Bureau. In addition, she worked with high-profile event planners in the fashion, interior design and luxury industries in Europe, Asia and the Caribbean.

Sylvie received a degree in marketing and mass communication at the École Supérieure de Commerce College in France and was designated a certified event planner and public relations professional by the European Federation of Higher Education. In addition, she is fluent in French, English and Spanish, and converses in Portuguese and Japanese.

A French-Caribbean native, tango dancer and world traveler, Sylvie enjoys architecture, interior design, art and cultures around the globe.

Willie D. Tate

Vice President, Private Client Manager
U.S. Trust
Bank of America

Lavon Washington

Senior Consultant
Strategy & Change – Public Sector
IBM Global Business Services

Willie Tate joined the Private Banking Group of Bank of America in the winter of 2006. He is part of a team that specializes in strategic wealth management and works closely with high-net-worth individuals, families and foundations to formulate and structure the most efficient financial plan. He utilizes the Integrated Advice Model to deliver preferred banking, comprehensive investments, world-class credit, and trust and wealth transfer advice to clients.

Willie holds an accredited asset management specialist certification from the College for Financial Planning. He has an undergraduate degree, a marketing major and theology minor, from Georgetown University. He also holds a Master of Business Administration degree in management and a master's degree in marketing from the University of Maryland University College.

A member of Alpha Phi Alpha Fraternity, Inc., Willie is an INROADS alumnus and former chair of its D.C. alumni chapter. He is a stalwart member of Team Bank of America, and has served as president for both the Greater Washington and St. Louis Diversity Networks. Willie serves as the president for the Bank of America Greater Washington/Greater Baltimore Black Professional Group chapter.

Lavon Washington is a senior consultant with IBM Global Business Services, public sector – strategy and change practice area. In this role, he is assigned to the education industry and provides clients with solutions offerings that help utilize technology to enhance teaching and learning, streamline administrative processes and build a strong infrastructure.

As a member of the National Black MBA Association, Washington serves as a mentor for the organization's high school mentoring program, Leaders of Tomorrow (LOT). He coached the winning LOT National Case Competition team in 2005, and founded the first black business student organization at his alma mater, Rice University.

Washington received a Bachelor of Science degree in computer information systems from the University of Nebraska-Kearney in 2001, and a Master of Business Administration degree from Rice University in 2006.

A native of Shreveport, Louisiana, Washington was raised in Houston, Texas, and relocated to Washington, D.C. He enjoys traveling, reading and working out. The son of Cheryl Brown, Washington has two younger brothers, Lavelle and Aaron.

Charlisa Watson

Executive Director
Unison Health Plan of the
Capital Area, Inc.

William L. Wilson Jr.

Director
Servicing Risk Strategy
Fannie Mae

Charlisa Watson is executive director of Unison Health Plan of the Capital Area, an AmeriChoice/UnitedHealth Group Company. In this position, she is responsible for the overall performance of the market, including profit and loss responsibility, managing a state-based operation, and partnering with corporate teams and sister segments to deliver various support services.

With nearly 20 years of health care experience, Charlisa has analyzed, developed and implemented policies and programs to improve managed care health plans serving Medicaid and other special needs populations. She is a recognized leader in both the health care and nonprofit industries for her energized vision and keen management skills, and has worked extensively in partnership with private and public sector companies, employers, health care management organizations, and health care professionals, as well as with state and local government officials.

Charlisa was awarded a Master of Science degree in health care administration from Central Michigan University. Married to Andre Watson, she is the proud mother of four children and resides in suburban Maryland.

William (Bill) Wilson Jr. is director of servicing risk strategy in Fannie Mae's National Servicing Organization Credit Loss Management division. In this role, he is currently responsible for identifying strategic initiatives to reduce Fannie Mae's credit losses, improve servicer's loss mitigation effectiveness and minimize incidence of default via pursuit of alternatives to foreclosure.

Prior to joining Fannie Mae in 2002, Wilson worked in the Financial Advisory Services division of Deloitte & Touche, LLP. He currently holds 15 years of experience in mortgage finance, consulting and commercial banking.

Wilson earned a Master of Business Administration degree in finance from the Robert H. Smith School of Business, University of Maryland at College Park and a Bachelor of Arts degree in economics from Dartmouth College. He has held Series 7, Series 63 and Series 3 licenses in prior positions. Wilson currently resides in Silver Spring, Maryland, with his wife, Kimberly, and their two sons, Jacob and Joshua.

Donna L. Woodall

Community Outreach Director
Mid-Atlantic District & Public Sector
Microsoft Corporation

Donna L. Woodall is the community outreach director for Microsoft's Mid-Atlantic District and public sector. She is responsible for managing and developing the strategy for Microsoft's community awareness in the six states that comprise the Mid-Atlantic area, in addition to Microsoft's public sector practice in Washington, D.C.

Since joining Microsoft in 2002, Donna has served as a consulting services sales manager and an engagement delivery manager for Microsoft's Mid-Atlantic District. Previously, she served as a marketing consultant in the White House Office of Public Liaison, supporting ethnic programs and marketing communications programs at the American Embassy in Vienna. In addition, she has held positions with Cambridge Technology Partners and Merant, Inc.

Donna is a graduate of Brown University, where she received a Bachelor of Science degree in computer science. She holds an international executive MBA degree from Georgetown University.

Donna is active in the community, fostered through her role as Microsoft's community outreach director. She was recently named to the advisory board at BHA Education Consultants. Her favorite hobbies include playing the piano and swimming.

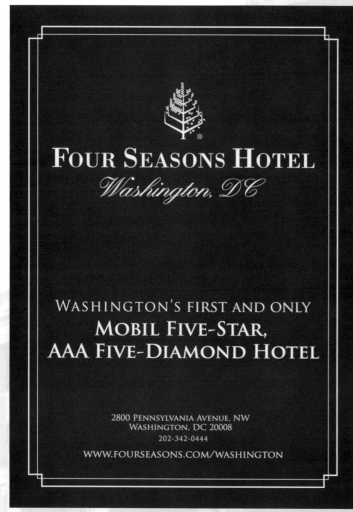
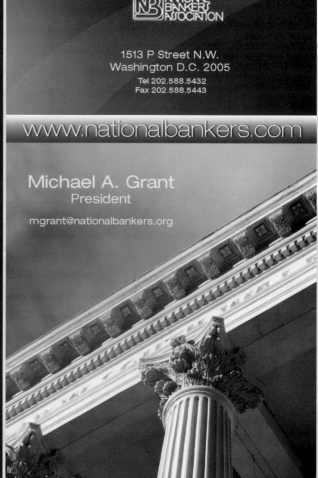

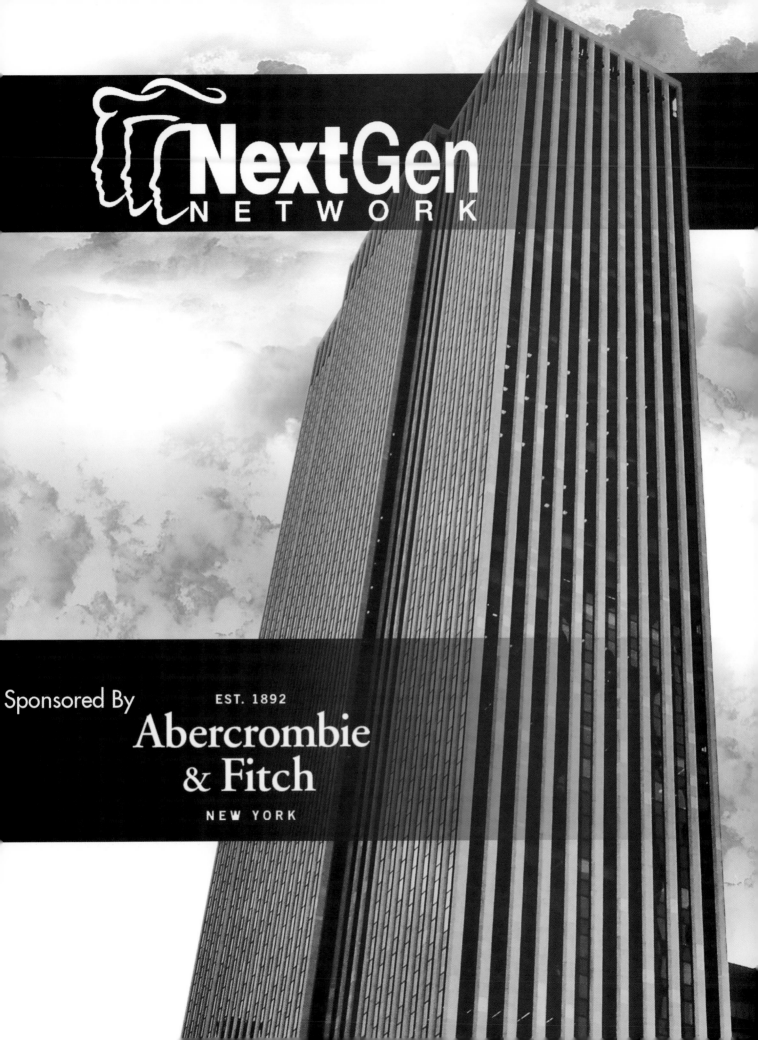

In the 10 years since NextGen Network was founded, we have evolved into the premiere affiliate of The Executive Leadership Council for developing the next generation of African-American executive leadership in corporate America. As we celebrate our 10th anniversary, we celebrate our achievements over the past years while acknowledging the great potential of our future. We are also thankful to The Executive Leadership Council and Abercrombie & Fitch in recognizing the contributions of NextGen Network members to their companies and to the NextGen Network organization.

The NextGen Network leadership team believes in the mandate behind the mission of NextGen Network, which is to serve as the partner-of-choice for developing the best and brightest African-American executive leaders in corporate America. We endeavor to accomplish this task by providing our members with leadership and career development programming, mentorship and coaching by senior executives, community outreach activities, as well as networking and relationship building opportunities. We are committed to and excited about NextGen Network's continued success and growth. Our membership currently stands at over 125 members and continues to grow rapidly. We accept one class per year in the spring with the application process starting in the fourth quarter. This application process is highly competitive given the limited number of membership slots available each year and the value through career/professional enrichment we offer to those invited to join.

The NextGen Network leadership team and committee chairs have worked diligently to expand our organization's reach to its key constituents including our membership, our pipeline, and our sponsors. As a result of these efforts, we have firmly positioned NextGen Network for success well into the future. Each year we evaluate our organizational objectives against our five key goals set forth as part of the NextGen Network strategic plan created in 2008, which are the following:

- Enhancing our financial stability
- Strengthening our member value proposition
- Increasing our marketing and communication efforts
- Improving our infrastructure and operations
- Advancing our community outreach programs

In 2009 and 2010, the leadership team will continue to ensure our organization objectives and other strategic organizational initiatives align with the goals of the strategic plan. In addition, we will be hosting events in major cities across the country to commemorate our 10th year anniversary. Please contact us at info@nextgennetwork.com if you would like to receive information about these activities.

As we look to the next 10 years, we believe the influence that NextGen Network members hold in corporate America will only multiply and the list of accolades will continue to grow. We remain excited and confident that our goals will continue to be realized as more of our members enter the senior executive ranks as the next generation of leaders in corporate America!

Joy Booker
Joy Booker
President, NextGen Network

Michael Watson
Vice President, NextGen Network

Joy Booker

Vice President
Institutional Sales & Marketing
Madison Square Investors, LLC

Pamela Hardy

Diversity Recruiting Manager
Booz Allen Hamilton

Joy Booker is vice president of the institutional sales and marketing division of Madison Square Investors, LLC (formerly New York Life Investment Management). She serves as a relationship manager for Madison Square Investor's $2.3 billion client portfolio.

Booker has international business experience in Asia and Europe. She began her career as a management consultant with the firms of Deloitte Consulting LLP and Price Waterhouse. She focused on large-scale e-commerce projects related to strategic technology planning and implementation for the financial service industry.

Columbia University awarded Booker an MBA degree and she received a Bachelor of Science degree in computer science from Binghamton University. She is a graduate of The Executive Leadership Council's (ELC) Strengthening the Pipeline: Critical Factors for Successful Leaders program. In 2007 Booker was elected president of the ELC's NextGen Network, and in 2005 she was a panelist at the ELC's Mid-Level Managers' Symposium. Recently, she was selected as one of *The Network Journal*'s 2009 40 Under Forty. This award celebrates her outstanding achievement, contribution, leadership and influence in the corporate and nonprofit arenas, along with service to the African-American community.

Based in Virginia, Pamela Hardy is a member of Booz Allen Hamilton's People Services Team. She leads the firm's diversity recruiting team, which is responsible for attracting top talent from diverse sources and strengthening the firm's brand as an employer of choice.

Prior to joining Booz Allen Hamilton, Pamela worked in recruiting and consulting roles within the consulting industry. As a consultant, she has partnered with organizations to develop leadership programs, succession planning workshops, and diversity recruiting strategies and techniques.

A member of the League of Black Women and the NextGen Network, Pamela holds a master's degree in human resources from Marymount University and a bachelor's degree in English from Virginia Union University. She enjoys cooking, reading and spending time with family and friends.

CORPORATE SPOTLIGHT

Reginia Brown Hester

Director, Corporate &
Public Sector Marketing
Global Transaction Services
Citi Corp

Kevin N. Hinton

Consultant

Reginia Brown Hester is the North America corporate and public sector marketing director of Global Transaction Services (GTS), a division of Citi Corp. As the senior point of contact for all North America corporate and public sector marketing, she leads a team that introduces and establishes the importance of GTS to the corporate and public sector, offers a full range of marketing services, and provides strategic marketing direction and program implementation to clients. She also analyzes corporate and public sector market performance to inform marketing strategy and identify new business opportunities.

Reginia supplements her corporate activities by incorporating her hobbies of interior decorating and fashion into contributions to her community. She paints newly-constructed, affordable housing with Habitat for Humanity and lends her time and talents in organizing clothing drives for Dress for Success, a not-for-profit organization that advances women's economic and social development.

A graduate of the University of Virginia with a Bachelor of Arts degree in government, Reginia studied abroad at the University of Valencia in Spain. She resides in Oakton, Virginia, with her husband, Gharun, and their daughter, Lena.

Kevin N. Hinton is a Washington, D.C.-based consultant with more than 15 years of experience in strategy development and execution, technology product management, financial analysis, and team leadership. Since 2005, he has provided business and product strategy consulting services to executives in industries including K-12 education, online media, business services and nonprofit services. In addition, he is an accomplished speaker and writer on topics such as product strategy, business plan development and leadership.

Previously, Kevin held management positions with market leaders in both the for-profit and nonprofit sectors, including vice president of the National Association of Investment Companies, senior manager of Marriott International, Inc., and business projects manager for global ecommerce channels for Discovery Education.

Kevin earned a Master of Business Administration degree from New York University Stern School of Business and a Bachelor of Arts degree from Williams College. A member of NextGen Network (NGN) since 2000, he was recognized for outstanding service by NGN's leadership team in 2007.

Shani Hosten

Director of Marketing
Pfizer Inc.

LaToya Lang, Esq.

State Legislative Director & Counsel
Marketing Research Association

Shani Hosten is director of marketing for Pfizer Inc.'s Southeast Regional Business Unit, where she manages strategic marketing development, program planning and campaign implementation for all the Primary Care Division's brands across eight states and the District of Columbia. She is responsible for establishing Pfizer's local brand presence, leading cross-functional teams and the development of marketing plans, strategies and tactics, including management of a multimillion-dollar budget.

Prior to her 11 years at Pfizer, Shani worked as a pharmaceutical sales representative with Eli Lilly and Company, and in several brand manager positions at Nabisco Foods Group. Additionally, she was director of marketing at Georgetown University Hospital, gaining a greater appreciation for the nonprofit sector, where she launched several innovative campaigns for Georgetown's oncology and transplant service lines.

Shani received a Bachelor of Science degree in marketing from Hampton University and an MBA degree from Columbia Business School. She enjoys running, biking and most outdoor activities with her family. A native of Richmond, Virginia, Shani currently resides in Potomac Falls, Virginia, with her husband, Terence, daughter Taylor, 9, and son Nicholas, 4.

LaToya Lang, Esq. is the state legislative director and counsel for the Marketing Research Association. She serves as the executive for proactively responding to state legislative issues impacting the survey research profession for all 50 states and the District of Columbia. Additionally, she provides legal education on issues impacting survey research activities.

LaToya has the fortunate pleasure of numerous legislative victories, including authoring law in the state of Louisiana and assisting in the creation of an exemption for survey research companies in a Massachusetts law.

The University of Cincinnati awarded LaToya a Bachelor of Arts degree in political science and she received a juris doctorate degree from the University of Cincinnati College of Law. She is currently attending the American University Washington College of Law as a Master of Laws degree candidate. LaToya serves as the corporate governance chair for the NextGen Network, and is a member of the Ohio State Bar Association and The District of Columbia Bar.

CORPORATE SPOTLIGHT

Michael Watson

Vice President
Strategy & Development
JPMorgan Chase

Michael Watson is vice president and president-elect of NextGen Network, Inc. NextGen Network's focus is to facilitate executive leadership and professional development for African-American professionals and to create opportunities for leadership development in communities, particularly those that are underserved and underprivileged, to help build the diverse pipeline of talent necessary to achieve long-term, sustainable business success for African Americans in corporate America.

Additionally, Mike is a vice president at JPMorgan Chase in the Strategy and Development Group. He has the responsibility of partnering with JPMorgan Chase's lines of business to evaluate and execute business and technical strategies for the Internet and mobile channel. He has supervised the deployment of JPMorgan Chase's award-winning mobile banking solution via the mobile browser, as well as the groundbreaking U.S. Open text messaging sweepstakes.

Mike graduated, cum laude, with a Bachelor of Arts degree from Wake Forest University, and received a Master of Arts degree in history from The Ohio State University. A native of Roosevelt, New York, he is the husband of Michelle Watson and the proud father of two sons, Spencer and Samuel.

Washington, D.C.

ACADEMIA

PERFORM

ELEVATE

PHENOM

SCHOLAR

PRODIGY

MENTOR

MERIT

VALUE

ATTAIN

Renaisa S. Anthony, M.D.

Assistant Research Professor
Department of Public Health & Services
School of Public Health & Health Services
The George Washington University

Erika H. Bunton

Clinical Counselor
Maya Angelou Public
Charter School – Evans Campus

A Detroit native, Dr. Renaisa S. Anthony witnessed the health disparities that afflict racial and ethnic minorities, and dedicated efforts to improve health outcomes in such populations. She earned a medical degree from The University of Chicago and a master's degree in public health from Harvard University. She completed obstetrics/gynecology intern training at Vanderbilt University.

Anthony migrated to Washington, D.C., as an American Association for the Advancement of Science Health Policy fellow at the National Institutes of Health (NIH) and the Office of the Surgeon General. She was honored by the surgeon general for her outstanding contribution to the Surgeon General's Conference on the Prevention of Preterm Birth.

Appointed as an assistant research professor at The George Washington University School of Public Health and Health Services, Anthony teaches courses on women's health and health disparities. She is the principal investigator on the NIH-supported chronic hypertension in pregnancy study, and a women's health consultant to NIH, the U.S. Department of Health and Human Services, the District of Columbia Department of Health, and Capitol Hill.

Anthony enjoys theater, karaoke and traveling internationally on medical missions

Erika Bunton is a clinical counselor for the Maya Angelou Public Charter School – Evans Campus. In this position, she provides individual and group psychotherapy to at-risk youth.

For her dedication in supporting District of Columbia youth within the child welfare system, Bunton was awarded the Child and Family Services Spirit of Support Award in July of 2006. She is a member of the National Association of Social Workers and Zeta Phi Beta Sorority, Inc.

Bunton received a Bachelor of Arts degree from The George Washington University in 1998 and a master's degree in social work from Howard University in 2002. She also received certifications in dialectical behavioral therapy from Behavioral Tech, LLC and adolescent trauma treatment from the University of Maryland, Baltimore.

A native of Philadelphia, Pennsylvania, Bunton continues to mentor urban teens, and now works as a youth advisor for First Baptist Church of Glenarden.

Derwin L. Campbell

Lecturer
Morgan State University

Jodi Anneliese Cavanaugh

EEO Officer
Office of Diversity &
Equal Employment Opportunity
Morgan State University

Derwin Campbell is a lecturer and doctoral candidate at Morgan State University (MSU) in Baltimore, Maryland, where he teaches Freshman Composition I and II, and Humanities I and II. In addition, he serves on the freshman English Curriculum, Hospitality and Humanities committees.

Derwin received the MSU part-time tuition assistance award while pursuing a doctorate degree in English. He is currently writing his dissertation prospectus focusing on the presentation of the down-low phenomenon in literature. His current area of expertise is multiculturalism and gender studies.

A member of the College Language Association, Derwin is also a member of the Phi Beta Sigma Fraternity, Inc. Delta Kappa Sigma Chapter, which hails from Sumter, South Carolina. He received Bachelor of Arts and Master of Arts degrees from Fayetteville State University. While there, he was recognized by *Who's Who in American Colleges and Universities*, graduate students, and received All-American Scholar honors. Derwin currently resides in Baltimore, Maryland.

Jodi A. Cavanaugh is currently employed in the Office of Diversity and Equal Employment Opportunity at Morgan State University in Baltimore, Maryland. She is also an attorney and specializes in mediation, tort and family law.

Jodi earned a Bachelor of Arts degree from the College of Notre Dame of Maryland and a juris doctorate degree from the University of Maryland School of Law. She is currently studying to earn a Doctor of Philosophy degree in higher education at Morgan State University.

A resident of Baltimore, Maryland, Jodi is the proud mother of one daughter, Evan, and one son, Adam.

Audrey Jean Childs

Teacher
Truesdell Educational Center

Julie Doar-Sinkfield

Co-Founder & Executive Director
The William E. Doar Jr. Public Charter
School for the Performing Arts

Audrey Jean Childs is a District of Columbia Public Schools teacher at Truesdell Educational Center, where she has modeled and promoted accomplished teaching for 17 years. She has chaired committees, coordinated summer and spring break programs, and directed annual musicals. She teaches courses in the development of pre-service and in-service teachers at American University through its certification and master's degree programs.

Jean directed the chorus at a local Catholic school, which performed in Canada, at the Kennedy Center for the Performing Arts and on FOX news. She attained national board certification and was one of the recipients of the 2005-2006 Metropolitan Organization of Black Scientists Teacher of the Year Award. Additionally, she is a member of Zeta Phi Beta Sorority, Inc., Beta Zeta Chapter.

A native of Washington, D.C., Jean attended public schools and received a bachelor's degree from Howard University. She was awarded a Master of Arts degree in teaching from the University of the District of Columbia. Jean is the wife of the Reverend Robert G. Childs and the proud mother of three young adults, Robert, Glenn and Regina.

Responsible for policy development, strategic planning, reporting, fundraising and organizational growth, Julie Doar-Sinkfield has managed three construction projects, negotiated financing, and raised more than $800,000 in grants and donations since opening. She has supervised school growth from one campus of 153 Pre-K through 5th grade students and a staff of 23 in 2004, to three campuses and 630 Pre-K through 11th grade students in 2008. She also coordinated the school's accreditation in its fourth year and is now working on a $23 million financing package.

Doar-Sinkfield served as interim principal at Children's Studio School Public Charter School, director of the Southeast Academy of Scholastic Excellence Public Charter School and middle school director of The Newport School. She holds instructional experience in a variety of academic settings and grade levels, including as an adjunct online professor at Strayer University.

Doar-Sinkfield has a Bachelor of Arts degree from Wesleyan University and a Master of Arts degree from Northeastern University. A native of New York City, she lives in Washington, D.C., with her husband, Rick Sinkfield, and three children, Hunter, Colette and Carmen.

Lorenzo L. Esters, Ed.D.

Vice President, Office for Access & the
Advancement of Public Black Universities
APLU

Sharon Fries-Britt

Associate Professor
University of Maryland

Dr. Lorenzo Lamar Esters is vice president of the Office for Access and the Advancement of Public Black Universities for the Association of Public and Land-Grant Universities (APLU). In his role for APLU, Esters works with the leadership of public historically black colleges and universities, including historically black land-grant institutions, as well as Native-American and Hispanic-serving institutions. He also provides support and leadership to the Commission on Access, Diversity and Excellence, and works to promote and advance access and equity across all APLU member institutions and throughout public higher education.

Prior to assuming this role, Esters was senior adviser to the president at Dillard University in New Orleans. Prior to joining Dillard University, he served as a management and program analyst in the Office of the Assistant Secretary at the U.S. Department of Education. Esters has more than ten years of experience as a career federal public employee. Additionally, he is a member of Alpha Phi Alpha Fraternity, Inc.

A native of the Mississippi Delta, Esters is single and when he is not working, he enjoys working out, reading and traveling.

Sharon Fries-Britt is an associate professor at the University of Maryland (UMCP). From 1998 to 1999, she served as a visiting professor at the Harvard Graduate School of Education. Prior to her academic career, she served as a senior administrator at UMCP.

As a research consultant for the national societies for black and Hispanic physicists, she studies minorities in science. She was a CO-PI from 2004 to 2006 on a grant funded by the Lumina Foundation to study race, equity and diversity in the 23 southern and border states. A national speaker and independent consultant on issues of race, equity and diversity, her current projects include work with Johns Hopkins University, Princeton University, MIT and several federal agencies.

Sharon received the University President's Award for outstanding contributions, the Outstanding Minority Staff Member Award, the first Woman of Color Award and the Outstanding Achievement Award as a black faculty member.

Sharon earned bachelor's and doctorate degrees at the University of Maryland, and a master's degree at The Ohio State University. She is married to Ned Britt Jr. and has one daughter, Katura Britt.

Doran Gresham, Ed.D.

University Supervisor & Project Director
The George Washington University

Maloney Rhonda Hunter-Lowe, Ed.D.

Faculty
University of Phoenix

D r. Doran Gresham is a university supervisor and project director at The George Washington University, where his chief duties are to provide clinical supervision and feedback to graduate interns who aspire to teach students with emotional and behavioral disabilities.

Gresham earned a Bachelor of Arts degree in English from the University of Virginia, and a master's degree in education with a concentration in learning disabilities and emotional disturbance from The College of William & Mary. Dedicated to community service, he is a proud member of Guerilla Arts Ink, a grassroots organization that brings artists and educators together.

In 2004 Gresham was awarded the Elliott Hair Man of the Year award from 100 Black Men of Greater Washington, D.C., Inc., where he is a member. This award recognizes efforts from within the chapter that have made a difference in the District of Columbia metropolitan area. Additionally, he is the director of instruction for CaseNEX, LLC, and serves as a founding board member of Achievement Preparatory Academy, where he is the current chairman of the Academic Performance and Accountability Committee.

D r. Maloney Hunter-Lowe believes that true education is the interaction of ideas and practice, and she facilitates with an integration of theory and practice to help bring new insights to all learners. She holds an associate degree in business, a Bachelor of Science degree in psychology, a Master of Science degree in elementary education and a Master of Science degree in school administration from Mercy College in Dobbs Ferry, New York. In addition, she completed a doctorate degree in educational leadership at the University of Phoenix.

Because she has studied in both the European (British) and American systems, Hunter-Lowe has come to learn and appreciate the strength of each model of education. She is a certified wedding officiant and serves as a notary public in her home and school community.

Teaching in public education for ten years, Hunter-Lowe has published her first book, *Qualitative Analysis of Disruptive Behavior and Leadership Influence in Two Urban K-6 Virginia Elementary Schools*. She was born and raised in Jamaica, West Indies.

William Hutchins

Retired Educator
District of Columbia Public Schools

Charles Jarmon, Ph.D.

Professor & Associate Dean
Howard University

William Hutchins was an educator with the District of Columbia Public Schools for 32 years, where he taught at the elementary level before retiring in 1995. He served as both a summer school teacher and administrator. Additionally, he served as school treasurer for several years and was responsible for all monies collected from the students.

During his tenure, William received numerous awards, including the Library Award and the Anacostia Museum Partnership Award. Upon retirement, he received the District of Columbia Public School Retirement Award and letters of accommodation from Mayor Marion Barry, the Honorable Eleanor Holmes Norton and Superintendent Franklin Smith.

William received a Bachelor of Science degree from the District of Columbia Teachers College in 1963 and a Master of Education degree from Bowie State College in 1972. He has been a member of Phi Beta Sigma Fraternity, Inc. since 1960, and is recognized as a prominent member of the Eastern Region.

William has been married to his wife, Barbara, since 1963. He has one son, Darin, a daughter-in-law, Angela, and two grandchildren, Quentin and Olivia.

Dr. Charles Jarmon is professor and associate dean at Howard University and a former chairman of the department of sociology and anthropology. Born in Kinston, North Carolina, he graduated from North Carolina College in 1965, continued further study as a James B. Duke graduate fellow at Duke University and received a Doctor of Philosophy degree from The State University of New York at Buffalo. He has taught at North Carolina College, Southern University, SUNY at Buffalo and Virginia Commonwealth University.

His consultancies include services to the African Development Fund, the U.S. Census Bureau, and the U.S. Senior Foreign Service selection board. Jarmon was a book review editor for the *Journal of African and Asian Studies* and a member of the editorial board of the *Canadian Review of Studies in Nationalism*. He has numerous publications on blacks in America and Africa, and his 1988 book, *Nigeria: Reorganization and Development since the Mid-Twentieth Century*, continues to be referenced in writing on African development. In 2008 the Association of Black Sociologists awarded him the Joseph Himes Award for Lifetime Achievement for a career of distinguished scholarship.

Judith Moore Kelly

Director
District of Columbia Area Writing Project
School of Education
Howard University

Eric Key

Director, Arts Program
University of Maryland University College

Judith Moore Kelly heads the District of Columbia Area Writing Project for the Howard University School of Education. In this position, she directs the local affiliate of the National Writing Project, a 200-site network of educators devoted to writing and the teaching of writing.

President of the Black Caucus of National Council of Teachers of English, Judith is also past president of the DC Council of Teachers of English/Language Arts, former chair of the Conference on English Leadership and a member of Delta Sigma Theta Sorority, Inc. She is a former public school teacher who has conducted workshops for educators nationally and internationally.

Her publications include teachers' guides to Chinua Achebe's *Things Fall Apart*, Harper Lee's *To Kill a Mockingbird*, Ken Burns' PBS *Jazz* series and articles in *The Journal of Negro Education*. Judith received a Bachelor of Arts degree from Saint Augustine's College, a Master of Education degree from Bowie State University and a Doctor of Philosophy degree from Bernelli University.

As director of the arts program at the University of Maryland University College, Eric Key manages the department, coordinates visual art exhibitions, manages and develops the university's art collections, and maintains a balanced budget through corporate development and grants.

Previously, Eric served as executive director of The Kansas African American Museum, Inc., and as curator and assistant director for the Museum of African American Life and Culture in Dallas. Additionally, he was program director for the Junior Black Academy of Arts and Letters, Inc.

Eric served as a panel reviewer for the National Endowment for the Arts, the Kansas Arts Commission, the City of Dallas Cultural Affairs, the Texas Commission on the Arts, and the Institute of Museums and Library Services. He is a member of the American Museum and the African American museum associations, and a lifetime member of the NAACP and Alpha Phi Alpha Fraternity, Inc.

Eric has a master's degree in museum studies and a bachelor's degree in political science from Hampton University. A native of Smithfield, Virginia, Eric is the proud single parent of Christopher L. Key, 18.

Christopher J. Metzler, Ph.D.

Associate Dean
School of Continuing Studies
Georgetown University

Charles P. Mouton, M.D.

Professor & Chair
Department of Community & Family Medicine
Howard University College of Medicine

Dr. Christopher J. Metzler is associate dean of human resources and diversity studies at Georgetown University. As such, he leads the graduate HR and diversity faculty in the master's degree program. Metzler is a highly regarded public intellectual and scholar who has appeared on ABC, BBC, Sky News and BBC Arabic, among other media outlets. He was also quoted in *The New York Times, The Washington Times* and others.

Metzler is a prolific writer, blogging for *"The Daily Voice"* and *"Diverse Issues in Higher Education."* Additionally, he is the author of *The Construction and Rearticulation of Race in a Post-Racial America* and the forthcoming "Jim Crow on Steroids."

Metzler earned a master's degree in international human rights from Columbia University in New York City. He holds a Doctor of Philosophy degree, with distinction, from the University of Aberdeen and is a member of the University of Oxford in Oxford, England, and Kellogg College at Oxford University.

An engaging scholar and global thought leader, Metzler has delivered lectures in Madrid, Paris, and the United Kingdom, as well as throughout the United States.

Dr. Charles P. Mouton is professor and chair of the department of community and family medicine at the Howard University College of Medicine in Washington, D.C. A native of New Orleans, Mouton holds degrees in mechanical engineering and medicine from Howard University and a master's degree in clinical epidemiology from Harvard University. He is a certified medical director, and board-certified in family medicine and geriatrics.

Mouton is founder of CPM Healthcare Consulting Group, LLC, providing health care, research, education and medico legal services. As an active researcher, he is co-investigator of the Women's Health Initiative, director of the D.C. Primary Care Research Network, and he leads studies on late-life domestic violence, practice-based research, exercise in minority elders and end-of-life care for older minorities.

Mouton has published extensively on a variety of topics, including health promotion, health disparities, ethnicity and aging, and domestic violence in older women.

Anthony C. Nelson, Ph.D.

Dean, College of Business
Bowie State University

Tracy M. Walton Jr., M.D.

Associate Professor
College of Pharmacy, Nursing &
Allied Health Sciences
Howard University

With nearly 20 years of higher education and corporate experience, Dr. Anthony C. Nelson is dean of the College of Business at Bowie State University. Prior to joining Bowie State University, he served as dean of the College of Business at Grambling State University, where he also taught. Currently, he serves on the board of directors of the Baltimore-Washington Corridor Chamber of Commerce.

His research interests include information systems personnel and the impact of information technology on society. Nelson has contributed to various journals, including *The American Review of Public Administration*, *Interfaces*, and *Information and Management*. He has also been a featured speaker on national television broadcasts regarding the impact of technology on society.

His academic credentials include a bachelor's degree in business management from North Carolina A&T State University, a master's degree in biblical studies from Dallas Theological Seminary and master's and Doctor of Philosophy degrees in business administration from the University of Pittsburgh.

A former three-time state champion and U.S. national champion in tae kwon do, Nelson enjoys martial arts. His passion is ministering to young men in juvenile detention centers.

Dr. Tracy Walton Jr. is an associate professor in the Howard University College of Pharmacy, Nursing and Allied Health Sciences, as well as the medical director of the physician assistant program. He was previously the medical director/advisor of the medical radiography program at the University of the District of Columbia and retired as the chief medical officer of the Radiology Division of the District of Columbia General Hospital in 1980.

Walton is board-certified by The American Board of Radiology. He has held several positions within the National Medical Association, is past president of the Medico-Chirurgical Society of the District of Columbia, past speaker of the Provisional House of Delegates and past board of trustees member of the Medical Society of the District of Columbia. Additionally, he is a member of the American College of Radiology.

An alumnus of Morgan State University and the College of Medicine – Howard University, Walton married the former Mae Yvonne Squires and has four children and several grandchildren. He is listed in the *Dictionary of International Biography*, *Who's Who in Medicine and Healthcare*, and *Who's Who in America*.

Washington, D.C.

ENTREPRENEURS

EXPLORER

INDUSTRIALIST

PIONEER

CAPITALIST

TYCOON

HEROIC

PHILANTHROPIC

HUMANITARIAN

ALTRUISTIC

Naleli Askew

President
Quintessential Consulting

N aleli Askew founded Quintessential Consulting, a private event coordination and jewelry consulting business. She has 15 years of experience in jewelry marketing and sales. Trained and certified by the Diamond Council of America, her expertise covers engagement and wedding ring designs, and acquiring special occasion jewelry. She has designed custom pieces and collaborated with craftsmen to cater to a diverse clientele in the Washington, D.C. area.

Naleli received a bachelor's degree from Marymount University, where she was president of the Black Student Alliance and planned fundraisers, fashion shows and social events. Since college, she has organized annual fundraising campaigns for Relay for Life, the March of Dimes, St. Jude's Children's Hospital and other community events, which has inspired her to venture into the event management business. Her portfolio includes fundraising, wine tasting, art/trade exhibits and weddings.

Born in southern Africa, Naleli attended high school at the Academy of Holy Cross. She is married to Joseph Askew Jr., Esq., and they have two children, Joseph Lefa III and Nala. She is a member of Nativity Catholic Church and the Marymount University Black Alumni Association.

George Brownlee

Founder & Chief Executive Officer
Ergo Solutions, LLC

A Howard University graduate, George Brownlee founded Ergo Solutions, LLC in 2000 with the vision of providing rehabilitation services, including physical therapy, occupational therapy and speech therapy, to local hospitals and nursing homes in Washington, D.C. Since Ergo Solutions' first contract in 2003 at Medlink Hospital, now known as The Specialty Hospital of Washington, the company is currently the rehabilitation provider at seven hospitals and nursing homes in the District of Columbia.

Currently, Ergo Solutions has four partners, including Olu Ezeani, co-founder and chief financial officer; Jason Henderson, chief information officer; and Courtland Wyatt, chief operating officer. In 2008 Ergo Solutions' gross revenue was more than $6 million.

Ergo Solutions has established itself as the largest outsourcing rehabilitation provider in Washington, D.C. The company has 86 total employees, and has recently developed Ergo Resolutions, a nonprofit company; Ergo Occ-Med; Ergo University; Ergo Out-Patient; and Ergo International. Each area concentrates on providing rehabilitation resources and services to those in need.

George is the husband of Gail Quinn Brownlee, and the proud father of three children, Donovan, Aniyah and Jessica.

Cheron Reed Burns is the owner/general manager of Rx Catering, Washington D.C., LLC and owner of Rx Catering, Baltimore, LLC. She manages the daily operations of the catering company located in Alexandria, Virginia, which is geared towards the pharmaceutical/medical, corporate and institutional industries.

As a former district sales manager with Pfizer, Inc., Cheron understands the importance of excellent customer service with quality products. She is the second vice president of Delta Sigma Theta Sorority, Inc. Northern Virginia Alumnae Chapter, and has a regional position on the Nominating Committee. Cheron has been an active volunteer for the past ten years with the National Black MBA Association Leaders of Tomorrow mentoring program, where she was awarded Volunteer of the Year in 2006 and Entrepreneur of the Year in 2008.

She received a Bachelor of Science degree from Florida A&M University, where she majored in business economics. A native of Minneapolis, Minnesota, and Champaign, Illinois, Cheron has a very supportive family and circle of friends whom she appreciates immensely as she continues to pursue her entrepreneurial endeavors.

Cheron Reed Burns

Owner
Rx Catering,
Washington, D.C., LLC

Tim Davis is founder, director and current owner of International Visions – The Gallery, LLC. As director, his objective has always been to exhibit and introduce highly accomplished international, national and regional artists to Washington, and to link people, cultures, beliefs and lifestyles through art.

Tim received a Master of Arts degree from the University of Illinois, where he studied sculpture and painting. He has had several years of experience in researching, consulting and arts education. Tim was honored by the National Endowment for the Arts (NEA) with an arts management fellowship in 1984 and continued to work with the Expansion Arts Program at the NEA for some years.

Additionally, he has worked as a consultant with the District of Columbia Commission on the Arts and Humanities, the D.C. Art Works Murals Project, the Council on Foundations and the Arlington County Arts and Planning Commission. He has been on numerous committees and boards throughout the Washington, D.C., area including, most recently, being appointed to the Dulles Corridor Metrorail Public Art Selection Panel.

Timothy A. Davis

Owner & Director
International Visions – The Gallery

Bernetta "Niecie" Draper

Franchise Owner
Priority Financial Services

Bernetta "Niecie" Draper is the franchise owner of Priority Financial Services (PFS) in Largo. She and her team provide residential and commercial real estate financing to families and businesses. Niecie publishes weekly newsletters to more than 5,000 subscribers delivering advice on personal finance matters such as borrowing, saving and investing money, wealth, equity, asset and debt management, credit repair, planning for college tuition, and the impact of current economic events.

With more than 15 years' experience in finance, Niecie began her career at AT&T. In her last role, she served as project manager in federal systems. She served with Fannie Mae for ten years, her most recent position being director of operations/chief of staff to the executive vice president. In addition to PFS, she has originated loans with CitiMortgage and American Home Mortgage Servicing, Inc.

Niecie earned a Bachelor of Arts degree in economics and a master's degree in finance from the University of Maryland. She also holds a master's certificate in project management from The George Washington University. Additionally, Niecie is a member of Zeta Phi Beta Sorority, Inc.

Danessa "Dee Dee" Drumgold

President
Motivations Extraordinaire

Dee Dee Drumgold is president of Motivations Extraordinaire. In this position, she has stood in various arenas coaching and encouraging individuals to confront obstacles and life challenges that will help them overcome. Her messages have taken her before audiences from junior/senior high school students to university adult education special development programs, programs designed to assist adults re-entering the employment market, and homeless shelters. She displays compassion and humor in her delivery.

Dee Dee has worked as a manager and director in the human resources profession for 24-plus years in the areas of consulting, legal and health care. She has been a member of the Society for Human Resource Management since 1996.

Dee Dee is also a licensed minister and psalmist – places of travel include various parts of the United States, the Caribbean, Europe and Mexico. Her joy is serving others and celebrating their successes.

Ofield Dukes has excelled in three careers as a journalist, a public relations executive and as an educator. A native of Detroit, Dukes received a Bachelor of Science degree in journalism from Wayne State University in 1958. As an editor and journalist, he won three National Newspaper Publishers Association awards for editorial, column and feature writing in 1964.

After serving three years on the staff of Vice President Hubert H. Humphrey, Dukes opened his own public relations firm, Ofield Dukes & Associates, currently celebrating 40 years. He won the Public Relations Society of America's (PRSA) Silver Anvil Award in 1975, and became the first African American to receive the highest individual award given in the public relations industry, the coveted PRSA Gold Anvil Award in 2001.

Dukes helped organize the public relations curriculum at Howard University, where he has taught as an adjunct professor for 25 years. He also taught public relations at The American University for eight years.

For years, Dukes was active with the Congressional Black Caucus and as a communications consultant in Democratic presidential campaigns.

Ofield Dukes

Owner
Ofield Dukes & Associates

Sandra Fowler is president of Brewton Enterprises, a commercial real estate development and consulting firm with a diverse portfolio of nonprofit and private sector clients. She has more than 27 years of experience in the commercial real estate and construction industry, and has been responsible for a variety of building projects. Two noted projects managed by Fowler include the reconstruction of the prestigious and award-winning The Army and Navy Club, located in Washington, D.C.'s exclusive Farragut Square, and the redevelopment of the 18th Century Forrest-Marbury Court in historic Georgetown.

In 1995 Fowler received an appointment from President Bill Clinton as a delegate to the White House Conference on Small Business. She received a Bachelor of Science degree in architecture from Tuskegee University and studied communications at the University of South Carolina.

Fowler is a Legacy Life member of the National Council of Negro Women. A native of Spartanburg, South Carolina, she is the proud mother of one daughter, Keeona Diamond, and two grandchildren, Akayla and Clifforn Jr.

Sandra R. Fowler

President & Chief Executive Officer
Brewton Enterprises, Inc.

John A. Glover

President & Chief Executive Officer
Strategic Fundraising Solutions, LLC

John A. Glover is president of Strategic Fundraising Solutions, LLC, a fundraising consulting practice with an eye toward teaching smaller nonprofit organizations how to create, manage and implement effective resource development operations with limited staff resources and budgets. His use of short-term and long-term strategic planning permits organizations to develop at a pace that teaches the basic strategies of resource development.

As a development professional and manager for more than 35 years, John has served as vice president of resource development for the Congressional Black Caucus Foundation; chief development officer for the National Council of Negro Women; director of resource development and corporate relations for the National Association of Black Accountants; executive vice president of Jarvis Christian College; executive vice president of Tougaloo College; and regional vice president of the UNCF.

John served as senior account executive with Who's Who Publishing Company for the inaugural edition of *Who's Who Black In Washington, D.C.*®.

John received a Bachelor of Science degree in business administration from Livingstone College and performed graduate studies at the Hunter College School of Social Work in Manhattan, New York.

Scott E. Glover

President & Chief
Business Development Manager
Opulent Living, LLC

Born and raised in Cleveland, Ohio, Scott E. Glover is president and chief business development manager of Opulent Living, LLC. A premier Washington, D.C.-based interior development firm, Opulent Living provides exclusive interior and architectural design solutions for residential and commercial projects.

A former Citibank business banker, Scott has utilized his corporate skill sets and expertise in sales and marketing to position Opulent Living to become one of the most sought-after names throughout Washington, D.C.'s interior development society.

In September of 2000, Scott launched Urban Link Promotions, an event promotions company that emphasized linking urban professionals through social networking. Through Urban Link Productions, he was able to establish youth mentoring programs, as well as aid in securing critical funding for a number of Cleveland's local nonprofits.

Always believing the keys to success to be determination, the ability to stay focused and old-fashioned hard work, Scott has never let a lack of opportunity limit his progress. He attended Livingstone College (an HBCU), where he majored in business administration.

A native Washingtonian, Ayo Handy-Kendi serves as a certified transformational breath facilitator, certified stress manager, breathologist, Reiki I and II, Rasekhi II, Qi Gong I and II, aromatherapist and diversity healer through her holistic health service, PositivEnergyWorks.

Ayo is founder and director of the African American Holiday Association, a nonprofit membership organization offering storytelling, performances, workshops, lectures, celebration and ritual facilitation, and affordable special events management.

Considered an authority on cultural holidays and stress management, she has appeared on radio and television, and in print, most recently appearing on *The Steve Harvey Morning Show*. Ayo is the author of three books, a play, and has organized more than 30 national marches. She has received numerous recognitions, such as the Ambassador of Peace Award, the Kool Achievers Award, the Anheuser-Busch Profile in Excellency Award, and recognition in Benin, West Africa.

Ayo has an associate degree as a counselor from Washington Technical Institute and a bachelor's degree in community organizing from Antioch College. She is spiritually degreed in overcoming childhood abuse, homelessness, addiction, domestic violence and the murder of her teenage son.

Ayo Handy-Kendi

Chief Executive Officer
PostivEnergyWorks

After the loss of his job in 1999, Rodney Hawkins realized an opportunity to start his own IT consulting firm and founded the Washington Technology Group, Inc. (WTG). Celebrating ten years as a multimillion-dollar business, WTG provides IT support service for federal and commercial customers, including the FBI, NASA Goddard Space Flight Center, the U.S. Air Force, the Executive Office of the President and several U.S. government departments.

Rodney volunteers at Calvin Coolidge High School, and has served as a mentor and computer trainer for youth ages 8-16 in the Prosperity Media's Summer Media Arts Program. He mentors young men in the District of Columbia's juvenile detention center and speaks to youth on the importance of making the right choices. Additionally, he has donated thousands of dollars to youth programs.

A native Washingtonian, he received an associate degree from Washington Technical Institute, a bachelor's degree from Howard University and completed graduate study at George Washington University. An avid golfer, Rodney spends time relaxing on area golf courses and reading. He lives in northwest Washington, D.C., with Cheryl, his wife of 18 years.

Rodney G. Hawkins

Founder
Washington Technology
Group, Inc.

Shonda Hurt

President
SDH Professional Services, LLC

E vent planner extraordinaire Shonda Hurt is well versed on the ingredients required to create events that strengthen an organization's brand, and help influence the overall perception of a company's products and services. With more than ten years' experience in planning and executing hundreds of corporate events under her belt, she began SDH Professional Services, LLC in 2007.

Some of Shonda's most memorable projects include the Remy Martin Louis XIII midnight tasting during the *Food & Wine's* Aspen Classic, *Sister 2 Sister* magazine's annual Anniversary Gala held in New York City and the Automotive Rhythms' Urban Restyln' Salon held during the Washington, D.C., Auto Show.

Shonda works as a consultant with a laundry list of clients, including event and design firm K.I.M. Media, LLC, and Automotive Rhythms Communications, LLC, an automotive media and publishing company. Additionally, she was responsible for assisting in the creation and execution of the Why Can't We All Just Buckle Up campaign, a joint partnership with the National Highway Traffic Safety Administration.

Shonda majored in business and communications at the University of Pittsburgh, where she received a bachelor's degree.

Sharon Jarrett

President & Chief Executive Officer
Jarrett Affairs & Productions, LLC

S haron Jarrett arrived from New York just two years ago. After 16 years at IBM, she left to pursue her passion full time, and as president and chief executive officer of an event management and public relations firm, her heartbeat is the flawless execution of a well-designed event plan. With solid corporate experience in finance, audit and marketing, Jarrett Affairs is where business expertise and creativity meet to create events on time, on target and on budget.

Jarrett Affairs coordinated Jack and Jill of America, Inc.'s Pink, White & Blue Children's Inaugural Ball at the Ritz-Carlton, Pentagon City, which was attended by nearly 1,000 children and adults. Some of Sharon's other clients include Chicken Soup for the Soul and the National Black MBA Association, Inc. Her company recently produced Pretty In Pinstripes, a women's power luncheon celebrating exceptional women in business and government from our communities, and featured Judge Glenda Hatchett. In addition, Jarrett Affairs recently received the 2008 Best In Show award for exhibit design from the Prince George's Chamber of Commerce.

While pursuing juris doctorate and MBA degrees at Georgetown University, award-winning jazz pianist Marcus Johnson independently produced his first album, *Lessons in Love* in 1996. The album helped him launch his career as a renowned jazz musician and chief executive officer of Marimelj Entertainment Group, LLC (MEG).

Noting Johnson's business savvy and musical ambition, BET founder Robert L. Johnson invested in MEG. MEG's label, Three Keys Music, established its own full-service recording studio, Studio 8121, and music publishing companies, Marimelj Music and Three Keys Music.

His latest album, *Poetically Justified*, reached No. 5 on the Billboard Contemporary Jazz Charts within 15 days of its release on June 2, 2009. Johnson's previous projects were the groundbreaking Billboard Top 20 Contemporary Jazz FLO series, *FLO: Chill, FLO: Romance* and *FLO: Standards* in September of 2008, as well as his solo record, *The Phoenix* in July of 2007.

Johnson intends to bring his love of jazz to the masses. His ambition and ideas are the rock on which he stands, raising the art of jazz to the upper echelon of the music industry.

Marcus Johnson

Chief Executive Officer
Marimelj Entertainment Group, LLC

Dr. Daemon Jones completed her undergraduate education in economics at Northwestern University, where she graduated in 1992. "Dr. Dae," as she is affectionately called, completed her naturopathic medical training at the University of Bridgeport College of Naturopathic Medicine in 2002.

Jones founded Healthydaes Naturopathic Medical Center in Washington, D.C., in 2003. As a naturopathic physician, she is turning her life's passion of the pursuit of vibrant health into her life's mission for others. She uses private consultations, cooking demonstrations, lectures and workshops as a hands-on way to help people enjoy learning about improving their health.

The author of *Daelicious! Recipes for Vibrant Health*, published in 2007, Jones is a faculty member of the Smith Farm Center for Healing and the Arts and the Food As Medicine Professional Nutrition Training Program.

Daemon Jones, N.D.

Naturopathic Physician
Healthydaes Naturopathic
Medical Center

Melanie Lamar

President &
Director of Home Care
Right at Home, Inc.

Melanie Lamar is president and director of home care for Right at Home, Inc. Having always carried a passion for the nursing profession, Lamar credits her experiences growing up in a military family as her inspiration for a career in the care community.

Holding herself to a standard of excellence, Lamar oversees an army of private duty care professionals who have been trained, oriented and tested under her careful supervision. Currently, Right at Home, Inc. is flourishing with an ever-expanding roll call of clients and care professionals.

In 2000 Lamar earned a Bachelor of Science degree in nursing from Old Dominion University before embarking on a career in health care. She held staff positions at several hospitals in the District of Columbia area before branching out to launch Right at Home, Inc. Lamar founded the company after recognizing the need for an alternative for seniors who preferred to stay in the comfort of their own homes.

Jamail Larkins

Founder
Larkins Enterprises, Inc.

From the ripe age of 12 when Jamail Larkins stepped inside an airplane and co-piloted his first flight with the Experimental Aircraft Association (EAA) Young Eagles Program, he was hooked for life.

At 16 Jamail became the national spokesman of the EAA Vision of Eagles Program. He also became the first and youngest student pilot to solo in a Cirrus SR20, and one of the youngest air show aerobatic performers in the United States. Jamail founded his first company at 15, Larkins Enterprises, Inc.

By fall of 2004, the FAA signed Jamail as the first official ambassador for aviation and space education. He has flown with the Navy's prestigious Blue Angels, been featured in the Franklin Institute, and received a certificate of special recognition from the U.S. Congress.

Today, at 25 years old, Jamail serves on the board of two large aviation nonprofit organizations and is the chairman of the Careers in Aviation board. He continues to grow his primary company, Ascension Aircraft, Inc., and hopes to double the amount of planes the company currently owns in the next year.

Ron LeGrand is president and chief executive officer of LeGrand & Associates. In addition to legal services, LeGrand & Associates provides consulting expertise in government relations, diversity and inclusion, as well as structures operating, funding, marketing and strategic alliance strategies for nonprofit and small businesses. He also designs and executes programs and facilitates strategic fundraising with an emphasis on promoting the growth of nonprofit and small business clients.

A member of the District of Columbia and the Commonwealth of Pennsylvania bars, Ron won awards for outstanding performance during his tenure with the U.S. Department of Justice. In addition, he received numerous awards for community service, including the Most Valuable Player Award from the Congressional Black Caucus Foundation and the President's Award for Service from the National Bar Association.

Ron received a Bachelor of Arts degree in English literature and secondary education from the Boston College Lynch School of Education and a Doctor of Jurisprudence degree from Boston College Law School.

A Jersey City, New Jersey, native, Ron is the proud father of five sons, Ron, Justin, Aaron, Brian and Christopher.

Ronald A. LeGrand, Esq.

President & Chief Executive Officer
LeGrand & Associates

Donnell Long is executive chef and owner of Olde Towne Inn in Upper Marlboro, Maryland.

After graduating at the top of his class from the Washington School of Culinary Arts, where he specialized in French cuisine, Long worked as an apprentice to Chef Andre, the head instructor of the Baltimore Culinary Institute and owner of Le Marmiton. To define his unique cooking style, he also studied under Chef Nacho Perez in London, England. Of the cooking styles at which Long excels, he most enjoys creating delectable seafood dishes.

A product of the foster care system, Long continuously contributes to those less fortunate than he. He hosts an annual Thanksgiving dinner for children in the foster care system, where he serves a full meal and distributes gifts, blankets and non-perishable food items. His successes motivate and inspire the children. Long no longer lowers his head when reminded of his humble beginnings. He is proud of his many attainments and he serves as a wonderful example for youth.

Donnell Long

Executive Chef & Owner
Olde Towne Inn

Quinta Ann Martin

Co-Founder, Board
Chair & President
Institute for Progressive
Leadership

Quinta Martin is co-founder, board chair and president of the Institute for Progressive Leadership, an international training organization that builds the capacity of state and national leaders who have an active role in national and international public policy development.

Previously serving as senior director of Leadership Development Programs, Conferences & Special Events for the Center for Policy Alternatives, Quinta was responsible for all training, including the renowned Flemming Leadership Institute and Summit on the States. She has served as an association executive and consultant through Quinta Martin Consulting Services to several national professional, civic, social and military organizations.

Quinta received a Bachelor of Science degree from The University of Tennessee – Knoxville and pursued a master's degree in nonprofit organization management at Case Western Reserve University. She is a Harvard University John F. Kennedy School of Government certified master trainer and recognized as an association executive by the American Society of Association Executives.

A native of Nashville, Tennessee, Quinta is a member of Alpha Kappa Alpha Sorority, Inc. She is the proud mother of William Martin Pickrum and favored daughter of Ida Kathryn Martin.

Risikat "Kat" Okedeyi

Founder
Lil Soso Productions

Risikat "Kat" Okedeyi is founder of Lil Soso Productions, a College Park, Maryland, artists and event management company. Lil Soso Productions embodies Kat's international flair and is a throwback to her Nigerian-American roots.

Kat has created a series of signature events, including When Harlem Came to Paris, an artistic exploration of Harlem's most prolific artists in 1930s Paris; Soul Overdose, an interactive concert featuring independent and emerging artists; and In the Artist's Studio, a candid discussion and performance event with industry tastemakers, including artists and producers.

Kat recently launched the Be You campaign, which will expand Soul Overdose and In the Artist's Studio into a monthly series at featured venues throughout Washington, D.C.

Bernadine Okoro, a first-generation Nigerian American, is an actress, engineer, educator and author.

A fifth-year educator, Bernadine teaches chemistry at Woodrow Wilson Senior High School, the largest public high school in Washington, D.C. She currently participates with the Center for Inspired Teaching, a yearlong professional development program for teachers that conducts research on the process of teacher growth. Bernadine is also a recipient of the National Endowment for the Humanities grant, where she will be studying the Maritime America in the Age of Winslow Homer (Summer Institute for Teachers at the University of Massachusetts Dartmouth) in Boston, Massachusetts.

Bernadine received a Bachelor of Science degree in chemical engineering from Drexel University. She also holds two master's degrees in producing film and video, and teaching from American University.

Her debut novel, *Peculiar Treasures*, an urban inspirational, spins a dramatic tale about female relationships set in Washington, D.C.

A native Washingtonian, Bernadine acts, sings and directs stage plays.

Bernadine Okoro

President & Chief Executive Officer
Zoe Edutainment Enterprises

A certified life management coach, Victori I. Paige is founder and chief executive officer of the Journey of Life Foundation (JOLF). JOLF is a 21st century answer to engaging, empowering and developing youth executive leaders and entrepreneurs in communications. Her venture exposes youth not only to the myriad of careers in the industry, but also marketing and media tactics that shape the thinking of consumers, communities and the world at large.

Paige has more than 20 years of entrepreneurial and nonprofit experience in life skills training and career development. She studied business administration at Ball State University and served as a U.S. House of Representatives staff assistant to the late Congresswoman Julia Carson. Additionally, she co-hosted a cable television show and radio talk show.

Paige believes in capturing the essence of life in all that she does. Some activities that keep her moving to the beat of her own drum are traveling, reading, journaling and the dramatic arts. Paige knows no limit to life, and encourages everyone, most importantly the youth, to live healthy, abundantly wealthy and amazingly happy.

Victori Isis Paige

Founder & Chief Executive Officer
Journey of Life Foundation

Kimatni D. Rawlins

President & Publisher
Automotive Rhythms
Communications, LLC

Kimatni D. Rawlins is founder of Automotive Rhythms Communications, LLC, a lifestyle automotive media and marketing portal consisting of Internet, network television, online video, print, radio and event properties. He established the company to serve as the communications liaison between automotive companies and the urban car-buying market. Previously, Kimatni served with On Wheels, Inc. and Jaguar Cars of North America, Inc. Within the video production world, he is the host and executive producer of Automotive Rhythms TV.

Kimatni is a recipient of the 40 Under Forty Achievement Award, and held urban spokesperson positions for Shell Oil in 2006 and 2007. He is a board member and president emeritus of the Washington Automotive Press Association. Kimatni has been interviewed and featured on The Discovery Channel, BET, XM, EURweb and Comcast. Additionally, he has been in *Ebony*, *The Washington Post*, *Smooth Magazine*, the *Michigan Chronicle*, *The Detroit News*, *The New York Times*, *The Los Angeles Times* and *The Florida Times-Union*.

Kimatni received a bachelor's degree in business, and minored in marketing and economics at the Georgia Institute of Technology, where he lettered in football.

Keith A. Ridley IV

President
Ridley Funeral Establishment, Inc.

Keith A. Ridley IV serves as president of the Ridley Funeral Establishment, Inc. A sixth-generation mortician, his ancestral lineage of service extends back to 1874. Under his leadership, the funeral establishment has been continually recognized for its distinctive reputation as boutique funeral directors.

Keith has been identified by the *Washington Business Journal*, *Regardie's Magazine*, *Ebony*, *Jet* and *The Afro American Newspaper* as a community leader of statesmanship and a humanitarian within the metro Washington, D.C., region.

He is a member of Alpha Phi Alpha Fraternity, Inc., the Washington, D.C. Council on Foreign Relations, the Federal City Mortician's Association, the NAACP (life member), Thebans, Inc. of Richmond, Virginia, and the United Nations Association of America.

A native of Petersburg, Virginia, Keith received a diploma of funeral service directing from the Pittsburgh Institute of Mortuary Science and an Associate of Applied Science degree in mortuary science from the University of the District of Columbia.

Amber Robles-Gordon is an artist and exhibit coordinator. In February of 2009, she was elected vice president of Black Artists of DC (BADC), where she curates art exhibits and publicizes BADC members, mission and events.

A mixed media collage artist, Amber has been influenced by the work of Alma Thomas, Romare Bearden, Diego Rivera and George Seurat. She focuses on topics such as womanhood, nature and her life experiences. She has exhibited in California, Maryland, New York, Iowa, Virginia and Washington, D.C.

In May of 2005, Amber completed a bachelor's degree in business administration from Trinity College. After completion of her undergraduate program, she has been dedicated to pursuing her art career and master's degree at Howard University. In December of 2009, she will receive a Master in Fine Arts degree.

Born in Puerto Rico, Amber was raised in Arlington, Virginia, and currently resides in Washington, D.C. She has an 11-year-old, deaf son and is fluent in American Sign Language. In addition, Amber teaches yoga and Pilates.

Amber Robles-Gordon

Artist & Vice President
Black Artists of DC

Lita T. Rosario is president and chief executive officer of WYZ Girl Entertainment Consulting, LLC, an Internet, intellectual property, entertainment law and consulting firm. After leaving the Wall Street law firm of Shearman & Stearling LLP, Rosario got her start in entertainment as co-owner of University Music Group. She has negotiated entertainment agreements with Warner Music Group, Sony/RCA, Universal Music Group, EMI/Capitol Records, Disney, UPN, BET, Viacom/MTV and Universal Pictures.

Rosario's client roster includes Missy Elliott, Tank, Sisqo, Dru Hill, Peaches & Herb, Crystal Waters, Afrika Bambaataa, Soul Sonic Force, BXC, Marky Def, Grind Mode, Chucky Thompson and Charlotte Burley. Her Internet clients include Haven Media Group, LLC (funded by Syndicated Communications, Inc.) and the Black Leadership Forum, Inc., an umbrella organization for black civil rights associations.

Rosario is barred in the District of Columbia, New York and Massachusetts, and in the federal courts of New York and the District of Columbia. She attended Howard University School of Law in Washington, D.C., where she was in the top 6 percent of her class.

Lita T. Rosario, Esq.

Founder & Chief Executive Officer
WYZ Girl
Entertainment Consulting, LLC

Cheeky "Chee Chee" Sasso

Event Producer & Managing Partner
Cheeky Sasso Entertainment &
Marketing Group

Cheeky "Chee Chee" Sasso is the event producer and managing partner of Cheeky Sasso Entertainment & Marketing Group, and marketing/advertising director for the District of Columbia region for *UPTOWN Magazine* in New York, New York. In these positions, he produces, arranges, manages and executes corporate, congressional, political and modern luxury events while marketing and advertising companies in *UPTOWN Magazine*.

Cheeky produced the Congressional Black Caucus Foundation, Inc.'s Sistahood Reception, the Seersucker and Sundress Rooftop Fashion Show, the Save the Last Dance Gala featuring Clinton Portis and Jason Taylor, the 2008 Crown Royal campaign events, The Chestnut Law Firm, LLC inauguration reception, and the HBO: Obama that One inauguration event.

Tuskegee University awarded Cheeky Bachelor of Science and master's degrees. He earned dual certifications in advance study of counseling psychology from the University of Virginia and Harvard University. A native of Vidalia, Louisiana, Cheeky is the proud son of former legendary basketball coach Shirley A. Walker.

Duane L. Smith

Co-Owner
Instructions Apparel

Duane Smith is an associate in the Contracts and Compliance Group with KGS, Inc. Additionally, he is co-owner of Instructions Apparel. After graduating from the University of Michigan with a political science degree, he received a juris doctorate degree from the Howard University School of Law. During law school, he interned for U.S. Senator Debbie Stabenow, was a member of the Huver I. Brown Trial Advocacy Moot Court Team and participated in a monthly Feed the Homeless program with a local Washington, D.C., shelter.

Founded by Duane and two college friends, Instructions Apparel was established as a solution to the personal style challenges experienced within the corporate world. The three men saved and planned to present Instructions Apparel, a shirt and tie clothier.

Duane is aware that he has been afforded many privileges and truly considers it a disservice for one not to reach for the stars. When not working, he enjoys a good book, traveling, and is an avid supporter of both the Detroit Pistons and his beloved alma mater's Michigan Wolverines football team.

Jackie and Derrick Thompson, native Washingtonians, started their entrepreneurial endeavors as private dealers, where they were actively involved in supporting and promoting those artists whose work they believe in. To their credit and to the artist, these works have steadily appreciated in value. After surveying the gallery scene for African-American art in the Washington, D.C., metropolitan area, they opened Overdue Recognition Art Gallery as a venue for artists to showcase their work.

Since its opening in 2004, more than 75 African-American artists have shown their work at Overdue Recognition Art Gallery, including notable artists Anthony Armstrong, John Holyfield, George Hunt, James Denmark and Calvin Coleman.

The gallery specializes in originals, serigraphs, giclees, and limited and open edition lithographs. Jackie and Derrick fulfill their educational goals through lectures, workshops, intimate gallery talks and exhibitions with the artist in attendance. They are committed to art as an essential part of life, and therefore exhibit, collect, preserve and encourage art.

Jackie and Derrick take the responsibility of providing private and corporate collectors with art that is high in aesthetic quality and strong in investment potential.

Jackie & Derrick Thompson

Owners
Overdue Recognition Art Gallery

President and chief executive officer Tanya Walker laid the groundwork for what would later become TW & Company, Inc. (TW) during her tenure at the University of Maryland, College Park, where she worked with several contractors and learned about doing business with the federal government.

Guided by her vision and leadership, TW & Company, Inc. has grown substantially from a small security company to one of the most respected security and facilities management services contractors in the industry since its inception in 1998. TW's reputation enabled it to obtain prestigious contracts, and recently assisted TW in being nominated Prime Contractor of the Year by the U.S. Small Business Administration.

TW has received the Minority Business Award and the U.S. Small Business Administration's Administrator's Award for Excellence. Additionally, TW was nominated by the General Services Administration White House Service Center as the Region III Small Business Prime Contractor of the Year.

TW & Company, Inc. is licensed nationally, and operates in 50 states and all U.S. territories. The company has won major military and government contracts under multiple states and jurisdictions.

Tanya Walker

President & Chief Executive Officer
TW & Company, Inc.

Neville R. Waters III

Founder & President
The Waters Group

Neville Waters III has extensive experience in marketing, communications, entertainment, production and management. He has utilized his multifaceted skills in various business spheres, including professional sports, radio and television production, event and facilities management, and partnership development. His background includes the management of various creative artists, a long-term assignment with the United Way managing their NFL partnership, stints with the WNBA and the NBA Development League, Marriott Hotels and the DC Sports & Entertainment Commission. In addition, he has produced a radio magazine show, a local Washington, D.C., community affairs television program and an online newsletter entitled The Point.

A sixth generation Washingtonian, Waters graduated, magna cum laude, from Springfield College and received a master's degree from there two years later. Additionally, he earned an MBA degree from Georgetown University.

Waters received the NBC Fellowship Award, the National Black MBA Scholarship, the Walter Kaitz Foundation Award, the Achievement in Radio Award and an Addy Award. He also received an Effie Award, the Adrian Award from the Hospitality Sales and Marketing Association and Jack the Rapper's Radio Program Director of the Year.

W. Eric Whitehead

Chief Executive Officer
KrisKera, Inc.

W. Eric Whitehead is chief executive officer of KrisKera, Inc., and general manager and owner of JazzNSoul Café. As an entrepreneur dedicated to social and business enterprises that embrace values of community, quality service, professionalism and opportunity, Eric endeavors to provide unique, upscale entertainment to the residents of the District of Columbia and its vicinity.

In addition to owning a 5LINX telecommunications company, Eric is also a U.S. Army veteran and former counselor for the District of Columbia Department of Corrections. His memberships in various social organizations, such as the River East Emerging Leaders (R.E.E.L.) and Brothers and Sisters of Jazz, communicate his appreciation of leadership, legacy and music.

Eric has 20 years of experience in the entertainment and music business. With KrisKera Inc. and JazzNSoul Café, he continues to pursue conscientious approaches that contribute to economic and community development in Washington, D.C., and positions himself as a viable business leader in the mid-Atlantic region.

A native of Virginia and member of Pilgrim Baptist Church, Eric is the proud and devoted father of Eric K. and Chakera.

Named one of the most recognizable conservative voices in America by *The Washington Post*, Armstrong Williams is founder and chief executive officer of The Graham Williams Group, an international public relations firm and The RightSide Production, Inc., which produces the nationally syndicated television show *The RightSide with Armstrong Williams*.

In addition to appearances on the *Today* show, *Good Morning America*, *Charlie Rose*, CNN and MSNBC, Williams is also a commentator on NPR and *The Russ Parr Morning Show*. He is a syndicated columnist for *The Washington Times*, where his column appears weekly and his blogs appear daily for *The Hill*. *The Armstrong Williams Show* broadcasts daily on WGCV 620 AM.

Williams served on the President's Commission on White House Fellowships and is a member of several boards, including the Carson Scholarship Foundation and the Independence Federal Savings and Loan Bank board.

A native of Marion, South Carolina, Williams received a bachelor's degree from South Carolina State University and is a lifetime member of the Phi Beta Sigma Fraternity, Inc.

Armstrong Williams

Founder & Chief Executive Officer
The Graham Williams Group

Natalie Williams began her career as a television editor in 1989. She successfully combined her knowledge of mass media and public relations to become chief executive officer and president of her own company, BlitzAssociates, LLC, a full-service public relations firm. Her company focuses on the areas of media representation, internal and external communications, integrated marketing communications, event management, and image development. Past and present clients include First Lady Michelle Obama, the Congressional Black Caucus Foundation, Inc., the National Black Caucus of State Legislators and former District of Columbia Mayor Marion Barry.

Additionally, Williams is president of the Miss Black America organization, America's first pageant system for African-American women. During her career as a journalist, she has covered many unforgettable news stories and received numerous awards, including three Emmys and one Associated Press Award.

Williams holds a bachelor's degree in English with a concentration in journalism. She is a member of Delta Sigma Theta Sorority, Inc., the National Association of Black Journalists and the Public Relations Society of America. Williams calls her rise to the top a constant work in progress.

Natalie C. Williams

President & Chief Executive Officer
BlitzAssociates, LLC

George Worrell

Fashion Designer
GMW Enterprises, LLC

George M. Worrell of GMW Enterprises LLC "has been putting his stylish imprint on DC for the past 15 years" wrote *DC Modern Luxury* in their latest "People You Should Know" issue.

GMW Enterprises has collaborated on Mid-Atlantic promotional events with the Coca-Cola Company and The Ronald H. Brown Foundation, which featured former President William Clinton. Worrell and GMW Enterprises have been a major part of some of the most historic events to happen in DC's recent history including planning the groundbreaking ceremony for the Washington National's Ballpark with more than 1,500 VIP guests in attendance, as well as coordinating the inaugural events for Washington, D.C.'s Mayor Adrian Fenty, which included the Inaugural Ball with 20,000 guests in attendance, the prayer breakfast and swearing-in ceremony.

Additionally, Worrell has produced shows for some of the most sought-after designers, including the b.michael trunk show for Saks Jandel. Bringing the fashions of a growing list of Manhattan designers like Tracy Reese, Rachel Roy and Carolina Herrera to "the highest stratosphere of local government," Worrell has become a true style icon.

Taz Wube

Owner & Marketing Director
Suite 202

Taz Wube arrived in Washington, D.C. looking for something fresh. He teamed up with none other than mogul business proprietor Marc Barnes to present some of the grandest events in the city. They formed their following from Republic Gardens and transcended into Dream, which later became known as Love Night Club. The duo has held outlandish events at Super Bowl and all-star cities, as well as the Essence Festival Weekend, traditionally held in New Orleans.

Taz has since launched his own premier entertainment marketing company, Suite 202, which presents Taz Events. As marketing director, he extends his touch beyond the borders of the United States by hosting and planning international celebrity events and concerts in Ethiopia, Nigeria, Dubai and Kenya.

Continuing to command the nightclub circuit, Taz is never far from the action around the country. Adding the Midas touch to his events each week, no expense is ever spared and no corners are ever cut to bring patrons the finest entertainment experience.

With more than 35 years of health care management experience, F. Robert Yates is founder and chief executive officer of Children's Pediatricians & Associates, a subsidiary of Children's National Medical Center, which has more than 45 providers in 11 sites. He served as a senior executive at several other reputable health care organizations and is a management and acquisition/merger expert.

Yates holds a bachelor's degree in biology and chemistry, and a master's degree in health care management from Howard University. He is a fellow and board-certified by the American College of Healthcare Executives (ACHE) and the American College of Medical Practice Executives. Yates is a member of the National Association of Health Services Executives and served as the ACHE regent for the District of Columbia from 2006 to 2010, and on the ACHE Council of Regents. In addition, he also serves on the board of National Capital Healthcare Executives and presents on several important health care industry topics.

A native of Washington, D.C., Yates is married to Agnes Alexander Yates, Esq. They have three children, Francis III, Jason, and Kara, and eight grandchildren.

F. Robert Yates Jr.

Vice President
Children's National Medical Center

Collaborate

Align

Perform

It takes a leader to know how to align business objectives and resources. Working together, we have created an inclusive culture that benefits our entire firm community.

Diversity and inclusion are core values at Andrews Kurth. We maximize the effectiveness of diverse, high-performance teams, which results in a professional and energetic environment. Andrews Kurth congratulates all *Who's Who in Black Washington, D.C.* honorees. For straight talk about diversity and inclusion, visit **andrewskurth.com.**

ANDREWS
ATTORNEYS **KURTH** LLP

STRAIGHT TALK IS GOOD BUSINESS.®

Andrews Kurth LLP • 1350 I Street, NW • Suite 1100 • Washington, DC 20005 • 202.662.2700

Andrews Kurth LLP • 600 Travis • Suite 4200 • Houston, TX 77002 • 713.220.4200

Austin   Beijing   Dallas   Houston   London   New York   The Woodlands   Washington, DC

Washington, D.C.

COUNSELORS AT LAW

BENEVOLENT

PRINCIPLED

VESTED

DEMOCRATIC

ACCOMPLISHED

MEDIATOR

ADVOCATE

LITIGATOR

ARBITER

Lewis I. Askew Jr.

Partner, Attorney at Law
Watt, Tieder, Hoffar &
Fitzgerald, L.L.P.

Marilyn D. Barker

Counsel, Attorney at Law
Bryan Cave LLP

Lewis Askew Jr. is a partner with Watt, Tieder, Hoffar & Fitzgerald, L.L.P. His practice is primarily focused upon matters involving complex public and private construction and government contracts. He provides a full range of counseling and services related to contract drafting and negotiation, dispute resolution and complex litigation.

His client base includes sureties, owners, architects, engineers, general contractors and subcontractors. In many instances, the matters have involved multimillion-dollar claims, and have related to complex structures such as processing facilities, professional and collegiate sports stadiums, major highways, hotels, commuter rail systems, schools and tunnels. Lewis also speaks and writes regularly as a subject matter expert.

A graduate of the University of Maryland Clark School of Engineering with a bachelor's degree in mechanical engineering, Lewis was a member of the football team and named AV Williams Scholar Athlete of the Year. He earned a juris doctorate degree, cum laude, from Howard University School of Law.

An active member of Leadership Greater Washington, Lewis presently sits on boards for The National Center for Children and Families, and the Cinderella Foundation.

As an attorney at Bryan Cave LLP, Marilyn Barker focuses her practice on counseling financial services institutions on Bank Secrecy Act regulatory and compliance matters, including those involving anti-money laundering compliance, as well as on stored value and other electronic payment issues. She is admitted to the bars of both the District of Columbia and California, and is also a certified anti-money laundering specialist.

Marilyn received a bachelor's degree, cum laude, in Latin American studies from Yale University in 1983, a juris doctorate degree from Columbia University in 1987 and a Master of Laws degree in international private law from Stockholm University in 1992.

She previously worked at the U.S. Department of the Treasury's Financial Crimes Enforcement Network, where she provided advice and guidance, and developed policy for the administration of the Bank Secrecy Act regulations for financial institutions. During her tenure, Marilyn frequently lectured to foreign delegations from Europe, Asia, Africa and Latin America on the United States' regulation of money services businesses. Additionally, she worked at the Securities Exchange Commission and the Federal Reserve.

Clifford E. Barnes

Partner, Attorney at Law
Epstein, Becker & Green, P.C.

Johnine P. Barnes

Partner, Attorney at Law
Baker & Hostetler LLP

Clifford E. Barnes is a member of Epstein, Becker & Green, P.C., practicing in the area of health care law, representing clients in mergers, acquisitions and other affiliation transactions. He has the distinction of being one of the longest-employed minority partners in a major law firm, having been employed for more than 27 years and a partner for more than 19 years.

Barnes serves as faculty at the Saint Louis University School of Law Health Law Program and as a seminar presenter for Blue Cross Blue Shield, the National Association of Health Services Executives and the National Congress on the Un and Underinsured. He is a frequent publisher of professional and inspirational articles and books, including *What Am I Here To Do.*

Prior to law school, Barnes worked with the New York City Health Department and the Health Systems Agency of New York City. He received a Bachelor of Business Administration degree from Pace College, an MBA from Cornell University and a juris doctorate degree from the University of Virginia, where he served on the editorial board of the *Journal of National Resources Law.*

Johnine P. Barnes is a partner in the Washington, D.C. office of Baker & Hostetler LLP, where her practice areas involve employment and labor law and business litigation, including non-compete agreements, contract disputes, trade secrets, international disputes, white collar crimes, and property interest disputes and legislative matters.

Named by *Washingtonian* magazine as one of Washington, D.C.'s 40 Lawyers Under 40 in 2006, Barnes is a member of the District of Columbia Bar board of governors, a fellow of the American Bar Foundation and various bar associations, including the National Bar Association, where she was former deputy general counsel and special counsel to the president.

Barnes is an instructor of the court practice component of the mandatory District of Columbia Bar course and has been a speaker on employment law issues before the District of Columbia Bar. In addition, she is the author of *Lawyers, Managers and Agents: An Overview of Their Role* and *Inside the Minds: Entertainment and Media Law Client Strategies.*

Barnes received both bachelor's and juris doctorate degrees from Case Western Reserve University. Additionally, she is the mother of one son.

Sherri N. Blount

Partner, Attorney at Law
Fitch, Even, Tabin, & Flannery

Kevin P. Chavous

Partner & Attorney at Law
Sonnenschein Nath & Rosenthal

Sherri N. Blount is a partner in Fitch, Even, Tabin, & Flannery's Washington, D.C. office. Her practice focuses on intellectual property, entertainment and media issues in the manufacturing, industrial and retail industries. She represents Fortune 100 companies and nonprofit entities, with clients including media companies; national cable, television and radio networks; television and video producers; Web site operators; and wireless telephone companies, to name a few.

Previously, Blount was a partner with Morrison & Foerster, LLP. She served in various positions with the Public Broadcasting Service (PBS) and as an attorney advisor to a Federal Trade commissioner. Blount is a frequent speaker on entertainment, intellectual property law and other legal issues before the American Intellectual Property Law Association, the National Inventors Hall of Fame, the National Association of Black Owned Broadcasters, the American Bar Association and the National Bar Association.

The *Washington Business Journal* recognized Blount's professional achievements in 2007, when she was named the Top Intellectual Property Lawyer in Washington, D.C. Additionally she was named one of Washington's top intellectual property lawyers in 2006 and 2008 by the *Washingtonian*.

Kevin P. Chavous is a noted attorney, author and national school reform leader. He served on the Council of the District of Columbia from 1993 to 2005, and as chair of the Education Committee, he helped to usher charter schools and parental choice into the District of Columbia.

Chavous is a co-founder and board chair of Democrats for Education Reform, and an accomplished author, having published *Serving Our Children: Charter Schools and the Reform of American Public Education.*

Born and raised in Indianapolis, Indiana, Chavous graduated from Wabash College, where he was an All-American in basketball. He also graduated from the Howard University School of Law, where he was president of his graduating class.

Chavous lives in Washington, D.C., and enjoys spending time with his two sons, Kevin and Eric.

Joseph W. Clark

Partner, Attorney at Law
Jones Day

Karen E. Evans

Attorney at Law
Jack H. Olender & Associates, P.C.

Joe Clark is a partner at Jones Day with broad experience in white collar criminal matters, complex business litigations, and regulatory and enforcement proceedings. Joe is a former federal prosecutor in the District of Columbia and an accomplished trial attorney. He advises public, private and nonprofit entities on a broad range of legal and regulatory issues.

Joe handles substantial litigation matters involving securities and health care fraud, antitrust, contract disputes, construction litigation and consumer credit. His white collar defense practice includes significant experience in alleged violations of international trafficking in arms regulations, the Arms Export Control Act, export administration regulations and transportation security regulations. Joe has defended clients against allegations of bribery, providing an illegal gratuity, insider trading and kickbacks. Furthermore, he advises clients on issues of corporate compliance and governance.

He serves as a trustee on the District of Columbia Retirement Board, which invests, controls and manages the assets of District of Columbia teachers, police officers and fire fighters' retirement systems.

Joe earned a Bachelor of Arts degree from Morehouse College and a Doctor of Jurisprudence degree from Harvard Law School.

Karen E. Evans is an attorney at the malpractice law firm Jack H. Olender & Associates, P.C., where she handles catastrophic medical malpractice and personal injury cases. A registered nurse, she is a member of The American Association of Nurse Attorneys.

Evans is secretary of the Trial Lawyers Association of Metropolitan Washington, D.C. and is a member of their Executive Committee. She serves as the advisory director of the Virginia Commission on Women and Minorities in the Legal System, and is an adjunct professor at the University of the District of Columbia David A. Clarke School of Law.

Additionally, Evans is a volunteer mediator with the alternative dispute resolution programs of the Washington, D.C. Superior Court and the U.S. District Court for the District of Columbia. In 2007 Evans was named a Super Lawyer by *Washington, D.C. Super Lawyers* and is listed in *The Best Lawyers in America 2009*.

Anthony Graham Sr.

Founding Partner
Smith Graham & Crump, LLC

Edward W. Gray Jr.

Partner, Attorney at Law
Fitch, Even, Tabin, & Flannery

Anthony Graham Sr. is an experienced attorney who is qualified as a skilled advocate by the sheer number of successful trials under his belt. He practices primarily in the areas of personal injury and medical malpractice. As a veteran trial attorney, this past founder of The Capitol Legal Group has represented many personal injury clients to the benefit of large awards. His dedication, tenacity and passion for representing the common citizen and to protect their constitutional rights have proven him to be a true advocate for the people. He is a founding partner of Smith Graham & Crump, LLC.

Graham has a juris doctorate degree from The Catholic University of America Columbus School of Law, and is licensed to practice law in Washington, D.C., and Maryland. He also practices in the following federal courts: the U.S. District Court for the District of Columbia, the U.S. District Court for the District of Maryland, the U.S. Court of Appeals for the Fourth Circuit, and the U.S. Court of Appeals for the District of Columbia.

Edward W. Gray Jr. is a partner in Fitch, Even, Tabin, & Flannery's Washington, D.C., office. His practice focuses on intellectual property evaluation and strategy, trade secret programs, corporate technology management, licensing, patent strategy, trademark prosecution, and IP litigation.

Gray is extremely knowledgeable about business transactions, sales, manufacturing and government contract matters. His extensive experience includes practice in the private sector, various in-house positions and government service. He served in vice presidential roles at R.R. Donnelley & Sons Company and the Federal-Mogul Corporation, and in the senior executive service at the U.S. General Accounting Office for the president's Commission on Executive Exchange.

Active in the legal community, Gray currently serves as president-elect of the National Inventors Hall of Fame, and counsel to the National Knowledge and Intellectual Property Management Taskforce, a division of the Center for Advanced Technology in Austin, Texas. The *Washingtonian* recognized his longstanding record of professional excellence and client-oriented services when he was named one of Washington, D.C.,'s top intellectual property lawyers. Additionally, Gray is an AV peer reviewed-rated attorney by Martindale-Hubbell.

Roscoe Howard

Partner, Attorney at Law
Troutman Sanders LLP

Derrick A. Humphries

Partner, Attorney at Law
Humphries & Partners, PLLC

Roscoe Howard is a partner in the Washington, D.C., office of Troutman Sanders LLP. He brings extensive litigation and special investigation experience to the firm. His practice focuses on corporate compliance and ethics issues, white-collar criminal matters and complex litigation.

Howard served as U.S. attorney for the District of Columbia from 2001 to 2004. He previously served as a tenured, full professor at The University of Kansas School of Law, where he taught from 1994 to 2001. Howard has taken numerous cases to trial relating to various criminal violations, handled grand jury investigations and argued before the District of Columbia Court of Appeals and the U.S. Court of Appeals for the Fourth Circuit.

He received a Bachelor of Arts degree from Brown University in 1974 and a Doctor of Jurisprudence degree from the University of Virginia School of Law in 1977. Howard is currently on the boards of directors of the Canada-U.S. Fulbright Program and the Roger Williams University School of Law.

Derrick A. Humphries is a founding partner of the law office of Humphries & Partners, PLLC, based in Washington, D.C. He is legal counsel for several global professional associations, including the National Dental Association, the National Black Nurses Association, the National Alliance of Black School Educators, the Association of Black Psychologists, and the National Black Caucus of State Legislators Labor Roundtable.

Honored with many awards and recognition of his successes, Derrick has initiated a series of critical thinking conferences involving students and parents at the University of Michigan, the University of Virginia and other think-tank environments.

A graduate of the University of Michigan and the Wayne State University Law School, Derrick is a member of The District of Columbia and Michigan bar associations. He has served as an adjunct professor of law at Howard University School of Law and as legal counsel for the Congressional Black Caucus Foundation, Inc. A native of Detroit, Michigan, Derrick is the husband of Jonca Bull and the proud father of three sons, Taylor, Alexander and Auguste, and one daughter, Jonna.

Amos Jones

Attorney at Law
Bryan Cave LLP

Jerry L. Malone

Of Counsel
Lewis & Munday, P.C.

As an associate in Bryan Cave LLP's International Trade Group, Amos Jones counsels clients on matters involving export-control regulations, the Foreign Corrupt Practices Act and the Foreign Agents Registration Act. He advised legal practitioner-scholars in the Republic of Georgia on the liberty provisions of that country's constitution drafted after the Rose Revolution of 2003.

Prior to joining Bryan Cave in 2007, Amos was a Fulbright scholar and visitor to the Faculty of Law at the University of Melbourne in Australia. While a news copy editor for *The Charlotte Observer* in 2000-2001, he performed professionally in the Charlotte Philharmonic Orchestra on viola.

A 1999 Harry S. Truman scholar and member of *USA Today*'s 2000 All-USA College Academic First Team, Amos was an American delegate to the Academy of Achievement's 2000 summit in London, England. He currently serves on the national board of advisors of the Academy of Preachers.

A native of Lexington, Kentucky, Amos earned a juris doctorate degree from Harvard University, a master's degree in journalism from Columbia University and a bachelor's degree, cum laude, in political science from Emory University.

Jerry L. Malone, of counsel, has been a licensed attorney for more than 22 years. He served as a commercial litigator representing banks, railroads, school districts, insurance companies, publicly traded corporations, privately held corporations, government agencies and other entities. Additionally, he served as chief counsel of the Federal Highway Administration and chief of staff of the U.S. Department of Transportation.

Malone served five years as general counsel to the chief financial officer for the government of the District of Columbia, where he managed, directed and supervised all legal operations of the Office of the Chief Financial Officer. This included tax and revenue, budget formulation and execution, revenue estimation and fiscal impact, congressional appropriations, public finance transactions, contracts and procurement, human resources and labor relations, accounting, and internal audits.

With a bachelor's degree in public administration and a juris doctorate degree, Malone is licensed to practice in Arkansas and the District of Columbia. He is admitted before the U.S. District Courts for the Eastern and Western districts of Arkansas, the Eighth Court of Appeals, and the U.S. Supreme Court.

Darrell Gilbert Mottley

Principal Shareholder
Banner & Witcoff, LTD

Anthony T. Pierce

Partner In Charge
Akin Gump Strauss Hauer & Feld

Darrell G. Mottley is a principal shareholder of Banner & Witcoff, LTD in Washington, D.C. He advises clients on strategic intellectual property law protection, focusing on patent and trademark cases, including opinions, licensing and litigation. Prior to joining Banner & Witcoff, he was an engineer in private practice and in the federal government, where he earned a Silver Medal. He also served as a commissioned officer in the U.S. Air Force, where he earned a medal for meritorious service.

Mottley is a contributing author of the *Annual Review of Intellectual Property Law Developments: 2006-2008* and the *Public Contract Law Journal*, both publications of the American Bar Association. Additionally, he is a fellow of the American Bar Foundation.

The George Washington University awarded Mottley a law degree, with honors. He earned a Master of Business Administration degree and a bachelor's degree in engineering, both from Virginia Tech, where he was Phi Kappa Phi. He is admitted to practice before the U.S. Patent and Trademark Office and in the District of Columbia, Virginia, New Jersey and the Federal and Fourth Circuits.

Anthony T. Pierce is a litigator who has handled a variety of complex disputes in state and federal courts, including commercial litigation, trade secrets, trademark, copyright, counterfeiting and piracy, software licensing and employment matters. He is the partner in charge of Akin Gump Strauss Hauer & Feld's Washington, D.C. office.

The *Washington Business Journal* named Pierce as the 2008 winner of Top Washington Lawyers in the category of corporate litigation. He was selected from a pool of almost 500 nominations and was one of three finalists in the same category in 2007. He is routinely named by *Virginia Business* magazine to its list of Legal Elite in the area of civil litigation.

Pierce is a member of the board of directors of the Greater Washington Board of Trade and is past president of the Legal Aid Society of the District of Columbia. Additionally, he is a member of the Leadership Washington Class of 2002.

Carlean Ponder

Principal
The Ponder Law & Advocacy Group P.L.L.C.

Shemin Proctor

Managing Partner, Attorney at Law
Andrews Kurth LLP

Carlean Ponder founded The Ponder Law & Advocacy Group P.L.L.C., a civil rights firm, because she recognized a need for top-notch legal services at an affordable rate amongst working communities, a need largely unmet. The practice is unique in that it combines traditional legal skills with an understanding of community advocacy and an appreciation for how skilled use of the law can better affect people locally.

Ponder has years of civil rights experience working on behalf of people and organizations in Washington, D.C., and Illinois. Prior to attending law school and practicing law, she served as a community organizer for various organizations, including women's rights groups, anti-poverty groups and local politicians.

Her legal experience includes serving clients in matters such as family law, landlord tenant law, labor disputes, employee/employer severance agreements and small business contract negotiations. She has represented clients in both state and federal courts. Ponder received a bachelor's degree from the University of Michigan and a juris doctorate degree, cum laude, from the University of Illinois College of Law.

Shemin Proctor is managing partner of the Washington, D.C., office of Andrews Kurth LLP, an international law firm with more than 100 years representing a diversified client base and more than 400 attorneys in nine offices. She was elected to the firm's Policy and Executive committees, and divides her time between offices in Washington, D.C., and Houston.

Shemin represents major energy companies, including natural gas pipelines, energy marketing and trading companies, and midstream service providers, in proceedings before the Federal Energy Regulatory Commission and has represented natural gas pipelines before the federal courts. Representative matters include rate, tariff, certificate and complaint proceedings before the Federal Energy Regulatory Commission. She also works with clients seeking to develop natural gas storage and liquefied natural gas facilities.

She received a Bachelor of Arts degree from Harvard-Radcliffe College in 1987 and a Doctor of Jurisprudence degree from Harvard Law School in 1990. Shemin is a member of the American Association of Blacks in Energy, the American Bar Association, the Energy Bar Association, the National Bar Association and the Women's Council on Energy and the Environment.

Cynthia L. Quarterman

Partner, Attorney at Law
Steptoe & Johnson, LLP

Vanessa Scott

Associate, Attorney at Law
Sutherland Asbill & Brennan LLP

Cynthia Quarterman is a partner at Steptoe & Johnson, LLP in the Regulatory and Industry Affairs Department. Her practice focuses on litigation and administrative law in the energy, natural resources and transportation areas. The author of several publications, Quarterman has testified before Congress and speaks widely. She was a member of the Obama Transition Team at the Energy Department and was director of the Interior Department's Minerals Management Service. Previously, she served as an engineer with IBM.

Quarterman is the recipient of the Interior's Unit Award for Excellence and the Tahirih Justice Center Certificate of Appreciation. She is a member of *Natural Gas*' editorial advisory board and the Institute of Energy Law's Executive Committee. Additionally, she is past president of the Columbia Alumni Association of D.C.

Quarterman obtained a Doctor of Jurisprudence degree from Columbia University and a Bachelor of Science degree from Northwestern University. A native of Savannah, Georgia, she is the wife of Pantelis Michalopoulos and the proud mother of one daughter, Charis.

Vanessa Scott is a member of the Tax Group at Sutherland Asbill & Brennan LLP. She focuses her practice on tax compliance issues involving employee benefit plans, executive compensation arrangements, and domestic and international corporate transactions.

In 2003 Vanessa was tapped by Congressman Artur Davis to join his legislative team as counsel for tax and judiciary issues. Following her stint on Capitol Hill, she served as legislative counsel and corporate secretary for the ERISA Industry Committee.

Currently, Vanessa is chair of the National Bar Association's Tax Section and vice chair of the American Bar Association Section of Taxation's Diversity Committee. A former ambassador to the American Bar Association's Business Law Section, she is a former member of the Birmingham YWCA junior board of directors.

Vanessa holds a bachelor's degree from Duke University, a Doctor of Jurisprudence degree from the Vanderbilt University School of Law, and a Master of Laws degree in taxation from the Georgetown University Law Center.

A native of Brooklyn, New York, she is the wife of Dr. Quentin E. Scott and the mother of Quentin II and Taylor Scott.

Makan Shirafkan

Attorney at Law
Law Office of Shirafkan & Associates

Jennifer P. Streaks, Esq.

Attorney at Law

Makan Shirafkan is the founder and managing partner of the Law Office of Shirafkan & Associates. His practice includes personal injury, licensing and contracts; debt collection and settlements; insurance; and labor law disputes. Shirafkan also serves as general counsel for the DC Nightlife Association.

His experience of 12 years in D.C.'s entertainment industry has made him an expert in the field. He began as security in 1997. Shirafkan later acted as chief executive officer of Dream nightclub before he served as the chief adviser to entertainment mogul, Marc Barnes. During his tenure, he has produced hundreds of concerts and special events while managing more than $100 million and securing more than 5 million patron attendees.

Shirafkan holds a Bachelor of Science degree in business administration from James Madison University and a juris doctorate degree from the Howard University School of Law. He is a member of Phi Alpha Delta Law Fraternity, The International Honor Society Beta Gamma Sigma, the National Association of Criminal Defense Lawyers and the American Association for Justice. He also serves on the D.C. Police Foundation board of directors.

Jennifer P. Streaks is a financial services attorney who has continuously worked to develop programs that teach basic financial strategies to everyday people. Additionally, Streaks is finishing the last chapters of a consumer target book, "Digging Your Dreams Out of Debt."

A frequent guest on news talk shows, Streaks has hosted political news television show *News/ Counterpoint*, and served as a financial expert for *U.S. News & World Report*. She is also a financial contributor for *Mind Over Money*, a financial news program on WUSA-TV.

Streaks was appointed under the Bush Administration to the bi-partisan President's Commission on the U.S. Postal Service. In the community, she has raised numerous dollars, and is currently serving with The Washington Ballet Women's Committee, the Smithsonian Young Benefactors and the Trust for the National Mall. She also volunteers for the Washington Area Women's Foundation and the Washington Leadership Council.

Streaks received a bachelor's degree in political science from the College of Charleston, a juris doctorate degree from Howard University School of Law, and a Master of Business Administration degree from the Johns Hopkins University Carey Business School.

Ashley L. Taylor Jr.

Partner, Attorney at Law
Troutman Sanders LLP

Donald M. Temple

Principal, Attorney at Law
Donald M. Temple, P.C.

Ashley Taylor Jr. devotes his consumer law and complex litigation practice to defending companies in investigations initiated by state attorneys general, and representing companies in administrative law matters and business-related litigation.

In 2008 Ashley was recognized as one of the 50 Most Influential Minority Lawyers in America by *The National Law Journal.* He has been recognized as a Virginia Super Lawyer in Civil Litigation Defense, Business Litigation and Administrative Law by *Super Lawyers* magazine since 2006.

Ashley graduated from the Virginia Military Institute in 1990 with a Bachelor of Arts degree. He received a juris doctorate degree from Washington and Lee School of Law in 1993. Before joining Troutman Sanders LLP in 2001, he served as a law clerk for the U.S. District Court and as deputy Virginia attorney general. Ashley currently serves as a commissioner for the U.S. Commission on Civil Rights and as chair of the state attorneys general sub-committee for the American Bar Association.

Donald M. Temple, principal of Donald M. Temple P.C., practices civil and commercial litigation, with an emphasis on police misconduct and race discrimination.

Temple serves with the Congress Heights Community Development Corporation, Archbishop Carroll High School, the Columbia Heights Youth Center and the Kaiser Family Foundation's Barbara Jordan Health Policy Scholars Program. A member of the National Bar Association and Kappa Alpha Psi Fraternity, Inc., he is a graduate of Leadership Greater Washington. Additionally, he has appeared on numerous radio and television programs.

He received the Cora T. Walker and Gertrude E. Rush awards, the Howard University Community Service Award and the Ollie Mae Cooper Award. He was recently honored as one of Thurgood Marshall Center Trust Inc.'s Phenomenal Men 2009.

Temple received a master's degree from Georgetown University Law Center, a juris doctorate degree from Santa Clara University and a bachelor's degree from Howard University. He is admitted to practice in the District of Columbia and Pennsylvania, the U.S. District courts in Maryland and Michigan, the Third, Fourth and Federal circuit courts of appeal, and the U.S. Supreme Court.

Benjamin F. Wilson

Managing Principal, Attorney at Law
Beveridge & Diamond, P.C.

Benjamin F. Wilson is the managing principal of Beveridge & Diamond, P.C., the country's oldest and largest environmental, litigation and land use law firm. His environmental litigation practice encompasses a wide range of activities in both state and federal courts. He has been lead counsel in complex commercial and environmental litigation matters for major corporations, developers and a number of municipalities. Wilson has represented a number of cities and local government agencies on the enforcement of the Clean Water Act and wetlands development matters.

Wilson is an adjunct professor in environmental justice at the Howard University School of Law. From 1990 to 2004, he served as chairman of the District of Columbia Board of Elections and Ethics. Additionally, he served two terms as co-chairman of the Washington Lawyer's Committee for Civil Rights and Urban Affairs.

Wilson graduated, magna cum laude, from Dartmouth College, where he received a Bachelor of Arts degree in 1973 and was elected to Phi Beta Kappa. Additionally, he received a Doctor of Jurisprudence degree from Harvard Law School in 1976.

Washington, D.C.

COMMUNITY
LEADERS

NOBLE

CARING

SELF-SACRIFICING

GENEROUS

EMPOWERING

HEROIC

PHILANTHROPIC

HUMANITARIAN

ALTRUISTIC

Karen Y. Arrington

Founder & Chief Executive Officer
Miss Black U.S.A. Pageant, Inc.

A social activist, and an inspirational and motivational speaker, Karen Arrington has dedicated her life to the empowerment of young African-American women. She is founder and chief executive officer of the Miss Black U.S.A. Pageant and Scholarship Foundation, Inc. The nonprofit corporation is the premier pageant for women of color and has awarded more than $500,000 in scholarships to deserving young women.

A tireless humanitarian, Karen has taken the term "girl power" to new heights. She co-founded the first diabetes awareness campaign in The Gambia, where diabetes is the No. 1 disease affecting Gambian people. She is the creator of an online women's health resource dedicated to improving the quality of life of women in Prince George's County, Maryland. In addition, Karen developed a national partnership with the HeartTruth campaign to bring awareness of heart disease, the No. 1 killer of women and disproportionately affects women of color.

An expert on women's empowerment, Karen has received numerous honors and awards including a Lifetime Achievement Award from the family of Kunta Kinte (*Roots*). In 2007 she was appointed a Goodwill ambassador to The Gambia.

Edna Harvin Battle

President
Heritage Chapter
Blacks In Government

E dna Battle is president of a highly visible chapter of Blacks In Government, working for equity, excellence and opportunity for all Americans. She is also past national president of the Federally Employed Women Legal and Education Fund, Inc., a 501(c)(3) organization that defended human and civil rights through education and legal representation.

Edna is past national executive vice president of Federally Employed Women, a nonprofit organization working to eliminate sex discrimination and to the advance women in government. During this time, she managed the operations of a management association company and shared in the leadership of a diverse 3,800-plus international member organization made up of women in the federal, state and local governments, and private sector.

Retired from the federal government, Edna is an avid member of various organizations and leads a very active life in sharing her skills and services with the community. A native of Washington, D.C., she was educated in the public school system and continued her education in the telecommunications management field at Golden Gate University. Edna is the proud mother of three married children, Charles Jr., Brian and NyKisha.

V ercilla A. Brown is serving her first term as president of one of the most established and oldest chapters of Zeta Phi Beta Sorority, Inc., Beta Zeta Chapter in Washington, D.C., chartered February 20, 1925. An accomplished association executive, her career has traveled different avenues through Capitol Hill to include the House and Senate, corporate and nonprofit organizations, and included a five-year tenure as Zeta Phi Beta Sorority, Inc.'s sixth international executive director.

Beta Zeta Chapter is a powerful advocate for the community stakeholders' interest, and delivers programs and services from the empowerment of its community leaders, members, alliances and partners. Chapter initiatives focus in the areas of scholarship, health and economic services, youth and collegiate leadership development, community and social outreach and political advocacy.

In her leisure time, Brown possesses a true passion for movies (mainly independent films), and enjoys sports, good conversations, learning new things, traveling and community service. Married for 23 years to Rickey J. Brown, she attends Metropolitan Baptist Church. A dedicated community service advocate, she works tirelessly through her sorority ensuring continued deliverance in community-focused programs and services.

Vercilla A. Brown

President
Beta Zeta Chapter
Zeta Phi Beta Sorority, Inc.

J ulie A. Cunningham is president and chief executive officer of the Conference Of Minority Transportation Officials (COMTO), and most recently served on President Barack Obama's Transition Team/ Agency Review Group for the U.S. Department of Transportation.

Cunningham offers more than 20 years of hands-on experience as an agent of change in executive program management, strategic communication, operational leadership, workforce development and process improvement. She is nationally known for her talent in building effective partnerships, as well as her strong advocacy for a level playing field and maximum employment participation for minorities, women and the economically disadvantaged. She has ensured COMTO's continued partnerships with congressional representatives to co-host legislative forums, emphasizing the importance of equality in the transportation industry.

A native of Cleveland, Ohio, and a U.S. Army veteran, Cunningham graduated from Hiram College with a Bachelor of Arts degree in business management. She is a member of the American Society of Association Executives and the Association for Conflict Resolution. She also serves as first vice chair of the Black Leadership Forum, Inc.

Julie A. Cunningham

President & Chief Executive Officer
Conference Of Minority
Transportation Officials

Deirdre A. Curtis

Education Specialist
Edward C. Mazique Parent Child Center

Deirdre A. Curtis was initiated into Zeta Phi Beta Sorority, Inc. in 1982. A life member and a legacy, Dee has held elected positions in the Beta Zeta Chapter, the D.C. State, the Eastern Region and on the National Executive Board.

Originally from Cleveland, Ohio, Dee holds degrees from Alabama A&M University and Michigan State University. She is working on a doctorate degree in curriculum and instruction at West Virginia University.

She belongs to the Association of Curriculum and Development, the National Association for the Education of Young Children, the National Alliance of Black School Educators and Phi Delta Kappa International. She is also a distinguished Johnson and Johnson/UCLA Anderson School of Business Head Start Management fellow. Additionally, she is an education specialist for the Edward C. Mazique Parent Child Center.

Dee has four nieces and one nephew. She enjoys music of all genres, particularly jazz and hip-hop. She can sometimes be found sitting in with local jazz musicians at HR 57 playing her flute. In her free time, she enjoys traveling, playing tennis, reading and going to the movies.

Dwayne Dawson

Account Executive
District of Columbia
Department of Employment Services

Dwayne Dawson is a public administrator and account executive for the District of Columbia Department of Employment Services Transitional Employment Program, a planner, and a social service advocate with more than 20 years' experience communicating the concerns of citizens to government leaders. His expertise is in connecting available assistance programs with ex-offenders, domestic violence survivors, hard-to-serve youth, and individuals and families living in at-risk, low-income communities.

Dwayne was elected to the Prince George's County, Maryland, City Council as the youngest representative in 1987. A recognized representative of unbiased regional needs, he is a trusted advisor to local, state and federal officials.

Dwayne has studied at Bowie State University, The George Washington University and will attend Lincoln University in the fall of 2009 to earn a Master of Human Services degree. He has served in the U.S. Navy and was part of a special forces Terrorists Attack Team on the *USS Ponce*. In 1982 he was selected as honorman of his company and awarded a Navy achievement ribbon, and in 1984 he received a Navy Expeditionary Medal and a Navy Meritorious Unit Commendation.

Charles Debnam, a highly skilled and versatile business executive, has extensive leadership experience within the health education industry. He is an accomplished health education services deputy director and offers more than a decade of accomplishment. He brings valuable insight and knowledge regarding the leadership and management challenges faced by a small start-up and growing nonprofit organization. His capabilities in strategic planning are highlighted by accomplishments in the community, where he has been able to utilize his knowledge of the corporate industry.

Demonstrating initiative, Charles pioneers in business management and management techniques. He has been recognized for his business acumen with numerous competitive advantages secured for major organizations. His approach to retaining customers and ability to leverage solid internal and external relationships is reflected in his work as deputy director of health education services at the American Lung Association of the District of Columbia.

Charles received a Bachelor of Arts degree in business management from Fisk University and an associate degree in computer science from American University. He is active in Kappa Alpha Psi Fraternity, Inc. and resides in Washington, D.C.

Charles R. Debnam

Deputy Director
Health Education Services
American Lung Association of the
District of Columbia

Deborah Foster is executive vice president of strategic alliances and chief diversity officer for United Way, the nation's largest charitable organization. Debbie is responsible for leading relationships with key stakeholders and partners, including organized labor and nonprofit organizations. A frequent presenter on nonprofit management topics, including diversity and career development, her work extends globally as a trainer and consultant with the United Way affiliates in West and South Africa.

An active community leader through Delta Sigma Theta Sorority, Inc., Debbie is the current president of the Northern Virginia Alumnae Chapter. She serves on the board of trustees of Bennett College in Greensboro, North Carolina, and is a former fellow and board member of the National African-American Women's Leadership Institute. Additionally, she is a member of Alfred Street Baptist Church in Alexandria.

Debbie received a Bachelor of Science degree in education and human development from Syracuse University, and a master's degree in social work from Temple University. A native of Philadelphia, she is the proud wife of Leon Foster, mother of two adult children, Tiffany and Marc, and the grandmother of Cassidy.

Deborah W. Foster

Executive Vice President
Strategic Alliances
United Way Worldwide

Ivonne Fuller

Associate Executive Director
National Medical Association

I vonne Fuller is the associate executive director for the National Medical Association, representing 30,000 minority physicians. In this position, she promotes the visibility of the organization, serves as the corporate liaison-development officer and implements outreach programs. She has shaped policy, developed programs, and consulted and served on boards addressing numerous health issues. She has also raised more than $20 million for programs and special events.

Ivonne was a contributing author to *The Journal of Pain* and a writer for "Racism in Medicine and Health Parity for African Americans," which led to the Institute of Medicine's "Unequal Treatment" report. She was an executive committee member and contributing author for the "Vital Report on Global Health" and the "Global Opinions on Global Health."

A certified prevention professional, Ivonne is a member of the Society for Industry Leaders and the Gerson Lehrman Group health care council. She attended Harvard University's Training Institute for Women of Color as Leaders in Public Health and Health Policy. Her academic background includes a master's degree in public health administration and undergraduate studies include a bachelor's degree in international business.

Kenneth Furlough

Executive Director
Government Affairs
Strategic Seven Government Relations

K enneth Furlough is a government affairs consultant and community affairs advocate in the Washington, D.C., metropolitan area. He works and has worked for the National Federation of Independent Business, Georgetown University, Time Warner, where he was the first professional black male in the government affairs division, and Capitol Hill.

During his time at Capitol Hill, Kenneth was a legislative aide and advisor for U.S. Representative Corrine Brown, and directed the business and industry, telecommunications, and social science legislative agendas.

His interests include attending sporting events and theater, traveling, mentoring, reading and jazz music. Kenneth is a Baptist church member and an active member of Alpha Phi Alpha Fraternity, Inc., where he serves as chair of the Public Policy Committee, on the chapter's executive board, and as a chapter officer.

A Little Rock, Arkansas, native, Kenneth holds two Bachelor of Arts degrees in political science and history from the premier urban campus of the University of Arkansas. He is a graduate of historic Little Rock Central High School.

As chief executive officer of the national Parent Teacher Association, Byron V. Garrett brings a combination of experiences from the nonprofit and governmental sectors. He has served in positions with the Office of Public Affairs in the U.S. Customs and Border Protection agency and the National 4-H headquarters within the U.S. Department of Agriculture. Previously, Garrett served in various positions as an education advocate.

Garrett is currently co-chair of the Smart Television Alliance, a trustee of the America's Promise Alliance, and a member of the advisory boards for both *Parenting* magazine and *the.News*. An author of several books and an accomplished speaker, he has been a guest on the *Dr. Phil Show*, and featured in *The Wall Street Journal*, *USA Today* and *Jet*. In 2009 *Ebony* named Garrett to its Power 150, an annual list of the most influential black Americans.

Born, raised and educated in the Carolinas, Garrett holds a bachelor's degree from High Point University, a master's degree from the University of Phoenix, and has completed doctoral coursework at Pepperdine University in the educational leadership, administration and policy program.

Byron V. Garrett

Chief Executive Officer
Parent Teacher Association

Beverly Harrison Griggs is president of the Martin Luther King Jr. DC Support Group, Inc., where she organizes the Annual Luncheon & Fashion Show. Since 1972, the Martin Luther King Jr. DC Support Group has developed a humanitarian service award bestowed annually upon a deserving individual for their dedication to peace and justice for all.

Involved in the civil rights movement since 1963, she assisted in lobbying Congress to make Dr. King's birthday a national holiday. Further, she has volunteered for The Congressional Black Caucus Foundation, Inc.'s prayer breakfast since 1983. She became treasurer of the InterFaith Conference Committee for the Dr. King program, and in 2008 became treasurer of New Bethel Baptist Church. Additionally, she organized the hostesses for the First African Inaugural Ball honoring President Barack Obama.

Beverly was born in Washington, D.C., the fourth of seven children born to Tom and Susie Harrison. Educated in the District of Columbia's public schools, she graduated from Strayer College with an accounting degree. Beverly married the late James E. Griggs. Currently, she works as an educator in the Montgomery County Public Schools.

Beverly Harrison Griggs

President
Martin Luther King Jr.
DC Support Group, Inc.

Christine Hart-Wright

Executive Director
STRIVE DC

C hristine "Chris" Hart-Wright is executive director of STRIVE DC, a local community-based nonprofit organization and affiliate of the nationally recognized workforce development program, STRIVE. As executive director, Chris elevated STRIVE DC from an unknown start-up organization to a well-known, highly respected resource for individuals in need of training and employment. Annually, STRIVE DC places 200 program graduates into employment opportunities throughout the metro District of Columbia area.

She received the Hero Award from the Women's Institute for a Secure Retirement and the Gelman, Rosenberg & Freedman EXCEL Award, recognizing excellence in nonprofit chief executive leadership with an honorable mention. In response to the high mortality rate of cancer victims from wards 7 and 8, she founded the Mocha Walk, a 5K cancer awareness walk.

Chris received Bachelor of Arts and Master of Arts degrees from Howard University. She is a member of Zeta Phi Beta Sorority, Inc. and the Holy Christian House of Praise. A native Chicagoan, she is the wife of Anthony Wright and the proud parent of Malaijah Brinkley-Tyson. Chris enjoys reading, cycling and discovering new adventures.

Bernard L. Jackson

President
National Naval Officers Association

B ernard Jackson is president of the National Naval Officers Association (NNOA), which actively supports the U.S. Navy, Coast Guard and Marine Corps in the development of a diverse officer corps through recruitment, retention, professional/career development, mentoring and enhanced cultural awareness in order to contribute to overall operational readiness. NNOA is the largest affinity group sanctioned by the Secretaries of the Navy and Homeland Security.

Bernard is a retired U.S. Navy captain whose assignments included Commander Destroyer Squadron Fourteen, commanding officer of the USS McFaul (DDG 74), member of the Strategic Plans and Policy Directorate joint staff, and deputy director of military plans and policy (OPNAV N13). He is currently a general associate with Strategic Insight, a privately owned consulting firm headquartered in Arlington, Virginia.

A native of Macon, Georgia, Bernard received Bachelor of Science degrees in chemistry and math from Savannah State University. In 1995 he was awarded a master's degree in national security and strategic studies from the U.S. Naval War College. In addition, Bernard is the proud father of Anthony and Nichole.

The Reverend Louis B. Jones II is pastor of Pilgrim Baptist Church. He holds a Bachelor of Arts degree in business administration from Antioch University, and attended Talbot and Fuller theological seminaries in California. In addition, he received a Master of Arts degree in theological studies from Eastern Baptist Theological Seminary in Pennsylvania.

Mentored by the late Reverend Dr. Edward V. Hill of Los Angeles, Jones was inspired to feed his sheep and the community spiritually and through economic empowerment. With prayerful guidance, the church has purchased nine residential and six commercial properties located near and on H Street, an impetus to the revitalization of the corridor.

Jones' religious and professional associations include the Progressive National Baptist Convention, Project Bridges, the Promise Keepers, chair of the Nannie Helen Burroughs Scholarship Fund and board member of the Alliance for Retired Americans. He is former president of the Missionary Baptist Minister's Conference of Washington, D.C., and Vicinity, and has licensed five ministers and two evangelists. Jones is a spiritual inspiration to all who come to know him.

Rev. Louis B. Jones II

Pastor
Pilgrim Baptist Church

William A. Keyes IV is founder and president of The Institute for Responsible Citizenship, an intensive leadership program for high-achieving African-American male college students.

Keyes serves on the National Selection Committee of the Coca-Cola Scholars Foundation and is an auxiliary board member of the Alfred Street Baptist Church Foundation. He served on the local boards of the YMCA, Goodwill Industries International, the Fellowship of Christian Athletes and as a board of trustees secretary of Landon School. Additionally, Keyes is a member of the African American Nonprofit Network board, an organization that matches talented African-American professionals with governing board and executive opportunities in Washington, D.C.'s, nonprofit community.

Active with the University of North Carolina at Chapel Hill, Keyes serves on the board of visitors, and the boards of the School of Journalism and Mass Communication, The Graduate School and the Leadership Institute, which he helped found.

Keyes is a member of Sigma Pi Phi Fraternity, Beta Nu Boulé. He is married to Lola Green Keyes, and has two children, Lola Elizabeth Keyes and William A. Keyes V.

William A. Keyes IV

Founder & President
The Institute for Responsible Citizenship

Almeta Faye Richards Keys

Executive Director
Edward C. Mazique
Parent Child Center, Inc.

With more than 30 years' experience in education, Almeta R. Keys serves as executive director of the Edward C. Mazique Parent Child Center, Inc. She supervises 88 employees and oversees the operation of five Head Start and Early Head Start centers with a diverse population of 280 children and a $5 million-plus budget. She is a recognized expert in program administration, parent involvement, governance and community partnerships in Head Start communities across the country.

A UCLA/Johnson & Johnson Head Start Management fellow, Keys received the UCLA/Johnson & Johnson Management Improvement Plan Award. In addition to her appointment to the National Head Start Fellowship Program, her Head Start agency was invited by Nancy Pelosi to participate in the signing of new Head Start legislation.

Keys received associate, bachelor's and Master of Education degrees at the University of Louisiana at Lafayette. She serves on the Council for Early Childhood Recognition and is a member of the National Head Start Association board. Her most recent accomplishments include roles in organizing the DC Healthy Marriages and Strengthening Families Initiative and revitalizing the District of Columbia Head Start Association.

Ronald L. Moten

Chief Operating Officer
Peaceoholics, Inc.

Ronald L. Moten is a fifth-generation Washingtonian who attended Roosevelt Senior High School. Currently, he serves as chief operating officer and co-founder of Peaceoholics, Inc., which was established to combat violence among youth and promote peace. He is responsible for the program operations of the organization and specializes in strategically engaging youth to understand the importance of education, peace and economic empowerment.

Moten is a skilled trainer in conflict resolution and has negotiated many truces between male and female gangs and crews. He has assisted the nation's capital in developing numerous initiatives to combat violence. Moten has trained government, local and national leaders on the best practices and strategies to develop programs that support successful outcomes. Serving as an advisor to government and national leaders, he has strengthened the work to move young people from a life of violence to peace, from despair to hope and from no skills to self-sufficiency.

Moten has received awards from the NAACP and Common Ground, which has awarded others such as President Jimmy Carter and Muhammad Ali.

H.D. Odom Jr. serves as director of the Office of Returning Citizens Affairs. In this position, he works with Mayor Adrian Fenty's office, and networks with district and federal agencies, and civic associations. He also works alongside ANCs and community-based organizations to provide assistance to citizens in the Washington, D.C., area to improve their quality of life.

Odom encourages everyone he meets to do and be his or her best, no matter the circumstances. He inspired many to improve their quality of life and to believe in themselves, their community and their future. As an instructor, he believed in the quote, "If they do not learn the way that you teach them, then teach them the way that they learn."

Listed in *Outstanding Young Men of America*, Odom received a Bachelor of Arts degree from the University of the District of Columbia and is currently working on two books to be released by 2011. He partners with his wife as a photojournalistic photographer.

The native Washingtonian is the husband of Sandy Odom, and the proud father of three daughters, Mia, Taylor and Krystian Odom.

H. D. Odom Jr.

Director
Office of Returning Citizens Affairs

John E. Saunders III is executive director of the National Forum for Black Public Administrators (NFBPA), headquartered in Washington, D.C. A professional membership association dedicated to the advancement of black leadership in the public sector, NFBPA is the nation's premier association of black public leadership, with more than 2,700 members representing more than 350 jurisdictions in 40 states.

John holds Bachelor of Arts and Master of Arts degrees from Central State University and Lincoln University, and an honorary Doctor of Laws degree. He is a certified association executive, a National Academy of Public Administration fellow and an American Leadership Forum senior fellow. John served with the U.S. Army in both Vietnam and Germany. His career also includes serving as president and chief executive officer of the Urban League of Greater Hartford and Connecticut state deputy labor commissioner.

His current activities include the Consortium for International Management Policy and Development; the National Academy of Public Administration international standing panel, social equity panel and Africa working group; the Black Leadership Forum; and the National Urban Fellows, Inc.

John E. Saunders III

Executive Director
National Forum for
Black Public Administrators

COMMUNITY LEADERS

Tim Seay

Senior Pastor
Crossover Church

Tim Seay is founder and senior pastor of Crossover Church, a cross-cultural, interracial and multigenerational assembly. Established in October of 1987, Crossover Church remains a vibrant, growing expression of believers, driven by the mission of "changing lives, changing families, changing the world."

Seay serves the body of Christ with great passion and a commitment to seeing people advance in the purpose of God. His 25 years of ministerial experience include serving as a youth pastor, singles pastor and Bible school teacher. He can be seen on the weekly television broadcast *Living Now*, a show committed to the clear presentation of God's word driven by the objective of practical application.

A methodical, insightful and humorous communicator, Seay can leave a truth lodged in the hearts of those who hear him. His book, *15 Qualities of A Mature Woman*, demonstrates his ability to present biblical truths with clarity and insight. A native of Washington, D.C., Seay celebrates life daily with Robyn, his wife of 24 years, and their two children, Noel and Timothy Destiny.

Ron Simmons, Ph.D.

President & Chief Executive Officer
Us Helping Us, People Into Living, Inc.

Dr. Ron Simmons is president and chief executive officer of Us Helping Us, People Into Living, Inc., a nonprofit AIDS service organization. He is a member of the D.C. Board of Medicine and the HIV Prevention Community Planning Committee.

Simmons received a Bachelor of Arts degree in Afro-American studies, a Master of Arts degree in African history and a Master of Science degree in educational communications from The State University of New York at Albany. He also holds a Doctor of Philosophy degree in mass communications from Howard University, where he served on the faculty of the Howard University School of Communications for 12 years.

His published works include "Some Thoughts on the Challenges Facing Black Gay Intellectuals" in the anthology *Brother To Brother: Collected Writings By Black Gay Men*; "Sexuality, Television and Death: A Black Gay Dialogue On Malcolm X" in *Malcolm X: In Our Own Image*; and "Baraka's Dilemma: To Be Or Not To Be" in *Black Men on Race, Gender and Sexuality*. Additionally, he was a field producer, photographer and cast member of the award-winning documentary film *Tongues Untied*.

Gloria Simon is president of the Blacks in Government Veterans Affairs (VA) Headquarters Chapter, Region XI. She is responsible for chapter operations at the VA Central Office (VACO) in Washington, D.C., and serves as one of three regional representatives on the Region XI Council. The chapter is committed to offering programs and activities that enhance employee's professional and personal development for the improvement of pubic service, as well as promoting equity, excellence and opportunity in the work place.

Gloria served as the 2008 National Training Conference (NTC) co-chair of the customer service subcommittee, which provided conferees one-stop informational services. She also served as the VA forum chairperson for 2007 and 2008 at NTCs held in Nashville and New Orleans, respectively. In this capacity, she coordinated full-day training sessions for VA employees designed to enhance advancement and promotional opportunities.

The University of Maryland, College Park awarded Gloria with a Bachelor of Arts degree. She received a Master of Science degree in law and society from American University, and a juris doctorate degree from American University Washington College of Law.

Gloria C. Simon

President
Veterans Affairs Headquarters Chapter
Blacks In Government

Stephen Tucker is senior pastor of New Commandment Baptist Church and co-founder, president and chief executive officer of Jobs Partnership of Greater Washington. He is the recipient of the U.S. Department of State's George Schultz Award for community service, presented to him by former Secretary Colin L. Powell.

Featured on the front page of *USA Today* for his work in rescuing young people from gang life, Tucker is a national speaker on issues concerning ex-offender re-entry, pre-release workforce development and training youth to avoid the prison system. He has made presentations at the Brookings Institution, the National Press Club and the president's faith-based initiative conference.

Tucker received a bachelor's degree from Ball State University and a master's degree from St. Mary's Seminary & University and Ecumenical Institute of Theology. A native of Indianapolis, Indiana, he is the husband of the former Roberta Cornell and the proud father of two daughters, Kimberly and Steffani.

Stephen Tucker

Co-Founder & Chief Executive Officer
Jobs Partnership of Greater Washington

Brandon J. Wallace

Senior Vice President &
Chief Operating Officer
Motley Management LLC

B randon J. Wallace graduated, magna cum laude, from Howard University in May of 2007 with a bachelor's degree in communications and culture. While at Howard University, he served as president of the John H. Johnson School of Communications Student Council and as the international second vice president of Phi Beta Sigma Fraternity, Inc. He is currently seeking a master's degree in public administration at Howard University.

Brandon is senior vice president and chief operating officer of Motley Management LLC, an entertainment management company with a focus on community service and involvement. He also serves as the newly appointed executive director for The William Kellibrew Foundation and ROOT Inc., a nonprofit organization dedicated to providing support for victims of violent crime, gun violence and domestic abuse.

Currently, Brandon works for the Environmental Protection Agency (EPA), implementing the Memorandum of Understanding between Howard University and the EPA. This agreement was formed after Hurricane Katrina displaced university students across the gulf coast, and has grown into a blossoming partnership providing internships and opportunities to current Howard students and recent alumni.

Amber P. Waller

Board Member At-Large
Prince George's County Public Schools

A mber Waller is a board member at-large with Prince George's County Public Schools. In this elected position, she is actively engaged with board members to ensure the necessary tools are in place so that all graduating students are career and college ready. She seeks to reframe education as a collaboration between neighborhoods and schools.

As a community activist and strong advocate of education, Amber has served in various roles with the county and state Parent Teachers Association, the Multi-Cultural Alliance of Prince George's County, Inc. and Kiwanis. She has received several awards while serving as vice president of the NAACP Washington, D.C., Branch. As an active parent, she received the Prince George's County Public Schools Outstanding Volunteer Award. Prior to serving on the board of education, Amber was elected to the Maryland Democratic Central Committee. In 2008 she was appointed by the governor to serve on the Youth Camp Safety Advisory Council.

A native of Roanoke, Virginia, Amber was selected as one of nine students to integrate the schools. Additionally, she is the proud mother of Cullen and Alva Waller.

Inita Harper Winkey is founder and chief executive officer of ATWINDS Foundation, Inc. (A Teacher's Work Is Never Done Services) and a public school teacher. ATWINDS' purpose is fostering families to become productive citizens. She received a response letter from President Obama within his first 100 days of office for her six-year advocacy of medical record awareness and was invited to attend a live town hall health care conference call with the president.

Selected as a *Who's Who Among America's Teachers*, Eunita received the Community Children Advocacy Award. She was nominated for a 2007 Philanthropy Award and honored by Pine-Sol for making a powerful difference in the community. A member of the Woman's National Democratic Club and DC for Obama Health Care Reform, she is also a panelist on *The Point* television talk show.

Eunita received a Master of Education degree in leadership from George Mason University and a bachelor's degree in business administration from Saint Augustine's College. She is a foster and adoptive parent, and resides in Pomfret, Maryland, with her husband, Marvin, son Nicholas and daughter Ashley.

Eunita Harper Winkey

Founder & Chief Executive Officer
ATWINDS Foundation, Inc.

Savannah Winston is the current president of the Washington, D.C., Chapter of the National Pan-Hellenic Council, Inc. (NPHC). In this position, she works with 15 chapters of the black Greek letter organizations as they come together to achieve many community service and scholastic giving efforts.

A member of Zeta Phi Beta Sorority, Inc., Savannah has been an active member of Beta Zeta Chapter, having held several positions, and chaired committees on the local (president and financial secretary), state (financial secretary and treasurer) and regional (ZOL trainer and Web site coordinator) levels.

Savannah is proud to have held the position of president (2004–2008) of the second-oldest chapter of the sorority, Beta Zeta Chapter, where she led the platform of Fostering Our Community Using Scholarship and Service (F.O.C.U.S.S.). As president of the NPHC's Washington, D.C., Chapter and a member of Zeta Phi Beta Sorority, Inc., she advocates for increased scholarship giving and serving the community.

Savannah thoroughly believes in putting her best foot forward to accomplish this mission. Passion, patience and perseverance are the three Ps that motivate her daily.

Savannah Winston

President
Washington, D.C., Chapter
National Pan-Hellenic Council

Who's Who In Black Washington, D.C.® | The Inaugural Edition   231

Keith D. Wright

Executive Vice President &
Chief Operating Officer
Congressional Black
Caucus Foundation, Inc.

Rev. Lennox Yearwood

President & Chief Executive Officer
Hip Hop Caucus

Keith Wright is executive vice president and chief operating officer for the Congressional Black Caucus Foundation, Inc. (CBCF), where he provides leadership, management and vision to ensure the financial strength and operating efficiency of the organization. An accomplished leader, Wright has spent more than 30 years leading organizations, developing strong teams, and delivering technology and homeownership products and services in communities around the country. Prior to joining the CBCF, he held positions with Citigroup, Fannie Mae, and The Port Authority of New York and New Jersey.

A native of New Jersey, Wright served as chair of the New Jersey Economic Development Authority, the YMCA Capital Campaign and the Mayor's Community Development Corporation. He received a Master of General Administration degree from the University of Maryland, a bachelor's degree from Rutgers University, and completed the program for management development at Harvard Business School.

Wright serves on the boards of New Covenant Tabernacle Ministry and The Hurston\Wright Foundation. He is married to the lovely Eureka A. Wright and has three adult children, Keisha, Keith and Khalid, and two precious grandchildren, Blair and Noah.

The Reverend Lennox Yearwood Jr. is a minister, community organizer and one of the most influential people in hip-hop political life. As one of the founders and current president of the Hip Hop Caucus, he works tirelessly to encourage the hip-hop generation to utilize its political and social voice.

Yearwood was a co-creator of the 2004 campaign Vote or Die with Sean "P. Diddy" Combs. During the 2008 election, he also led the award-winning Respect My Vote! campaign, a nonpartisan voter registration, education and mobilization campaign of the Hip Hop Caucus with Grammy Award-winning artist T.I. and Platinum-selling artist Keyshia Cole. This groundbreaking initiative registered more than 110,000 young voters around the country.

Born in Shreveport, Louisiana, Yearwood earned an undergraduate degree from the University of the District of Columbia in 1998 and a Master of Divinity degree from Howard University in 2002.

Yearwood has appeared on CNN, *BET Tonight,* the BBC, C-SPAN, MTV, AllHipHop.com and *Hardball with Chris Mathews,* and in *XXL Magazine, Newsweek* and *The Nation.* Additionally, he was featured in *The Washington Post, The New York Times* and *VIBE* magazine.

Washington, D.C.

GOVERNMENT
PROFESSIONALS

INTEREST

LIMELIGHT

ATTENTION

PROMINENCE

HIGHLIGHT

CELEBRATE

SKILLFUL

INFLUENTIAL

EXCELLENCE

Marcell K. Bishop

Program Analyst
Office of Criminal Enforcement,
Forensics and Training
U.S. Environmental Protection Agency

As a program analyst on the resources management staff of the Office of Criminal Enforcement, Forensics and Training, Marcell Bishop serves as the human resources official for the organization's special agents, and advises employees on federal benefits, and civilian and law enforcement retirement guidelines.

Additionally, Marcell directs the Fairness and Equity Program, which focuses on diversity recruitment outreach opportunities, minority internship opportunities and ensures that diversity recruiting initiatives are implemented. In addition, he mentors African-American adolescents residing in the Anacostia areas of southeast Washington, D.C., under the EPA's Earth Conservation Corps (ECC) program. This program, which has a close partnership with the Washington Nationals, recruits African-American adolescents to become sworn volunteers for the ECC and educates them on the importance of protecting the environment, while also teaching them basic life skills to become productive citizens.

Marcell's hobbies include bowling, football, basketball and attending church. During the bowling season, he coaches youth bowling on a part-time basis. A Washington, D.C., native, he is the proud husband of April Bishop, and the proud parent of two daughters and two sons, Kriston, Jasmine, Jordan and Christopher.

Yolanda Butler, Ph.D.

Acting Director/Deputy Director
Office of Community Services
Administration for Children & Families
U.S. Department of Health & Human Services

Dr. Yolanda J. Butler currently serves as acting director of the Office of Community Services (OCS) at the Administration for Children and Families, U.S. Department of Health and Human Services. As acting director of OCS since November of 2008 and deputy director of OCS since April of 2006, she serves as an executive manager and advisor for nine highly visible block grant and discretionary community and social services grant programs, including one presidential initiative program, that total some $8 billion.

Yolanda received a Doctor of Philosophy degree in political science, concentrating in American government and public administration, at Howard University in 2006. She completed a master's degree in American government and public administration at Howard University in 1996, and most recently received a certificate in public administration from the Key Executive Leadership Program at American University in 2008. In addition, she is a 1994 graduate of the W.E.B. DuBois Honors College at Jackson State University.

With more than 20 years of IT service, Kevin Cooke currently serves the U.S. Department of Energy (DOE), where he is responsible for all administrative functions of the Office of the Chief Information Officer (CIO), including audits, budget, contracting and human resources. Additionally, he manages acquisitions of enterprisewide agreements, and is responsible for the human capital management functions of the office.

Active on the Federal CIO Council Workforce and Human Capital for IT Committee and the DOE CIO Council, Cooke also serves on the board of the Government Information Technology Executive Council. He is a graduate of the Federal Executive Institute and the American Council for Technology/Industry Advisory Council Partners Program.

Cooke began his career at the National Security Agency and the U.S. Department of the Interior. After completing a bachelor's degree at Kentucky State University, he worked at the DOE Ohio Field Office. Since joining the DOE Office of the CIO, he has held several roles. *CIO Magazine* named Cooke as a CIO Ones to Watch honoree, bestowed upon rising stars in IT who bring leadership, innovation and value to their organization.

Kevin R. Cooke Jr.

Associate Chief Information Officer
Office of the Chief Information Officer
U.S. Department of Energy

Paris Dennard is a senior field representative for the Republican National Committee's Coalitions Department, serving as principal liaison of the division to RNC state parties and targeted campaigns.

Paris served in President George W. Bush's Office of Legislative Affairs and Public Liaison. He was the liaison to black churches, business, civic and fraternal organization leaders, and the families of the former presidents and vice presidents for the state funeral of President Ford. Paris coordinated and managed White House events, meetings and travel for President Bush, the first lady and members of the U.S. House of Representatives. He began his White House tenure as an intern in political affairs and was hired full-time after two months.

He has attended three consecutive Republican National Conventions since 2000; as a page, he was the youngest featured platform speaker at 17 in 2000; he was a delegate-at-large from Arizona; and he was serving in management of the VIP Surrogate Program.

Paris earned public relations and political science degrees from Pepperdine University in Malibu, California, in 2005. He studied in London, England, and traveled to eight countries.

Paris Dennard

Senior Field Representative
Coalitions Department
Republican National Committee

Major General Walter E. Gaskin Sr.

Vice Director, Joint Staff
U.S. Department of Defense

Major General Walter E. Gaskin Sr. serves as vice director, Joint Staff. His previous commands include 2nd Marine Division, commander of the II Marine Expeditionary Force (Forward) and commanding general of Multi-National Force West in Fallujah, Iraq.

In 2006 Gaskin assumed command of the 2nd Marine Division in Camp Lejeune, North Carolina. He oversaw preparation of the division's 22,000 Marines and sailors in support of operations in Iraq, Afghanistan and the Horn of Africa, supporting the global war on terrorism. In 2007 he deployed as the II Marine Expeditionary Force (Forward) commander, in support of Operation Iraqi Freedom, and headed the more than 35,000-member Multi-National Force West.

On May 1, 2009, it was announced that Gaskin was nominated for appointment as the next deputy chairman of the NATO Military Committee and to the rank of lieutenant general. If confirmed by the U.S. Senate, he will be only the third African American in Marine Corps history to achieve three-star grade.

Gaskin graduated from Savannah State University's NROTC Scholarship Program in 1974 with a Bachelor of Science degree.

Tamia Nicole Gordon, Esq.

Associate Deputy General Counsel
Office of the General Counsel
U.S. Department of Defense

Tamia Gordon is associate deputy general counsel with the Department of Defense Office of General Counsel. A top-notch attorney, she is responsible for *habeas corpus* litigation for several detained enemy combatants at Guantanamo Bay and consistently provides sound legal advice in connection with detainee litigation to other government agencies and private sector entities.

Tamia is an extraordinary leader whose superior performance was documented during her years of military service. She achieved the rank of major during her outstanding career as a judge advocate in the Marine Corps and successfully held several challenging billets, such as prosecutor, income tax center manager, immigration/naturalization officer, legal assistance attorney and Marine Corps liaison to the White House Commission. Additionally, she is a qualified Arabic linguist with training in Iraqi, Egyptian and Syrian dialects.

A native of Washington, D.C., Tamia attended American University, where she pledged Delta Sigma Theta Sorority, Inc. She was awarded a master's degree in organic chemistry from the University of Pennsylvania and a Doctor of Jurisprudence degree from the University of San Francisco School of Law.

L eonard L. Haynes III was named executive director of the White House Initiative on Historically Black Colleges and Universities in 2007.

He was a member of the U.S. Observer Delegation to the UNESCO World Conference on Higher Education in 2003, and a principal member of the U.S. Delegation to the 50th Anniversary AMIDEAST Conference in 2002 in Morocco.

Haynes earned a bachelor's degree in history from Southern University, a master's degree in American history from Carnegie Mellon University, and a doctorate degree in higher education administration from The Ohio State University. A career member of the Senior Executive Service, he is a member of *the HistoryMakers*, the Rotary Club of Washington D.C., Phi Delta Kappa, Sigma Pi Phi Fraternity, Omega Psi Phi Fraternity, Inc. and Asbury United Methodist Church. In May of 2006, he was the 16th recipient of the Excellence in Public Service Award from The Ohio State University's John Glenn School of Public Affairs and Management.

Residing in Washington, D.C., Haynes is married to the former Mary J. Sensley and they have four children and four grandchildren.

Leonard L. Haynes III

Executive Director
White House Initiative on Historically
Black Colleges & Universities

D r. James D. Key is a U.S. Army chaplain at Arlington National Cemetery and guest columnist for *USA Today*. Born in Los Angeles, California, he earned a Bachelor of Arts degree in speech communication from CSUN, and Master of Divinity and Doctor of Ministry degrees from the Howard University School of Divinity in Washington, D.C.

Key previously served as a staff assistant for Congressman Sander Levin and as a legislative assistant/office manager for Congresswoman Maxine Waters in the U.S. House of Representatives. He has also served as an executive director, pastor, prison chaplain and college adjunct professor.

Some of his awards include the Bronze Star Medal, the Meritorious Service Medal, the Army Achievement Medal, the National Defense Service Medal, the Iraq Campaign Medal and the Global War on Terrorism Service Medal. Key was also recognized in *Who's Who In Black Los Angeles*™ and received the Outstanding Young Men of America Award, the Outstanding Graduate Award from California State University, Northridge's (CSUN) Pan-African Studies Department and the Western Regional College Brother of the Year award from Alpha Phi Alpha Fraternity, Inc.

Dr. James D. Key

Chaplain & Captain
U.S. Army

Yemaya Lawson

Senior Human Resources Generalist
U.S. House of Representatives

Yemaya Lawson is a certified senior professional in human resources, who works as a senior generalist for the U.S. House of Representatives. In this position, she serves as a strategic business partner to the House by providing consultative services to management and staff regarding workforce planning, employee relations and human resources development. Additionally, she is a philanthropist with plans to establish a nonprofit organization that will focus on encouraging youth to dream, plan and take action to attain their goals.

Yemaya lends her expertise and time to give back by coaching and facilitating career development meetings to aid the growing population of professionals seeking entry-, mid- and executive-level employment opportunities due to the challenging economy.

Yemaya received a Bachelor of Business Administration Management degree from the Howard University School of Business. A native Washingtonian, she loves to travel and has participated in a medical mission trip to East Africa. Yemaya is a proud big sister to Aleeyia Henderson and the daughter of Aprileona King and Rick Henderson. She aspires to motivate others to dare to dream and see what materializes.

George M. "Mike" Parker

Deputy Director
Office of Grants & Transition Programs
Veterans Employment & Training Services
U.S. Department of Labor

George M. "Mike" Parker is deputy director at the Office of Grants and Transition Programs for the Veterans Employment and Training Service (VETS) of the U.S. Department of Labor. As such, he provides the day-to-day direction and oversight of various programs and operations. This includes the Jobs for Veterans State Grants Program, the Homeless Veterans Reintegration Program, the Transition Assistance Program, and REALifelines, among other special projects, as directed by the director of the Office of Operations Grants and Transition Programs.

Mike is a retired colonel from the U.S. Army and served from 1974 to 2004. He received a Master of Science degree in national security strategy and strategic studies from National Defense University in 1977 and a Bachelor of Science degree in political science from North Carolina A&T State University in 1974. In addition, he is a life member of Omega Psi Phi Fraternity, Inc.

A native of Raleigh, North Carolina, Mike is married to Almetta Parker. He is the proud father of two children, Michael and Stacie, and the grandfather of Kaia and Kaden.

A ngela Sailor is coalitions director for the Republican National Committee. She served as director of African-American affairs for the Republican National Committee and Victory 2000. Other political experiences include deputy chief of staff to the U.S. secretary of education and associate director for the White House Office of Public Liaison.

Her corporate experiences include serving as partner of the Watts Consulting Group; manager of the Detroit Regional Chamber of Commerce; a communications, sales and marketing strategist for BET; and in sales and marketing for Procter & Gamble Co. Sailor worked for Michigan appeals Judge Jeffery Collins, U.S. Senator Spencer Abraham, Michigan Governor John Engler and Detroit's Wayne County Commissioner Kathleen Husk. Her media experiences include serving as a radio host with WGTZ 93 and WCSU-FM 88.9, and a freelance producer with FOX *Morning News*, in Washington, D.C.

Sailor holds a Doctor of Jurisprudence degree from the University of Memphis Cecil C. Humphreys School of Law, a master's degree in broadcast journalism and public affairs from American University and a communications degree from Central State University. She is happily married with two children.

Angela Sailor

Coalitions Director
Republican National Committee

D on "Donnie" Simons is a senior manager with the Federal Aviation Administration (FAA). He is also the district manager for the Washington Air Traffic District, where he is in charge of all air traffic control towers in Maryland, Virginia and the District of Columbia. Additionally, he serves as the air traffic manager (tower chief) for the Ronald Reagan Washington National Airport air traffic control tower.

A dedicated mentor, Simons is a member of the Federal Manager's Association, the National Black Coalition of Federal Aviation Employees and the NAACP. He is the recipient of numerous awards, including the NBCFAE's prestigious Ronald E. McNair Award.

Simons is also the director of the Aviation Ministry at First Baptist Church of Glenarden in Upper Malboro, Maryland. He is a licensed private pilot, enjoys playing golf, and is an avid motorcyclist. He and his wife, Kendolyn, have two children. Their daughter, Donielle, is a senior and a Meyerhoff scholar at the University of Maryland, Baltimore County. Their son, Kenneth, is a sophomore at the University of Maryland, College Park. He and his family reside in Mitchellville.

Don R. Simons

Senior Manager
Federal Aviation Administration

George Soodoo

Chief of Vehicle Dynamics
U.S. Department of Transportation

George Soodoo, chief of the vehicle dynamics division at the U.S. Department of Transportation, has turned his lifelong passion for cars into an exciting career. The McGill University mechanical engineering graduate started his career at the Ford Motor Company in Dearborn, Michigan, as a development engineer. While at Ford, he earned a Master of Business Administration degree at the University of Detroit Mercy before moving on to the Kerr-McGee Corporation, a diversified energy company in Oklahoma City.

After several years at Kerr-McGee, Soodoo accepted the position of safety standard engineer at the National Highway Traffic Safety Administration in Washington, D.C. In his current position, he is responsible for developing regulations pertaining to motor vehicle brakes and tires. He was instrumental in developing standards for antilock brake systems on heavy trucks, tire pressure monitoring systems for cars and the global technical regulation for motorcycle brake systems.

Soodoo enjoys his position because he has a direct impact on people's lives. In his free time, he enjoys reading, working on cars and biking.

Washington, D.C.

MEDIA
PROFESSIONALS

ENLIVEN

RECREATE

INSPIRE

CAPTIVATE

DELIGHT

IMAGINE

AMUSE

ILLUMINATE

INNOVATIVE

Antonio

Radio Personality
93.9 WKYS FM

Donald L. Baker

President & Chief Executive Officer
Don Baker Photography Group

Antonio celebrates ten years as a radio personality for 93.9 WKYS. He also serves as director of the Street Team and has hosted thousands of community events, parties and concerts throughout his 12-year radio career.

Known as "The Cuban Cigar Smoker," Antonio is the only bilingual urban radio on-air personality in Washington, D.C., and is a sought-after special guest host for both Latino and African-American events. He believes strongly in strengthening the bonds between both communities, and his motto is "I love you because I love myself and I love myself because I love God."

Antonio entered Bowie State University (BSU) in Maryland on a basketball scholarship, where he also played football. He is a member of Phi Beta Sigma Fraternity, Inc. In addition, he served as president of the dormitory association and was the activities coordinator for the BSU student government.

Born in New York City and raised in Puerto Rico, his mother is from Santiago, Cuba. Antonio is a proud Cuban-African-American man, and he takes his responsibility to represent both heritages in a positive light very seriously.

A native Washingtonian, Donald Baker has been providing quality professional photography services for the past 34 years in the Washington, D.C., metropolitan area and internationally. He developed his love for photography during his high school years with his twin brother, Ronald. Following a military tour in Vietnam, he continued his quest for creating lasting images through photography courses and personal trial and error.

Donald has had the honor of working and interacting with the Congressional Black Caucus, presidents Barack Obama, William Clinton and Jimmy Carter, Tom Joyner, William Cosby, the Jacksons, U.S. House majority whips James Clyburn and William Gray and Dr. Dorothy I. Height. Additionally, he has worked with the late Dr. C. Delores Tucker, Rosa Parks, Dr. Betty Shabazz, Coretta Scott-King, Richard Pryor and Alex Haley.

Donald mentors students interested in photography careers. He and brother Ronald are planning a photo exhibit for 2010, and Donald is currently working on a documentary about the Foxtrappe Private Towne Club, Washington, D.C.'s first black-owned private social club.

The proud father of Joseph Baker, Donald is grandfather to 17-year-old princess Natia Baker.

Ronald G. Baker

President & Chief Executive Officer
Solid Image Photographic Service

Edgar Brookins

General/Circulation Manager
Washington, D.C. Area
The AFRO-American Newspapers

A native Washingtonian, Ronald followed the birth of his big brother, Donald, 15 minutes later on June 4, 1949. At 14, his mother, Bernice, gave him two-and-a-half books of top value trading stamps to purchase an Anscomatic camera that would be the launching pad for his entry into photojournalism.

Ronald officially established his small business, Solid Image Photographic Service, in 1974, one year following his military service during the Vietnam War. By 1975 he began to cover the performances of numerous high-profile entertainers.

Ronald's first book, *Solid Images...A Collection of Memories*, published in 1994, highlighted his first 19 years as a professional photojournalist. His most recent book collaboration paired him with author Tracey Gold Bennett and their book entitled, *Washington, D.C. 1963-2006*, was published in 2007. For the past 35 years, Ronald has made his mark as a photojournalist with photo credits appearing in *Billboard*, *Ebony* and *Jet* magazines.

Ronald and his lovely wife, Imogene, of 36 years, have a beautiful daughter, Kellee, who is the broker/owner of City Dwellers Real Estate Company and principal of the KB Law Firm.

Edgar Brookins is general/circulation manager for the Washington, D.C., *The AFRO-American Newspapers*. He is responsible for the day-to-day operations of the District of Columbia office, including the distribution and management of the circulation program, community outreach, editorial input for the Sophisticated Settings page and weekly appearances on WUSA9.

Edgar has received several awards from local churches, and community and military organizations for his support and commitment to youth and homeless veterans. He leads the annual celebration at the gospel service in Fort Myer, Virginia, and established the Patriotic Circle of Friends, which sends the *AFRO* to soldiers in Iraq and Afghanistan.

Awarded a bachelor's degree from Jackson State University, Edgar completed both the Armed Forces Staff, and the Command and General Staff colleges during his 20-year-plus career as an Army officer. He is a member of the National Black Public Relations Society, the National Association of Black Journalists, Omega Psi Phi Fraternity, Inc. and Veterans of Foreign Wars of the United States. A native of Benton, Missouri, Edgar is the proud parent of three daughters, Tara, Angel and Ciera, and one son, Dexter.

George E. Curry

President & Chief Executive Officer
George Curry Media

DJ Flexx

Assistant Program Director
WPGC 95.5 FM

George E. Curry is a public speaker, commentator and columnist for the *Philadelphia Inquirer* and the National Newspaper Publishers Association (NNPA) News Service. He is a former Washington, D.C., correspondent, the New York Bureau chief for the *Chicago Tribune*, editor-in-chief of *Emerge* magazine and editor of the NNPA News Service. In addition, he was also a reporter for *Sports Illustrated* and the *St. Louis Post-Dispatch.*

While serving as editor of *Emerge*, Curry was elected president of the American Society of Magazine Editors, the first African American to hold the organization's top post. In 2000 the University of Missouri presented him with the Missouri Honor Medal for Distinguished Service in Journalism. In 2003 the National Association of Black Journalists named him Journalist of the Year.

Curry is the author of *Jake Gaither: America's Most Famous Black Coach*, editor of *The Affirmative Action Debate* and *The Best of Emerge Magazine.* He wrote and served as chief correspondent for the *Frontline* television documentary "Assault on Affirmative Action."

Currently, he serves as chairman of the board of trustees at Knoxville College, his alma mater.

DJ Flexx is assistant program director and an on-air personality at WPGC 95.5 FM, a CBS radio station. As assistant program director, he assists in directing and coordinating all daily radio station operations. He also develops and supervises all productions and the airing of all programs.

Flexx is the creator of the *Hometeam*, a young urban hip-hop entertainment show. He and his co-host, Rane, serve as the District of Columbia's Metropolitan area portal to the entertainment world by delivering non-stop music, cutting-edge news and commentary, especially issues concerning today's young people.

When dealing with pressing issues that effect our youth, Flexx addresses them through speaking engagements, roundtable/panel discussions and town hall meetings, as well as lending himself to several nonprofit organizations. Most recently, he was awarded the Lifetime Achievement in Entertainment Award by Mayor Adrian Fenty.

A native of Washington, D.C., Flexx lives in Maryland with his wife and daughter.

Lori Hall

Director
Promotions & Marketing
WPGC 95.5 FM

Leon Harris

Anchor
ABC 7/WJLA-TV

Lori I. Hall is the promotions and marketing director for WPGC 95.5 FM. In this position, she is responsible for the overall marketing efforts of the radio station, which include everything from executing events to creating marketing campaigns. Most recently, she was selected for Mentoring and Inspiring Women in Radio.

Lori graduated from Fisk University in Nashville, Tennessee, with a Bachelor of Arts degree in English. Additionally, she received a master's degree in mass communications from the Walter Cronkite School of Journalism and Telecommunications in Tempe, Arizona.

Outside of work, Lori keeps busy in various organizations, including Mentoring and Inspiring Women in Radio, the National Association of Black Journalists, Alpha Kappa Alpha Sorority, Inc., and the Women in Entertainment and Empowerment Network, where she is the Washington, D.C., ambassador. She also had a television debut on HGTV's *My First Place*, where the search for her first home was captured on television and aired numerous times on the network.

Award-winning journalist Leon Harris anchors the 5 and 11 p.m. newscasts for ABC 7/WJLA-TV. He came to Washington, D.C., after 20 years at CNN's Atlanta headquarters, where he co-anchored *CNN Live Today* and *Prime News*, and hosted *CNN Presents* and *American Stories*.

Harris has covered the 9/11 terror strikes, the Oklahoma City bombing, the Asian tsunami of 2004, the explosion and crash of TWA Flight 800 and the Los Angeles riots. He has interviewed presidential candidates, and reported live from both the Republican and Democratic national conventions.

Harris' work has earned him multiple CableAce awards for Best Newscaster, and National Emmy awards for coverage of the 9/11 terror strikes, the Oklahoma City bombing and the 2000 presidential election. Additionally, he was honored with a National Headliner Award and a National Capital Area Emmy for Best Anchor.

A cum laude and honorary doctorate recipient from Ohio University, Harris is passionate about improving the lives of children, and serves on numerous charitable boards, including For Love of Children, Junior Achievement of the National Capital Area and MenzFit.

Norlishia A. Jackson

Writer & Editor

Kristy Johnson

Editor-at-Large & Founder
Shepreneur Magazine

Norlishia Jackson is a freelance writer and editor. For 22 years, she directed The YWCA Tower, a group home for teenage girls that was consistently rated as the city's No. 1 group home by the Youth Services Administration. Under her leadership, the residents met First Lady Hillary Clinton, attended Broadway plays and political conventions, and visited college campuses. Additionally, she ensured the girls registered to vote when they turned 18.

Norlishia edited national publications for Delta Sigma Theta Sorority, Inc. and wrote a newspaper column for the National Business League of Greater Washington. She has written for major organizations, including the Greater Washington Urban League, where she served as director of information. Norlishia's work has been published in *Essence*, *USA Today* and *American Visions*. Currently, she does research, writes and edits for various authors and organizations.

The YWCA National Capital Area awarded Norlishia the Centennial Leadership Award. She also received an award from the governor of Maryland for outstanding services to children. Norlishia earned a bachelor's degree in psychology from Howard University and a master's degree in counseling from The Catholic University of America.

Kristy Johnson is the founder and editor-at-large of *Shepreneur Magazine*. *Shepreneur Magazine* is designed for African-American business and executive women. Johnson supports black women in achieving their ambitions with regard to leadership to the potential that lies within them. She leads and teaches African-American women about their unleashed prospective in black America, and shows African-American women how to engage themselves with the people who matter most.

Johnson is also the owner and broker of Omega Realty Group, a residential real estate firm in Maryland, and has achieved many awards within her industry. Helping homeowners save their home from foreclosure and preserve their credit has always been a mission of hers, even before the economic crisis. She is very active in her community as an active member of the Greater Baltimore Board of Realtors and the Maryland Association of Realtors, where she sits on several committees.

A native of Baltimore, Johnson is the wife of radio host, screen writer and director Jermaine Johnson of Jer Joh Entertainment, and the proud mother of three little shepreneurs, Jazmyn (12), Mariah (10) and Mikenzie (6).

Guy Lambert

News Director
WPGC 95.5 FM

Justine Love

Director
Community & Public Affairs
WPGC 95.5 FM

Guy Lambert is the news director/news anchor for *The Donnie Simpson Show* on WPGC 95.5 FM, in Washington, D.C. In this position, he manages the daily operations of the newsroom. He also hosts *Community Focus*, a one-hour weekly community affairs show.

Guy started as an intern at WPGC ten years ago. He then ventured to New York, Connecticut and Houston, where he covered hurricanes Katrina and Rita. Guy also reported nationwide on numerous radio stations during 9/11. In 2005 he returned to Washington, D.C., at WPGC.

Among his many other duties, Guy is a continuous contributor to CNN, serving as a political analyst. He attended The University of Alabama and is a member of Kappa Alpha Psi Fraternity, Inc. Guy is an avid environmentalist who serves as president of the Capital Solar Condominium Association. A native of the District of Columbia area, he is the son of George Lambert and Linda Hardester.

Justine Love is director of community and public affairs for WPGC 95.5, Washington, D.C.'s CBS radio affiliate, and is an advisor to all CBS affiliates in the district on major community initiatives. She might be better known by her sultry voice and poignant insight as host of *Love Talk* and *Slow Jams*. She lives and breathes for the community, reaching out a helping hand whenever possible, especially to address youth, HIV/AIDS, violence prevention, domestic violence and other numerous health topics.

Justine has received numerous awards for her community service from national voluntary health organizations, sororities and fraternities. Most recently, she was given the prestigious awards of Lifetime Hero from Mayor Adrian Fenty and Citizen of the Year from the Metropolitan Police Department of the District of Columbia.

A graduate of The University of the District of Columbia, with a Bachelor of Science degree in health education/public health administration, Justine is a native Washingtonian and proud mother of a daughter, Kendall.

Wisdom Martin

News Reporter
WTTG FOX 5

Dave Owens

Sports Digital Correspondent
WUSA9

Wisdom Martin joined WTTG FOX 5 as a general assignment reporter in January of 2003. He also serves as host of the station's webcast, "Today's Voices," and "My Voice Roundtable."

While at FOX 5, Martin has been a part of some big news stories. He was the first reporter to report live, on-the-scene during the station's Emmy Award-winning coverage of the serial bank robbers. Additionally, he covered Hurricane Katrina, live from New Orleans, Louisiana, and the murder of Washington Redskins safety Sean Taylor, live from Miami, Florida.

Prior to his arrival in Washington, D.C., Martin served as a weekend anchor and reporter for four years at WKRN in Nashville, Tennessee. He has also worked for KSEE in Fresno, California, WRAL in Raleigh, North Carolina, and *CNN Headline News* in Atlanta, Georgia.

Martin graduated with a degree in broadcast journalism from Jackson State University.

Dave Owens serves as a sports digital correspondent for WUSA9, where he covers all of the major professional and collegiate sports teams in the District of Columbia area. Co-host of the Sunday *Sports Plus* program with Sara Walsh, he also films, writes, edits and produces weekly features of high school student athletes.

Prior to arriving at WUSA9, Dave served for two years in Shreveport, Louisiana, where he covered the Louisiana State University Tigers, the Arkansas Razorbacks, the New Orleans Saints, the Dallas Cowboys, and multiple local universities and high schools. Before working in Shreveport, Dave was the weekend sports anchor and reporter in Redding, California.

Dave was a multiple-sport athlete in Southfield, Michigan, but is no stranger to the Washington, D.C., area. He played two seasons of football for the Naval Academy and served in the U.S. Navy for six years. Dave received a master's degree in business administration from the University of Redlands in 2001.

Benjamin M. Phillips IV

Director, Global Markets
The AFRO-American Newspapers

Roz Plater

Reporter/Web Host
WTTG FOX 5

Benjamin Murphy Phillips IV is director of global markets and has overall responsibility for the circulation, distribution and marketing departments of the *Washington, D.C., AFRO-American* and *Baltimore AFRO-American* newspapers' weekly print and electronic products. A great-grandson of *The AFRO-American Newspapers* founder John H. Murphy Sr., he has served on the 117-year-old company's board of directors for more than two decades, and is currently a member of its Executive Committee.

After completing two years at Tennessee State University, Phillips transferred to Morgan State University in order to work full time at the paper as a writer, photojournalist, photographer and supervisor. Upon receiving a Bachelor of Arts degree in 1976, he became the communications director for the Greater Baltimore Urban League until 1981. Additionally, Phillips is a member of Omega Psi Phi Fraternity, Inc.

Phillips spent more than 24 years in the corporate world at IBM and Xerox Corporations as a systems engineer, specialist, systems analyst, sales executive and product manager. In 2007 the opportunity arose to rejoin the company and develop new initiatives in support of the chief executive officer's ambitious growth objectives.

Roz Plater is a reporter and Web host for WTTG, the FOX affiliate in Washington, D.C. She reports for the FOX 5 *News at Ten* and the *NewsEdge at 11*, and co-hosts "Today's Voices" and "My Voice Roundtable," shows that examine pop culture and provide political analysis. She helped launch both shows on the station's Web site dedicated to African-American news and culture.

A two-time Emmy Award nominee, Roz returned home to the District of Columbia in the fall of 2004. Prior to that, she served as a reporter/anchor in the San Francisco Bay Area for a decade. Additionally, she holds a master's degree in broadcast journalism from the University of Missouri – Columbia.

On her days off, Roz can be found out-and-about D.C. She is a big fan of the performing arts and the city's fine restaurants.

Zenitha Prince

Washington, D.C. Bureau Chief
The AFRO-American Newspapers

Dorothy Tené Redmond

Freelance Writer/Playwright

Zenitha Prince is the Washington, D.C., bureau chief for *The AFRO-American Newspapers*, a 117-year-old continuously published and one of the oldest black-owned newspapers in the country. In this position, she manages staff writers and interns, and is the chief national correspondent responsible for such beats as the White House and Congress.

A multiple award winner for her work on series such as Hurricane Katrina and its aftermath, the genocide in Darfur and more, Zenitha most recently covered the campaign and inauguration of President Barack Obama. She reported on the Democratic National Convention in Denver, Colorado, and conducted community-based reporting in states including Ohio, Pennsylvania and North Carolina on issues pertaining to the election.

Zenitha graduated, summa cum laude, from Morgan State University, and in 2004 was awarded a master's degree in journalism from the University of Maryland at College Park. A native of the twin-island Caribbean nation of Trinidad and Tobago, she has called the Baltimore-Washington, D.C., metro area home for the past ten years. Still an unabashed country girl, she enjoys hiking, swimming, rafting, outdoor activities, singing and reading.

Dorothy Tené Redmond began her love affair with writing at the age of 9 with her very first homemade journal. She launched her career as an on-air personality for CBS/UPN Detroit before transitioning into her current position as a freelance writer/playwright specializing in travel, entertainment and automotive beats.

Currently, Redmond contributes to 11 magazines throughout the globe, including *Heart & Soul*, *DC Modern Luxury Magazine*, *Ambassador* and *Intersection* magazine, based in London, England, just to name a few. She also contributes to newspapers such as the *Michigan Chronicle* and *The Michigan FrontPage*.

Redmond is founder of RedHaze Productions, an original theater production company. She has penned several stage-plays, including the award-winning *Mahogany Dreams*; *Love Is....*, starring FOX TV's Charles Pugh; *Hit 8 Mile*, starring Coleman Young Jr.; and *Good Girls Rarely Make History, The Life and Times of Rosa Parks*.

Redmond's motto is "Following your dreams is never easy, but it's always worth it!"

Rev. Dr. Barbara A. Reynolds

President
Reynolds News Service

Big Tigger

Host, Afternoon Drive
WPGC-FM

The Reverend Dr. Barbara A. Reynolds is president of Reynolds News Service that produces her books, news commentaries and television productions. An ordained minister and graduate of two seminaries, Reynolds teaches prophetic ministry at the Howard University School of Divinity and writes a religion-oriented column for the National Newspaper Publishers Association that is distributed to more than 250 African-American newspapers. She is executive producer of *The Point* television show aired on cable channels within Metropolitan Washington, D.C.

Reynolds is author of five books, which include her latest, *Doing Good in the Hood: The Life, Legacy and Leadership of Bishop Alfred Owens Jr*; her spiritual autobiography, *Out of Hell & Living Well: Healing From the Inside Out*; and the first unauthorized biography of the Reverend Jesse Jackson. She is currently writing a biography of Coretta Scott King.

In addition, Reynolds directs the Harriet's Anti-Drug Ministry in Washington, D.C., and teaches eschatology at Calvary Bible Institute. In 2009 she was a visiting scholar at Central State University, where she directed the honors program.

Big Tigger, official DJ for the Washington Wizards and host of WPGC 95.5's *Afternoon Drive*, is one of radio and television's most distinctive personalities. He reaches millions of fans weekly as host of the nationally syndicated radio show, *Live in the Den with Big Tigger*.

A broadcast veteran from the Bronx, Big Tigger was host of the longest-running nationally televised hip-hop show, BET's *Rap City: Tha Bassment*. Additionally, he served as host of BET's *106 & Park*, *BET Style* and the *BluePrint*. He has appeared in Reebok commercials with NBA All-Star Steve Francis and as a guest on *Chappelle's Show*. He has been featured on several albums, including "Snake" on R. Kelly's triple platinum album *Chocolate Factory* and "If You Don't Know, Now You Know" on Busta Rhymes' *Back On My B.S.*

As a community servant, Big Tigger founded the Street Corner Foundation to increase HIV/AIDS awareness and to improve the quality of life for youth. Through the foundation, he hosts a series of annual events, including an annual celebrity weekend attracting A-list celebrities and a motorcycle ride benefit.

Gwen Tolbart

Weather Anchor & Reporter
WTTG FOX 5

G wen Tolbart is a weather anchor and reporter at WTTG FOX 5, in Washington, D.C. She is a member of the National Association of Black Journalists and Women in Film & Video, and serves as a board member of the Juvenile Diabetes Research Foundation and Our House, a program for adolescent males.

Gwen won a shared Emmy Award, among several Emmy nominations, and multiple Associated Press awards. Her community commitment has been recognized with the Woman of Distinction Award, the National Association of Black Journalists' National Community Service Award, the Best Media Person of the Year Award, the Empower Program Voices Against Violence Award, the D.C. Chapter of Zeta Phi Beta Sorority, Inc.'s Woman of the Year Award and official commendations from the governor of Texas, the U.S. Congress and the Nova Scotia House of Assembly.

A native of Montreal, Quebec, Canada, Gwen is a graduate of Dawson College and holds a Bachelor of Arts degree in journalism from Concordia University. She is a motivational and keynote speaker who enjoys reinforcing positive direction in people and mentoring youth.

BIOGRAPHICAL INDEX

ADVERTISER'S INDEX